European Social Law and Policy

TAMARA HERVEY
Reader in Law
University of Nottingham

LONGMAN
LONDON AND NEW YORK

Addison Wesley Longman Limited
Edinburgh Gate
Harlow, Essex CM20 2JE
England
and Association Companies throughout the world

First published 1998

ISBN 0 582 29320-0 Paper

Visit Addison Wesley Longman on the world wide web at http://www.awl-he.com

British Library Cataloguing-in-Publication Data
A catalogue record for this book is
available from the British Library

Set by 7 in 10/12pt Sabon

Printed in Malaysia, PP

In memory of my father,
Sándor Hervey, 1 July 1942–3 August 1997.

Contents

Preface

This book aims to provide an introduction to European social law and policy. Many books about 'European social law' focus on European labour law. The idea of this book is to focus instead on *social* law and policy, in the sense of social security, welfare, health, education and other measures aimed (or at least ostensibly aimed) at the redistribution of resources from the wealthier to the poorer in society. There are books on European social policy which cover those matters. This book aims to introduce the *law* relating to and affecting European social policy: the legality (or legal basis) of its implementing measures, their content, scope and effect, and the impact of the EC's internal market laws on national social policies. The book will provide a source of reference for lawyers and political and social scientists who wish to pursue further the legal foundation of European social policy. The book does not cover the whole of Europe as a geographical entity, but is concerned exclusively with the Member States of the European Union (EU). As my focus is very much the EU level, the picture given by the book is incomplete: a more complete picture could only be gained by a detailed study of the relevant provisions of social policy in each of the fifteen Member States.

In writing this book, I have proceeded on the assumption that there is a difference between 'economic' and 'social' policy aims. While I recognise that economic and social *phenomena* are not always easy to disentangle, I think that policy *aims* may be assessed in terms of whether their main focus is economic or social, and that this may tell us something about whether policy outcomes are desirable. I have explained what I think desirable policy aims and outcomes for European social policy might be in more detail in Chapter 1.

I am indebted to many people who helped me while I was writing this book. Jo Shaw and Joanne Scott were both extremely generous with their time and energy, by reading drafts and providing helpful and thought-provoking comments and suggestions. Nick Hopkins kindly read and commented on the education chapter, and Jean McHale did the same for the chapter on health policy. My thanks to all of these people. The members of the 'extended NLDEU network' (as Joanne Scott calls it) continue to be a source of inspiration, support, information and excellent opportunities for the 'social dimension' of academic collegiality. Thanks are also due to Brian Willan, for his patience and continued enthusiasm for the project.

I would like thank my sister Stella, for her practical contributions (mainly in the domestic domain) to the completion of this book. Finally, I would like to record my gratitude to Phil, for his encouragement and for the emotional and practical support he gives to my work, instances of which are too many to elaborate.

Notes

The terms 'EC' and 'EU' are both used in the text. I have used EU generally to refer to the European Union as a whole, as established by the Treaty of Maastricht, as a geographical entity, and in particular to refer to the institutions of the EU. I have used EC to refer to the European Community established by the Treaty of Rome, as amended, the so-called 'first pillar'. It is in this 'pillar' that the institutions of the EU have competence to enact EC law. The term 'European social policy' refers to the 'policy space' created within the EU's 'multi-level system of governance'; these ideas are elucidated below.

At the time the manuscript of this book was finished, the Treaty of Amsterdam had not yet entered into force, although it had been signed by the Heads of State and Government in October 1997. Reference is therefore made in the text to the relevant amendments which will be made by the Treaty of Amsterdam, when (or if) it is ratified. However, in order to make clear the relationship between existing provisions and the proposed Amsterdam amendments, I have not used the new Article numbers of the renumbered Treaty of Rome. Readers are therefore referred to the 'Conversion Table', annexed to the Treaty of Amsterdam, for further information.

General Editor's Preface

The Longman European Law Series is the first comprehensive series of topic-based books on EC Law aimed primarily at a student readership, though I have no doubt that they will also be found useful by academic colleagues and interested practitioners. It has become more and more difficult for a single course or a single book to deal comprehensively with all the major topics of Community law, and the intention of this series is to enable students and teachers to 'mix and match' topics which they find to be of interest: it may also be hoped that the publication of this Series will encourage the study of areas of Community law which have historically been neglected in degree courses. However, while the Series may have a student readership in mind, the authors have been encouraged to take an academic and critical approach, placing each topic in its overall Community context, and also in its socio-economic and political context where relevant.

As its title indicates, this book contains not only a detailed analysis of the relevant law but also examines policy issues and the underlying concepts. As she explains in her own Preface, Dr Hervey takes a broad view of Social Law and Policy, and this is not simply a book on labour law. In particular, this book brings together in an innovative way considerations of education and training, health, and the EC structural funds, and draws attention to the distinction between social security and social assistance. Dr. Hervey's perceptive conclusion does not make entirely comfortable reading, though she does suggest a way forward through 'social citizenship'.

John A. Usher

Abbreviations

Bull EC	Bulletin of the European Communities
Bull EU	Bulletin of the European Union
CEDEFOP	European Centre for Development of Vocational Training
CMLRev	Common Market Law Review
CPAG	Child Poverty Action Group
CPMP	Committee for Proprietary Medical Products
DG	Directorate General
EAGGF	European Agricultural Guidance and Guarante Fund
EC	European Community
Ecofin	Economic and Financial Affairs Council
ECOSOC	Economic and Social Committee
ECR	European Court Reports
EEA	European Economic Area
EEC	European Economic Community
ELJ	European Law Journal
ELRev	European Law Review
EMEA	European Medicines Evaluation Agency
EMU	Economic and Monetary Union
ERDF	European Regional Development Fund
ESF	European Social Fund
ETUC	European Trade Union Congress
EU	European Union
EUC	Citizen of the European Union
GATT	General Agreement on Tariffs and Trade
GDP	Gross domestic product
GNP	Gross national product
ICLQ	International and Comparative Law Quarterly

IGC	Intergovernmental Conference
ILJ	Industrial Law Journal
ILO	International Labour Organisation
JCMS	Journal of Common Market Studies
JEPP	Journal of European Public Policy
JESP	Journal of European Social Policy
JPP	Journal of Public Policy
JSWFL	Journal of Social Welfare and Family Law
LIEI	Legal Issues of European Integration
MLRev	Modern Law Review
NGO	Non-governmental organisation
OJ	Official Journal of the European Communities
OJLS	Oxford Journal of Legal Studies
PQ	Political Quarterly
SAP	Social Action Programme
SEA	Single European Act
SPA	Social Policy Agreement
SPP	Social Policy Protocol
TCN	Third country national
TEU	Treaty on European Union (Treaty of Maastricht)
UEAPME	European Association of Craft, Small and Medium-Sized Enterprises
UN	United Nations
UNICE	Union of Industrial and Employers' Confederations of Europe
YEL	Yearbook of European Law

Table of Cases

xiv

TABLE OF CASES

TABLE OF CASES

TABLE OF CASES

Table of Legislative Provisions

CHAPTER ONE

Introduction

European Social Policy

> The Community shall have as its task ... to promote throughout the Community ... a high level of employment and of social protection ... the raising of the standard of living and quality of life, and economic and social cohesion and solidarity among Member States. (Article 2 EC)

> The Union shall set itself the following objectives: to promote economic and social progress ... (Article B TEU)

The aspirational provisions of the founding Treaties of the European Community and the European Union claim that the European Community and the European Union have a social dimension. This social dimension is expressed as both additional to, and consequent upon, the economic activities and objectives which are the main focus of the European Community. The social dimension of the European Union, and in particular its manifestation in law and policy, is the subject of this book.

Social policy is conventionally defined as government action concerned with establishing and maintaining the welfare state for the benefit of its citizens; that is to say with such matters as social security, health care, welfare services and social work, housing, community services and education.[1] T. H. Marshall[2] defined social

---

1. Marshall, *Social Policy* (Hutchinson, 1975) p 7; Titmuss, *Social Policy* (eds Abel-Smith and Titmuss) (Allen and Unwin, 1974) p 30; Rees, *T. H. Marshall's Social Policy in the Twentieth Century* (Hutchinson, 1985) p 11; Majone, 'The European Community: Between Social Policy and Social Regulation' (1993) 31 JCMS 153–169, p 158; Cahill, *The New Social Policy* (Blackwell, 1994) p 173; Spicker, *Social Policy: Themes and Approaches* (Prentice Hall/Harvester Wheatsheaf, 1995) p 3; Cochrane and Clarke, *Comparing Welfare States:*

I

citizenship as 'the whole range from the right to a modicum of economic welfare and security to the right to share to the full in the social heritage and to live the life of a civilised being according to the standards prevailing in society'. In the Europe of the 1990s, where free market capitalism has asserted its position as the principal organising ideology for national governments, it makes sense to see social policy as operating within the context of a wider public policy, in particular one in which the market has established its place as an integral provider of services.[3] Social policy is thus defined as interconnected with other policy areas such as regional policy, family policy and fiscal policy.[4]

The measures of social policy affecting individuals within the European Union are formed at both national and European Union level. Actions of the EU institutions have an impact on social policy regimes in the Member States; national social policy regimes affect the formation of EC social policy measures. The social policy regime in the EU is being created in the context of a 'multi-level system of governance' of which the EU is the central (although weak) level.[5] The aim of this book is to set out the main provisions of EC law which affect national social policy provision in the Member States. The book concentrates on EU-level activity in the social policy sphere, and therefore the picture it paints of the 'multi-level system' is incomplete. EC measures may have an effect on national social policies in various different ways: by deregulation, re-regulation, coordination or provision of finance.[6] Since the competence of the EC to act in the social sphere is contentious,[7] the book is also concerned with the legality or 'legal basis' of relevant legal acts of the EU institutions.

Britain in International Context (Open University Press, 1993) p 4; Majone, 'Which social policy for Europe?' in Mény, Muller and Quermonne (eds), *Adjusting to Europe: The impact of the European Union on national institutions and policies* (Routledge, 1996) p 127; for alternative (although similar) defin- itions, see Kleinman and Piachaud, 'European Social Policy: Conceptions and Choices' (1993) 3 JESP 1–19, p 3 and Gomà, 'The Social Dimension of the European Union: a new type of welfare system?' (1996) 3 JEPP 209–230, pp 209–10.

2. Marshall, *supra* n 1. 3. Cahill, *supra* n 1. 4. Titmuss, *supra* n 1.
5. Streek, 'Neo-Voluntarism: A New European Social Policy Regime?' (1995) 1 ELJ 31–59, p 31; Pierson and Leibfried, 'Multitiered Institutions and the Making of Social Policy' in Leibfried and Pierson (eds) *European Social Policy: Between Fragmentation and Integration* (Brookings, 1995) pp 15–19.
6. See further Chapter 3.
7. See further below, and Chapter 3.

The objective of social policy is generally understood to be the promotion of the 'welfare' of individuals.[8] Promotion of welfare has two senses; individual and generalised. Individual welfare provision focuses on the entitlement of individuals to rights or claims to welfare – a basic standard of living, health care, social security and so on. Generalised social policy programmes aim to create the external conditions of welfare for all in society; for instance to promote employment, to ensure protection of the environment, or to ensure a decent quality of life.

Traditionally, social policy has as its central concern the redistribution of resources, and the direct reduction of disadvantage.[9] In a traditional sense, although social policy has an impact on the economy, social policy goals tend to be expressed as concerned with social justice as a *political* aspiration, in terms of equity or solidarity within a community. According to T. H. Marshall, 'social policy uses political power to supersede, supplement or modify operations of the economic system in order to achieve results which the economic system would not achieve on its own ... [It is] guided by factors other than those determined by open market forces'.[10] In the EC context, on the other hand, the dominant explanation for social policy provisions has tended to be *economic*. At the heart of the EC's social dimension (with its historical basis of the European *Economic* Community) is the aim of creating and completing the internal market. Within this conception, social policy is a tool for the creation of an integrated and 'efficient' market, not a corrective for the inequalities produced by a free market system.[11]

The European Community is concerned with social policy in both an individual and a generalised sense, although arguably it is more focused on the latter sense. Provisions of EC law which refer to the individual *per se*, aiming to establish a basic floor of rights to social protection, do exist. But the main thrust of EC social policy measures is the promotion of welfare in general within the Member States. The EC has tended to be more concerned with the

8. Spicker, *supra* n 1, pp 18–20; 54.
9. Gold and Mayes, 'Rethinking a Social Policy for Europe', in Simpson and Walker (eds) *Europe for richer or poorer* (CPAG, 1993) p 28.
10. Marshall, *supra* n 1, p 15; but see eg Kleinman and Piachaud, *supra* n 1, pp 3–5 for other grounds, such as efficiency.
11. Deakin, 'Labour Law as Market Regulation' in Davies et al (eds), *European Community Labour Law: Principles and Perspectives* (Clarendon, 1996); Majone, *supra* n 1, p 156; Streek, *supra* n 5, p 40.

impact of economic integration on the broad issue of living and working conditions, than with specific personal needs of individuals and the operation of social services for social security, health, education, and personal welfare.[12] However, the distinction can be overstated. The two senses of promotion of welfare, though conceptually separate, may overlap a great deal when it comes to concrete social policy provision.

If 'social policy' is taken in the narrow sense of state provision of individual welfare, through redistribution of resources, the European Community cannot be said to have its own 'European' social policy.[13] By and large, social welfare provision remains firmly within the competence of the Member States. There is no 'European-level welfare state', nor is there likely to be, within the current Treaty framework and given the division of competence between EU and Member State-level institutions. Individuals who live and work within the territory of the European Union derive entitlement to social protection mostly in accordance with national law, not law emanating from the EC. However, some of these entitlements may be affected by provisions of EC law. These provisions form the European level of the multi-level regulation of social policy in the EU. 'European social policy' is meant in this sense.

The EC's social policy thus defined includes measures dealing with labour mobility, such as coordination of social security for migrant workers, the transferability of social benefits, vocational training and education, and provision for migrant workers' families. EC social policy also encompasses provisions of employment regulation, such as entitlement of workers to non-discrimination on grounds of nationality, protection for employees on restructuring of employing companies, sex equality in employment, regulation of the working environment, and industrial citizenship provisions.[14] Regulation in other areas could be included, for instance, consumer protection, product safety, and aspects of environmental policy.[15] Policy areas in which the EU

12. Collins, 'Policy for Society', in Lodge (ed), *European Union: The European Community in Search of a Future* (Macmillan, 1986) p 89; Collins, 'Social Policies', in El Agraa (ed), *The Economics of the European Community* (Philip Allan, 1990) p 346.

13. Although see Majone, *supra* n 1, p 162, who suggests that the CAP may be conceptualised as the EU's redistributive welfare system for farmers.

14. Employment regulation is not covered in this book, see Szyszczak, *EC Labour Law* (Longman, forthcoming 1998).

15. These areas are not covered in this book. See Weatherill, *EC Consumer Law and Policy* (Longman, 1997) and Scott, *EC Environmental Law* (Longman, 1998).

institutions play a coordinating role and provide finance, such as human health, education and promotion of employment, are also included. In addition, EC social policy includes measures taken by the EU institutions concerned with alleviating the disadvantage suffered by some groups of people and some geographical regions of the EU as a result of the technological, industrial and economic changes brought about by the creation of the EU's internal market. The structural funds (such as the European Regional Development Fund, the European Social Fund) and financial institutions such as the Cohesion Fund, are the most obvious manifestations of this aspect of EC social policy. This aspect of EC social policy is also reflected in the Commission's programmes to combat poverty, racism, unemployment and social exclusion, and to support the young, the elderly and the disabled.[16] There are also social aspects to the EC's policies in the spheres of agriculture, transport, competition (in the regulation of state aids to industry) and the environment, although these are covered only incidentally in this book.

Because of the link between European Community social policy and the creation of the internal market, through, *inter alia*, the establishment of an area within which labour may move freely, EC social policy has tended to be conceptualised as focused upon employment. For many, the most obvious justifications for taking social policy measures on a European level is to enhance labour mobility, and create a level playing field of competition for employers within the Member States. This focus on employment is reflected in many[17] texts which cover EC social law.[18] A focus on employment is also reflected in documents emanating from the European Commission; for instance, *Social Protection in the European Community*,[19] which stresses the link between social protec-

---

16. Collins, *supra* n 12, p 346; Montanari, 'Harmonization of social policies and social regulation in the European Community' (1995) 27 European Journal of Political Research 21–45, p 23; Room (ed), *Towards a European Welfare State* (SAUS, 1991) pp 3–6; Shaw, *European Community Law* (Macmillan, 1993) pp 326–9. See Chapter 8.

17. Though not all, see Shaw, *supra* n 16, pp 323–337; Nielsen and Szyszczak, *The Social Dimension of the European Union* (Handelshojskolens Forlag, 1997) pp 135–48, 250.

18. Cochrane and Clarke, *supra* n 1, p 253; see eg, Lasok, *Lasok and Bridge's Law and Institutions of the European Union* (Butterworths, 1994) pp 687–707; Craig and de Búrca, *EC Law: Text, Cases and Materials* (Clarendon Press, 1995) pp 792–885; Weatherill and Beaumont, *EC Law* (Penguin, 1995) pp 613–46; Burrows and Mair, *European Social Law* (Wiley, 1996).

19. COM(95) 457 final.

tion and work. The Commission's latest social action programme is grounded in the connection between competitiveness and social solidarity, and is firmly fixed upon job creation as the principal mechanism for social improvement.

But even this document admits that European social policy extends further: 'Community action in the social field cannot be restricted to the world of work.' Others have been more insistent in their calls for the extension of European social policy.[20] They argue that European integration has social consequences which extend to all individuals within the Member States, not just to employees. There is therefore perceived to be a justification for a European-level social dimension which treats the whole community, not simply the employed, and which treats those who are employed not simply as workers but as people.

This book adopts that broader view of European social policy. Although employment law provisions will be mentioned, their inclusion forms a backdrop, not the central focus.[21] The main organising principle of this book is the examination of areas where EC law and policy affects (or at least claims to affect) the national social policies concerned with welfare of individual human beings *primarily as people*, as social beings, rather than as economic units of production or consumption. It is this sense of European social law and policy – the law of a people's Europe – with which this book is concerned.

Is European-level social policy necessary or justified?

The traditional rationale for social policy, at least on a national level, is for the state to intervene by means of regulatory and redistributive measures, to reduce or correct the free play of market forces. The application of the principle of subsidiarity, and the concept of spheres of competence, can lead to the conclusion that social policy should not be the concern of the European Union institutions.[22] But the question then arises of how far the economic

20. Gold and Mayes, *supra* n 9, p 26; Begg and Nectoux, 'Social Protection and Economic Union' (1995) 4 JESP 285–302.
21. For discussion of the EC's employment law, see Barnard *EC Employment Law* (Wiley, 1996); Bercusson, *European Labour Law* (Butterworths, 1996); Nielsen and Szyszczak, *supra* n 17.
22. Spicker, 'The Principle of Subsidiarity and the Social Policy of the European Community' (1991) 1 JESP 3–14.

integration of the Member States of the European Union makes necessary a convergence of their social institutions, policies and laws. Given the interconnection between economic and social policies, is it realistic for each Member State to maintain a totally separate social policy within the internal market? From a *legal* point of view, this may be expressed as a question of whether the European Union institutions have a legal basis (competence) on which to enact (binding or hortatory) social policy provisions.

Although these questions have a legal significance, they are essentially *political* questions. The answer to them depends upon the political perspective on European intervention in the social sphere adopted by the person answering. There are four different types of basic perspectives or models which feature in political, academic and legal debates on the desirability or necessity of European social policy.[23] It is important to remember that these are *models*, not expressions of objective reality. Each model may, through time, find stronger support in a particular Member State or Member States, depending upon the dominant regime of national social policy.[24] Each model presented is necessarily simplified; a thumbnail sketch. The models are neither stable nor fixed, rather each is a 'product of [a] consensus of competing claims in reality'.[25] Support for each of the models can be found in the Treaty provisions on social policy.[26]

According to the *neo-liberal market tradition*, a social dimension is undesirable. Society is comprised of individuals, each of whom is to be enabled to compete within the marketplace.[27] No further state intervention is necessary or justified. Social regulation is 'burdensome' on business, and hinders the 'flexibility' needed by employers to enable them to compete in the global economy. This model tends to be associated with the former UK Conservative government. A variant on this model may be found in the view that there is no need for a European-level social dimension, because high social standards are 'rewards' for efficiency, not rigidities imposed on the market. For instance, if Germany can afford to

---

23. Room, *supra* n 16, pp 8–9; Hagen, 'The Social Dimension: A Quest for a European Welfare State', in Ferge and Eivind (eds), *Social Policy in a Changing Europe* (Westview, 1992) p 290.

24. See further Chapter 4.

25. Room, *supra* n 16, p 9.

26. Carter, 'The European Union Social Policy Debate' in Barbour (ed), *The European Union Handbook* (Fitzroy Dearborn, 1996) p 241.

27. See Spicker, *supra* n 1, pp 20–1, 25–6 and citations therein.

have high levels of social protection, that is because it has an efficient economy, and the social protection is a reward to those whose work makes it a success.

The other side of this argument is that EC social policy (especially in the form of regulatory measures) is detrimental to the long-term interests of the EU, and especially detrimental to the poorer Member States in the south. EC social policy is seen as a form of protection for the northern, richer Member States.[28] The reason for this is that the imposition of high social protection standards on southern Member States removes their competitive advantage in the internal market. This advantage arises from their comparatively low labour costs,[29] which might provide an incentive for investment in those Member States. This incentive is withdrawn if high social standards require higher wages or higher contributions to social security benefits. Therefore, it is argued that the EU institutions should not set European-level social standards, but should leave the internal market to function unimpaired.[30]

The *convergence model i*s related to the neo-liberal model, but is rather less ideologically based. The convergence or cooperation model adopts the position that interventionist European-level social policy is superfluous because political and economic forces within the internal market will themselves encourage a tendency towards convergence of national social policy standards. Member States need not be required by law to coordinate national social policies, but will do so for sound economic reasons, because of their ever closer economic integration. There is therefore no justification for a harmonised European-level social policy. Coordination of the co-operative efforts of the Member States is all that is required of the EU institutions.

The position of those who adopt a model of *conservative social cohesion* (or a social justice model) is that social policy measures are necessary to maintain and support the established social order. If the market is left to function unimpeded, this will produce

---

28. Barnard, 'The External Dimension of Community Social Policy', in Emiliou and O'Keeffe (eds), *The European Union and World Trade Law* (Wiley, 1996), pp 153–4.
29. Both direct labour costs, such as wages, and indirect labour costs, such as social security and other contributions, for instance to education and training.
30. Hagen, *supra* n 23, pp 298–9; Majone, *supra* n 1, p 160; Scharpf, *A New Social Contract? Negative and Positive Integration in the Political Economy of European Welfare States* (EUI Working Paper RSC 96/44, 1996) pp 6–7; for counter-arguments, see Barnard, *supra* n 28, pp 83–5.

threatening social dislocation, as the 'losers' in the free market no longer consider themselves to be part of the society. This view has links with an 'ordo-liberal' conception of the 'European economic constitution', within which constitutional protections guarantee a 'free and equal society', based on market transactions taking place in a framework of 'true' free competition.[31] Social policy measures are therefore justified as 'market correcting' or 'market creating' measures.[32] Conservative social cohesion has roots in Roman Catholicism, and is particularly associated with Germany and Austria. The model can be used to support the position that European-level social policies are necessary to preserve and promote a consensus in favour of European integration among Europeans.[33] The intensification of competitive pressures brought about by European economic integration, with the restructuring of European industries and services, could lead to more 'losers' in European society. The resulting unemployment and poverty could lead to social ills, such as crime and racism. This 'centrifugal force' will have a disintegrating, rather than integrating, effect, which needs to be corrected by social policy intervention.[34]

The conservative social cohesion model also draws on a phenomenon known in the European social policy debate as 'social dumping'.[35] The argument from 'social dumping' seeks to locate social policy firmly in the desire to create a European internal market governed by principles of free and fair competition. Social dumping is short-hand for several related ideas. It is argued that divergent social standards between the Member States will lead to 'trade distortions and price wars' as Member States with lower wages and social protections seek to restrain improvements in

---

31. Maduro, 'Reforming the Market or the State? Article 30 and the Economic Constitution: Economic Freedom and Political Rights' (1997) 3 ELJ 55–82, pp 61–3; Joerges, 'European Economic Law, the Nation-State and the Maastricht Treaty', in Dehousse (ed), *Europe After Maastricht: An Ever Cloer Union?* (Beck, 1994); Bercusson et al, 'A Manifesto for Social Europe' (1997) 3 ELJ 189–205.
32. Deakin, *supra* n 11; Chalmers, 'The Single Market: from Prima Donna to Journeyman' in Shaw and More (eds), *New Legal Dynamics of European Union* (OUP, 1995) pp 56–7, 62–3.
33. Wise and Gibb, *Single Market to Social Europe: The European Community in the 1990s* (Longman, 1993) p 131.
34. Gold and Mayes, *supra* n 9, pp 26–7.
35. Mosley, 'The social dimension of European integration' (1990) 129 International Labour Review 147–63, pp 160–1; Kleinman and Piachaud, *supra* n 1, p 6; Barnard, *supra* n 21, pp 81–7; Deakin, *supra* n 11, pp 81–2.

working and living conditions in order to increase exports to other Member States, or to protect their home markets.[36] Without some social harmonisation, employers in states with a high level of social protection would find themselves at a competitive disadvantage *vis-à-vis* employers in Member States with lower levels of social protection. The (perceived) resultant tendency would be for firms to relocate in areas of low social protection (and therefore lower employer overheads in terms of social contributions, or burdensome health and safety requirements, for instance). Member States with higher levels of social protection would therefore feel constrained to lower their standards in order to maintain their competitive position in terms of trade, and to safeguard employment and investment in the national economy. Thus a 'race to the bottom' – a general lowering of standards throughout the EU – would ensue. Obviously, for proponents of a social cohesion model of social policy, such a 'race to the bottom' is regarded as highly undesirable.

A more radical version of *social cohesion* or *social justice* emanates from the social democratic tradition of various European states. This model is particularly associated with the Scandinavian Member States and with French socialism. (It is also associated with the personality of Jacques Delors, former President of the European Commission.[37]) According to this model, social policy is necessary to 'humanise' the market, for reasons of fairness and distributive justice.[38] Economic efficiency must be balanced by welfare objectives, by the creation of a European social market economy. The model is based on notions of solidarity – a position which views social welfare as a collective activity rather than the responsibility of individuals[39] – and social citizenship – the normative claim that egalitarian provision of welfare needs is superior to individual neo-liberal provision.[40] An extreme variant of this model calls for the creation of a 'European welfare superstate' to

36. Carter, *supra* n 26, p 245.
37. Ross, *Jacques Delors* (Polity, 1995); Drake, 'Jacques Delors and the Discourse of Political Legitimacy', in Drake and Gaffney (eds), *The Language of Leadership in Contemporary France* (Dartmouth, 1996) p 248; Drake, 'Political Leadership and European Integration: the case of Jacques Delors' 140–60 18 West European Politics pp 146–7.
38. Spicker, *supra* n 1, p 11.
39. Spicker, 'Exclusion' (1997) 35 JCMS 133–43, p 135.
40. Shaw, *Citizenship of the Union: Towards Post-National Membership?* (Specialised course, Academy of European Law, Florence, 1995).

counteract the negative social effects of the processes of economic integration and creation of the internal market. Additional justification for the social market cohesion model may be found in the aspirational provisions of the founding Treaties. The avowed intention behind the European integration project is to produce social benefits. Those who espouse this model are of the view that pure economic integration is unlikely to deliver these benefits by itself. The internal market perpetuates and increases disparities and inequalities of those who are already socially disadvantaged, by its centralising effect, coupled with the lack of infrastructure in peripheral regions. Social policy measures are necessary to correct this tendency towards inequality.

The assumption underlying the approach in this book is that, if action of the EU institutions affects social policy provision in the Member States, then it should meet the standards of social cohesion or social justice models. It seems sensible for policy makers to behave as if there is such a thing as society (not merely individuals) quite simply because of people's essential interdependence in late twentieth-century society. Concepts of fairness and distributive justice resonate with founding principles of Western European socio-political philosophy such as equality and personal dignity. These principles are echoed in the EU's 'self image' – its claims and aspirations. Accordingly, this book adopts social justice models as the most appropriate position for the purposes of a critique of European social policy.

However, this does *not* mean adopting a position of ideological commitment to a limitless extension of EU-level social policy. There is much of value in national level social policy provision, reached through the democratic processes in each Member State, which would not necessarily be replaced by harmonised European-level social policy provision, and should be preserved. But where European-level intervention has already taken place in the social sphere, or where a case for intervention is made in terms of the principles of division of competence and subsidiarity, the standpoint taken is that the standard the EU should be tested against is that of social cohesion or social justice. As the European Union begins to claim for itself ever more of the 'badges of statehood' (for example, the claim that the EU has 'citizens', who have 'duties'),[41] it becomes increasingly viable to begin to compare the EU to a

---

41. Article 8 EC.

nation state, and to determine whether, and in what respects, it measures up to or falls short of the responsibilities of nation states to its citizens, and inhabitants. Some of this type of criticism is already very familiar in legal writing, for instance the critiques of human rights protection by the institutions of the EU.[42] According to a social cohesion model, one of the functions of a modern Western democratic state is to provide a social policy as a 'security net' for its citizens and others who live within its boundaries, to ensure basic human entitlements to a decent life, health, housing, education and so on. As the EC takes on some of the rights of a state, to regulate the lives of its 'citizens', and to redistribute their collective resources, questions may also be asked about the provision being made for the EC to take on some responsibilities for its citizens and other residents in its territory also. Therefore, it is contended in this book that it is appropriate to begin to understand the EC's social policy provision, and to see it as a conceptually separable part of the EU enterprise, in order to begin the task of its subjection to critical analysis.

However, before turning to the substantive provisions of social policy, some contextual perspectives are explored. The next three chapters aim to set European social policy in its historical, legal structural and institutional contexts. These may shed light on the following chapters, which cover substantive EC law, and may help to illuminate possible future lines of development for European social policy.

---

42. Coppell and O'Neill, 'The European Court of Justice: Taking Rights Seriously?' (1992) 29 CMLRev 669–92; Phelan, 'Right to Life of the Unborn v Promotion of Trade in Services: The European Court of Justice and the Normative Shaping of the European Union' (1992) 55 MLRev 670–89; de Búrca, 'Fundamental Human Rights and the Reach of EC Law' 13 OJLS (1993) 283–319; Weiler and Lockhart, '"Taking Rights Seriously" Seriously: The European Court and its Fundamental Rights Jurisprudence' (1995) 32 CMLRev 51–94 and 579–627.

CHAPTER TWO

The historical context

The historical development of EU-level social policy may be conveniently divided into five broad periods.[1] The development of European social policy at EU level appears to be cyclical, in the sense that periods of relatively significant activity are followed by periods of retrenchment during which few concrete provisions are enacted. The 'ebbs and flows'[2] of European social policy reflect institutional and political tensions, and the essentially contentious nature of arguments for and against social policy measures at EU level. Policy makers often show tendencies to revert to a minimalist approach, based on the neo-liberal or convergence models of European social policy, particularly in times of national difficulties. However, this tendency towards minimalism has been countered, at various stages in the historical development of European social policy, by particular constellations of those whose political perspective leads them to favour more interventionist social cohesion models.

Neo-liberalism or 'benign neglect' (1957–72)

The cautious beginnings of European social policy during the first fifteen years or so of the European Economic Community have

1. Kenner, 'Economic and Social Cohesion – The Rocky Road Ahead' (1994) LIEI 1–37, pp 7–20; Mosley, 'The social dimension of European integration' International Labour Review (1990) 129 147–63; Nielsen and Szyszczak, *The Social Dimension of the European Union* (Handelshojskolens Forlag, 1997) p 16–64; Cram, 'Calling the Tune without Paying the Piper? Social Policy Regulation: the Role of the Commission in European Social Policy' (1993) 21 Policy and Politics 135–46.
2. Shaw, *European Community Law* (Macmillan, 1993), p 329.

been described as a period of 'benign neglect'.[3] In general, faith was placed in a *laissez faire* approach to economic and social policy. The assumption was that the benefits of increased competition within the newly formed European Economic Community, based upon the freedom of movement of the factors of production, would spread to all geographical and social sectors of the EEC.[4] The founding fathers of the EEC were influenced by the conclusions of the International Labour Organisation's Report by the Ohlin Committee (1956)[5] that there was no need for Europe-wide harmonisation of social policy. The growth expected from the opening of the single market, with an assumed 'trickle down' effect, would ensure economic and social progress for all, without the need for social intervention in the market.

However, even during this period, there is evidence of some social policy activity at the European level. The experience drawn from the European Coal and Steel Community, the founding of which was already causing decline in coal and steel industries in some areas of the EEC, was one factor in the inclusion in the Treaty of Rome 1957 of Title III on 'Social Policy'. Article 117 EEC stressed the commitment of the Member States to the promotion of 'an improved standard of living for workers'. Article 118 EEC charged the Commission to promote cooperation between Member States in the employment field, including (implicitly) measures dealing with unemployment.[6] Another factor was French fears of competitive disadvantage, in particular as against German firms, arising from the more developed system of employment rights in France, which, for instance, included a right to equal pay for women with men. The provisions in Articles 119 and 120 EEC reflect these concerns. However, these provisions did not provide a legal basis for secondary legislation, and (it was thought[7]) were not directly applicable in national law. European-level activity

---

3. Mosley, *supra* n 1, p 149; Shaw *supra* n 2, p 329.
4. Kenner, *supra* n 1, p 7; Bercusson et al, 'A Manifesto for Social Europe' (1997) 3 ELJ 189–205, p 190.
5. See Barnard and Deakin, 'Social Policy in Search of a Role: Integration, Cohesion and Citizenship' in Caiger and Floudas (eds), *1996 Onwards: Lowering the Barriers Further* (Wiley, 1996) pp 178–80; Deakin, 'Labour Law as Market Regulation' in Davies et al (eds), *European Community Labour Law: Principles and Perspectives* (Clarendon, 1996) pp 65–70.
6. Wise and Gibb, *Single Market to Social Europe: The European Community in the 1990s* (Longman, 1993), pp 126–7.
7. The ECJ held that Article 119 is directly effective in Case 43/75 *Defrenne No 2* [1976] ECR 455.

remained limited to financing modest research, consultation and coordination between the Member States.

Other areas in which embryonic social policy provisions may be found during this period include the provisions on educational exchange schemes found in Article 50 EEC. The social dimension of the Common Agricultural Policy found expression in Article 39 EEC. This took the form of grants from the European Agricultural Guidance and Guarantee Fund, Guidance Section (EAGGF). The other mechanism for structural assistance during this period was the European Social Fund (ESF), established by Article 123 EEC. Due partly to the limited funds available, and partly to the limited legal base for developing EEC structural policies, the ESF was narrowly focused upon re-employment, retraining of redundant workers, and their resettlement in areas where employment was available.[8]

More significant (in particular for Italy, whose nationals stood to gain most from access to labour markets in the northern Member States) was the inclusion in the Treaty of Rome of the provisions on free movement of workers, found in Articles 48–66 EEC. Article 49 EEC provided a basis for the enactment of legislative measures to bring about the free movement of workers. The Commission interpreted this requirement broadly, enacting legislation to promote the free movement not only of workers themselves, but also of their families.[9] The principle of non-discrimination on grounds of nationality required that migrant workers were to enjoy the same social and tax advantages, including, for instance, access to vocational training programmes, as nationals.[10] Article 51 EEC provided a basis for European-level legislation in the social security field necessitated by the free movement of workers. Here the principles established by the relevant legislation – the principles of aggregation and transferability – reflected a policy of coordination, not regulatory harmonisation. Social security was to be 'an area of study and exchange of ideas',[11] not of European-level regulation.

Although it is possible to point to some efforts towards establishing a European Community social policy during this period, generally speaking, these remained peripheral Community activity,

---

8. Kenner, *supra* n 1, p 8.
9. Regulation 1612/68/EEC OJ Sp Ed 1968 (II), p 475.
10. Regulation 1612/68, Article 7. See further Chapter 5.
11. Hagen, 'The Social Dimension: A Quest for a European Welfare State', in Ferge and Eivind (eds), *Social Policy in a Changing Europe* (Westview, 1992), p 296.

and rather insignificant. In the conflict between neo-liberal assumptions of 'trickle down effect' and concerns about the possible social costs of the single market, the neo-liberal assumptions appeared to have won the day. In fact, partly as a function of this conflict, and an expression of the fundamental disagreement between Member States on the proper role of 'European social policy', the Social Affairs Council did not even meet between 1964 and 1966.[12] The result was that there were no significant attempts to generate any sort of common policy.[13] Even where there was activity, it tended to be coordination of national systems, to the extent required to ensure labour mobility, rather than creation of harmonised European-level regulations. Streek[14] claims that this position – of coordination rather than regulation – characterises the whole history of European social policy.

Social action: a 'human face' for the European Community (1972–80)

The European Council summit meeting in Paris in 1972 proved to be the catalyst for the dynamism which characterised the next period in the development of European social policy. Echoing the memorandum on social policy issued by the social democrat German Chancellor Brandt to the earlier summit meeting in the Hague, the Heads of State and Government called for the coordination of economic integration with social harmonisation. The European Community was to initiate activity in the areas of labour, environmental and consumer affairs. The EC was to develop its 'human face'.[15]

Various factors have been identified as contributing to the new 'social cohesion' or 'social justice' focus. The new social action initiative took place at a time of increasing instability in the international economic sphere, with the precursors to the 1973 oil

---

12. Holloway, *Social Policy Harmonisation in the European Community* (Gower, 1981) p 55; Cram, *supra* n 1, p 143; Wincott, 'Political Theory, Law and European Union' in Shaw and More (eds), *New Legal Dynamics of European Union* (OUP, 1995) p 303.

13. Hagen, *supra* n 11, p 296.

14. Streek, 'Neo-Voluntarism: A New European Social Policy Regime?' (1995) 1 ELJ 31–59, pp 40–1.

15. Communiqué issued at Paris summit 1972; Shanks, 'The Social Policy of the European Communities' (1977) 14 CMLRev 375–83, p 378.

crisis, and economic recession beginning to be felt across the Member States. This instability tended to undermine the neo-liberal, growth-based economic ideology which had hitherto provided the basis for Community economic policy, and therefore for the lack of concerted effort in the social policy field,[16] on the grounds that neo-liberalism had failed to deliver its promises. New social movements arising in the late 1960s ushered in changes in dominant political ideologies.[17] National economic and political groups (including, for instance, trade unions) began to see the benefits of organising on a European level. These groups may have found allies in the Community institutions, in particular the Commission, which was keen to seize the opportunity to coordinate social (and especially labour) policy.[18] The coalition of social democrat governments in key Member States, committed to social cohesion models of social policy, and perhaps seeking to preserve their high levels of national social protection by imposing them on the rest of the EEC, gave the necessary clout in the Council of Ministers, and at European Council level.[19] Added to these factors were public fears in the new Member States, the UK, Ireland and Denmark, over, *inter alia*, the lack of sensitivity in the EEC to the social dimension of its activities.[20] The effects of economic integration on geographical areas on the periphery of the newly enlarged EEC were a matter of particular concern. On the eve of enlargement, the EEC was keen to demonstrate its willingness to develop social policies as a counterbalance to the negative effects of economic integration.

In January 1974, the Council passed a Resolution on a Social Action Programme (SAP) for the EEC. The Commission's response was enthusiastic: the SAP 1974–76[21] followed. The focus of the SAP was on labour law, with four main areas of activity: equal treatment of men and women at work; harmonisation of labour law; common standards for working conditions; and supranational employment and regional policy.[22] However, although labour law was the main concern of this first SAP, reference was also made to

16. Collins, 'Social Policies', in El Agraa, (ed), *The Economics of the European Community* (Philip Allan, 1990) p 351.
17. Shanks, *supra* n 15, pp 378, 380.
18. Hagen, *supra* n 11, p 298.
19. Streek, *supra* n 14, pp 42–3.
20. Wise and Gibb, *supra* n 6, p 32.
21. OJ 1974 C 13/1; EC Bulletin 2/74.
22. Hagen, *supra* n 11, p 298.

the improvement of living and working conditions, to consultation between Member States on social protection, and to cooperation of the Community institutions with Member States' national systems to combat poverty.

The European Social Fund was reinvigorated, with the bulk of its resources being targeted upon vocational training programmes designed to improve living and working conditions. A new structural fund in the form of the European Regional Development Fund (ERDF) was established in 1975,[23] in particular to alleviate fears of regional disparities within the EEC which had been heightened by the accession of the new Member States.

Of the social legislation enacted during this period, the sex equality directives[24] proved the most successful in terms of their direct impact on individuals in the Member States. The Commission also enjoyed some success with the enactment of three directives on the rights of employees on the restructuring of companies.[25] A directive on the education of children of migrant workers[26] extended the existing Community legislation covering free movement of labour and contributed, albeit obliquely, to Community action in the sphere of education.

However, the early 1970s enthusiasm for social action at European Community level proved short-lived. Faced with economic recession,[27] governments of the Member States retreated into national solutions to the problems of rising inflation and unemployment, and falling rates of growth.[28] Pressures to compete with the more deregulated labour markets of the United States and Japan, and to adapt to new technologies, led to an increasing focus on labour market 'flexibility',[29] with a concomitant withdrawal from other social activities, as they were founded and focused on the labour market. Thus, various Commission proposals were watered down at Council level, or remained on the table, blocked by the lack of consensus in Council. As for the structural funds, the ERDF, which at this stage lacked a coherent, programmatic

---

23. Regulation 724/75/EEC; OJ 1975 L 73/1; see further Chapter 9.
24. Directive 75/117/EEC OJ 1975 L45/19; Directive 76/207/EEC OJ 1976 L39/40; Directive 79/7/EEC OJ 1979 L6/24; see further Chapter 5.
25. Directive 75/129/EEC OJ 1975 L48/29; Directive 77/187/EEC OJ 1977 L61/27; Directive 80/987/EEC OJ 1980 L283/23.
26. Directive 77/487/EEC; OJ 1977 L 199/32; see further Chapter 6.
27. For figures see Crijns, 'The Social Policy of the European Community', in *Social Europe* No 1/79 (Commission of the EC 1987) 51–62, pp 56–7.
28. Wise and Gibb, *supra* n 6, pp 134, 145.
29. Nielsen and Szyszczak, *supra* n 1, p 28.

approach, and was based upon national regional policies, became characterised by political rhetoric, rather than concrete action, and by battles over national quotas.[30] The European Social Fund quite simply lacked the necessary funds to respond to increasing unemployment.[31]

By the end of the decade, social action on the Community level had reached a stage of virtual stagnation. The necessity for unanimity in Council for enactment of social measures was the most significant contributing factor to this 'Euro-sclerosis'.

'Flexibility' and deregulation (1980–85)

The response of many of the Member States (and most notably the UK Conservative government under Thatcher) to increased pressures of global competition on the EEC during the late 1970s and early 1980s was to adopt a philosophy of deregulation of social and labour law. This position reflected a neo-liberal ideological commitment to labour market 'flexibility' – the philosophy of protecting employers (particularly small enterprises) from burdensome regulations. Neo-liberal deregulationists found natural allies in those nationalists in Member State governments who resisted Community intervention in any area (including social policy) which was regarded as a national preserve.[32]

As a consequence, very little social legislation was enacted during this period, with most Commission proposals[33] remaining blocked by Council. The lack of consensus in terms of models of social policy, and on the crucial question of whether the Community should adopt social policy measures at all, ensured stagnation in meetings of the Social Affairs Council.[34] But again, although the trend during this period was for relative inactivity, there were a number of developments. Rather than regulation by legislation, the emphasis tended to be upon 'soft law' – resolutions, opinions, other non-binding acts, action programmes and so on.

30. Kenner, *supra* n 1, p 9; Scott and Mansell 'European Regional Development Policy: Confusing Quantity with Quality?' (1993) 18 ELRev 87–108, p 91.
31. Kenner, *supra* n 1, p 9; Wise and Gibb, *supra* n 6, p 140.
32. Streek, *supra* n 14, p 43.
33. Eg COM(83) 686 final OJ 1983 C 333/6 on parental leave and leave for family reasons.
34. Carter, 'The European Union Social Policy Debate' in Barbour, (ed) *The European Union Handbook* (Fitzroy Dearborn, 1996) p 244.

Various measures of 'soft law' were proposed[35] and some resolutions adopted[36] by the Community institutions. The Commission also pursued various 'action programmes', for example on vocational training, and on positive action for women. In the sphere of education, the ERASMUS programme promoting exchanges between university students and teachers was established. However, it is fair to say that, generally speaking, the trend of inaction was reinforced during this period by the political complexion given to intervention in the social sphere by deregulatory nationalist ideologies which had found favour in the Community institutions.

The internal market and the 'Espace Sociale Européene' (1986–93)

By no means all the governments of the Member States gave whole-hearted support to the philosophy of flexibility and deregulation. The French socialist government under Mitterand began the process of revitalising the idea of Europe's human face in the early 1980s. Mitterand issued a memorandum to Council on the creation of a 'European social area', with three main objectives: giving employment problems a central place in Community endeavour; increasing dialogue between management and labour at Community level; and improving consultation and cooperation in social protection.[37] But it was not until the appointment of the new European Commission in 1984 under the dynamic leadership of Delors that these ideas found sufficient support to take effect. The contribution of Delors, with his French socialist background, to the development of European social policy at this stage, was significant.[38]

By this time, the Community had undergone two further enlargements in membership. A coalition of social democratic governments, with a particular focus on the German model of a 'social

35. Eg Draft Council recommendation on the reduction and reorganisation of working time OJ 1983 C 290/4; Draft Council recommendation on the principles of a Community policy with regard to retirement age OJ 1982 C 16/12.
36. Eg Council resolution of the representatives of the Governments of the Member States meeting within Council on the social integration of handicapped people OJ 1981 C 347/1.
37. Wise and Gibb, *supra* n 6, p 146.
38. Ross, *Jacques Delors* (Polity, 1995).

market economy' led to the predominance of the argument that the social regulation of markets was functionally necessary for success of the integration project.[39] At the same time, a recognition that social and economic phenomena are not divisible was gaining increasing credence within the EC institutions.[40] Carter characterises this as an 'economic reading of the social provisions of the Treaty': the Commission claimed that the Treaty made very specific provision for certain social policy provisions which were *necessary* for the economic functioning of the internal market.[41] These ideas found their expression in the social aspects of the 1992 programme on completing the single internal market.

The 1992 programme was significant in its general boosting of Community activity, and was successful in breaking the deadlock and stagnation which had characterised the Community through much of the preceding decade. The Treaty amendments introduced by the Single European Act (SEA) in 1986 provided new legal bases for Community action, crucially enabling enactment of legislation (under the cooperation procedure) without the need for unanimity in the Council of Ministers. While most of the 1992 endeavour was focused on the deregulatory and re-regulatory harmonisation of economic matters required to make the internal market a reality by the end of 1992, there was a recognition of the need for the Community to concern itself with the social effects of the programme.

The concern for the Community's social dimension found expression most famously in Delors' 'Espace Sociale Européenne' (European social area) speech:

> The creation of a vast economic area, based on the market and business cooperation, is inconceivable – I would say unattainable – without some harmonisation of social legislation. Our ultimate aim must be the creation of a European social area. (Delors 1986)

As one response to the fears of the potentially negative social effects of the 1992 programme, particularly in peripheral regions in the EC, the SEA introduced into the Treaty of Rome new provisions on 'economic and social cohesion' (Article 130a EC). The general force behind this provision was to narrow regional disparities through the mechanism of the Structural Funds. Regions

---

39. Streek, *supra* n 14, p 43.
40. Wise and Gibb, *supra* n 6, p 150.
41. Carter, *supra* n 34, p 244.

with a GDP per head of less than 75% of the EC average, regions with marked industrial deterioration, and regions with high unemployment (in particular high youth unemployment) would be given aid with a view to restructuring. The Structural Funds (ESF, ERDF, EAGGF) were better coordinated, better financed (with a doubling of the budget) and refocused upon economic and social cohesion.[42] The Common Agricultural Policy was reformed (Delors package), including a focus on structural problems in agriculture. A policy for the environment (Article 130r EC) was included in the Treaty for the first time.

New legal basis provisions[43] made use of the new legislative procedure (cooperation procedure) under which measures could be adopted with a qualified majority in Council. Article 118a provided for the first time a specific legal basis for the enactment of provisions on improvements to health and safety in the working environment. Article 100a provided a basis for enactment of provisions 'which have as their object the establishment and functioning of the internal market'. However, Article 100a(4) expressly excluded 'provisions ... relating to the free movement of persons [and] those relating to the rights and interests of employed persons', thus requiring the old legislative procedure (and unanimity) for such provisions, although the precise scope of this exclusion remained difficult to draw.[44]

A second response to the social effects of the 1992 programme eventually found its form in the Community Charter of Fundamental Social Rights for Workers 1989 (the Community Charter).[45] At the request of the European Council at the 1988 Hannover Summit, the Commission and ECOSOC[46] drew up a charter of basic social rights,[47] based on the European Social Charter, a Council of Europe document which many Member States had signed. The Community Charter was eventually signed by eleven of the twelve Member States (the UK being the exception). It is a non-binding declaration of intention. The Charter is largely based on the rights of *workers*, especially those who have exer-

---

42. Kenner, *supra* n 1, pp 12–20; Wise and Gibb, *supra* n 6, p 146; see further Chapter 9.

43. See further Chapter 3.

44. Vogel-Polsky, 'What Future is there for a Social Europe Following the Strasbourg Summit?' (1990) 19 ILJ 65–80, p 65.

45. See Watson, 'The Community Social Charter' (1993) 28 CMLRev 37–68.

46. OJ 1989 C 126/4.

47. COM(89) 248 final.

cised Community rights of free movement, although some reference to social protection for those with special needs (the young, the old, the unemployed and the disabled) is included.

However, proponents of the social cohesion or social justice models found diametrically opposite solutions to the social problems of the internal market being proposed by neo-liberal free-marketeers, for whom the solution was certainly not burdensome social regulation, but Community-wide deregulation in order to improve economic performance, which would eventually lead to economic and social benefits throughout the Community. The very essence of the internal market programme is fundamentally deregulatory: it is concerned with removing barriers to trade, especially regulatory barriers, thereby making the single internal market a reality. The tensions between these opposing viewpoints had been constantly present throughout the development of EC social policy, but their effects began to be increasingly obvious following the introduction of the 1992 programme.

One of the effects of this tension, coupled with the lack of a clear legal basis for EC social policy, has been a tendency for EC social policy measures (and this is particularly true of labour policy) to focus on process rather than substance. Thus, in lieu of a comprehensive substantive labour law, the Community initiated the social dialogue between management and labour, from which measures regulating employers and employees are to emanate.[48] Hagen characterises this as a shift from 'a bureaucratic to a corporatist process of supra-national decision-making'.[49]

Another feature of European social law and policy which came to the fore during this period was the effort to improve Europe's 'human face' in terms of its 'image'. Thus, for instance, the preamble to the SEA included an affirmation that the EC would respect the fundamental rights of citizens in the European Convention on Human Rights and Fundamental Freedoms, and (perhaps more significantly) in the European Social Charter. The EC's embracing of principles of 'freedom, equality and social justice' provided no concrete rights, nor even a basis for future ac-

---

48. There is a similar dialogue between consumers, producers and distributors of goods (see Kendall, *EC Consumer Law* (Wiley Chancery, 1994) pp 8, 13, 19–22) and an embryonic 'civil dialogue' between the Commission and various NGOs, charities and other voluntary organisations; see further Chapter 4.

49. *Supra* n 11, p 297; see also Cram, *Policy-making in the EU: conceptual lenses and the integration process* (Routledge, 1997) pp 100–1.

tion, but it may be seen as important as a statement of principle.[50]

Similar 'image-creating' may be found in the Adonnino Report to the European Council following the Fontainebleau Summit of 1984. This was largely concerned with boosting many areas of Community social activity which were already established, in particular free movement of persons. However, the report also called for new areas of social activity; for example, European-level activity in public health (for instance, supporting medical research programmes), and promotion of a European cultural identity (for instance, establishing European television and radio services and promoting contacts between national cultural institutions such as museums and libraries).[51] The adoption of a European flag and a European anthem completed the image of a Europe for its citizens. The matching of the image to the reality, however, remained (and remains) an aspiration (for some) for the future.

Maastricht, Amsterdam and beyond: continued tensions (1993–)

The amendments made to the Treaty of Rome by the Treaty of Maastricht (or Treaty on European Union (TEU)), which came into force in 1993, signal the beginnings of the latest stage in the development of EC social law and policy. Post-Maastricht European social policy remains characterised by unresolved contradictions and tensions, which is unsurprising given that no model for European social policy has gained predominance. New Articles 2 and 117 EC, introduced by the Treaty of Amsterdam, reflect the continuing tensions:

> The Community shall have as its task ... to promote ... a high level of employment and social protection, ... a high degree of competitiveness and convergence of economic performance ... (Article 2 EC)

> The Community and the Member States, having in mind fundamental social rights ... shall have as their objectives ... proper social protection ... with a view to ... the combatting of exclusion. To this end the Community shall ... take account of ...

50. Collins, *supra* n 16, p 349.
51. Collins, *supra* n 16, pp 352–3; Moxton-Browne, 'Social Europe', in Lodge (ed), *The European Community and the Challenge of the Future* (Pinter, 1993) pp 160–1.

> the need to maintain the competitiveness of the Community
> economy.   (Article 117 EC)

However, there are indications that this latest stage in the history of EC social policy may yield significant new developments.

The TEU further entrenched differences in approach to European social policy by their institutionalisation in the Social Policy Agreement, from which the UK 'opted out'. Unable to agree a new Social Chapter for the Treaty of Rome, the (then) twelve Member States agreed, in the Social Policy Protocol annexed to the Treaty of Rome, to 'lend' to the other eleven Member States the institutions of the European Union for the purposes of enacting measures provided for in the Social Policy Agreement (SPA). All Member States except for the UK adopted the SPA. Acts adopted under the SPA were inapplicable in the UK. The SPA therefore effectively created the 'novel and unfortunate precedent'[52] of a 'two-speed' or 'twin-track' Europe[53] with an inside track of Treaty-based provisions, and an outside track of provisions based on the SPA, in the social sphere.

The new 'social chapter' in the Treaty of Amsterdam will (when or if it comes into force) effectively restore social policy to the 'inside track'. This development was made possible by the election of a Labour government in the UK in May 1997. The Treaty of Amsterdam will (if ratified) repeal the SPA and replace Articles 117–120 EC with provisions based closely on those of the SPA. These provisions provide new legal bases for action of the EU institutions in the social field.[54] The focus is the field of employment, although new powers are given to Council to adopt directives in some welfare-related social policy fields, such as promotion of the 'integration of persons excluded from the labour market'. In the meantime, the UK Labour government has declared its intention to 'sign up' to the SPA,[55] and a political compromise has been reached, according to which the UK has been invited to give its views to the Social Affairs Council of the 14.[56] The continued full

---

52. Watson, *supra* n 45, p 488.
53. Shaw, 'Twin-track Social Europe – The Inside Track', in O'Keeffe and Twomey (eds), *Legal Issues of the Maastricht Treaty* (Wiley, 1994) pp 295–311.
54. Articles 118, 118a, 119 (3) EC; see further Chapter 3.
55. Barnard, 'The United Kingdom, the "Social Chapter" and the Amsterdam Treaty' (1997) 26 ILJ 275–82.
56. This deal was agreed at the Amsterdam Summit; see Burrows, 'Opting in to the opt-out' (1997) *Web Law Journal*.

participation of the UK in social policy affairs at EU level will presumably be effected in some way,[57] whether or not the Treaty of Amsterdam is ratified.

The Treaty of Maastricht made various changes to social policy provision found in 'statements of principle, substantive content and general emphasis'.[58] These are carried through, and in some cases further consolidated, in the Treaty of Amsterdam. Changes to the Preamble and other 'mission statements'[59] reflect a change of principle, at least at the level of rhetoric. The Preamble calls for promotion of economic *and social* progress, and specifically refers to 'cohesion' and 'environmental protection' for the first time. Article B TEU states that one of the Union's objectives is to be 'to promote economic and social progress ... through ... strengthening of economic and social cohesion'. These statements probably have symbolic significance, and may suggest a change in emphasis heralding new developments in the future.

The Treaty of Maastricht and (if ratified) the Treaty of Amsterdam introduce further changes to the content of EC social law and policy in some areas.[60] The development of EC competence in social affairs is especially obvious in the 'flanking policies'.[61] These are areas where the EU institutions are to 'make a contribution' to policies of the Member States, and where regulatory harmonisation is expressly excluded from EC competence. There has not, therefore, been a great upheaval from the intergovernmental activity which previously characterised these areas. However, the possibility for the Council to proceed on a qualified majority vote makes a difference from the necessity for consensus which characterises intergovernmental activity. 'Flanking policies' include education and vocational training,[62] public health[63] and strategic promotion of employment.[64] In the sphere of education, various innovations have followed the Maastricht amendments. For instance, the new Leonardo programme was adopted by the Social Affairs Council in 1994, establishing an action programme on EC vocational training policy for 1995–99; and the Socrates educational exchange programme (successor to ERASMUS) was adopted in 1995. The provisions on education reveal a new focus on the

57. Although this may not be straightforward; see Burrows, *supra* n 56.
58. Shaw, *supra* n 53, p 295.   59. Shaw, *supra* n 53, p 298.
60. Shaw, *supra* n 53, pp 305–10.   61. See further Chapters 6 and 7.
62. Article 127 EC; see further Chapter 6.   63. Article 129 EC; see further Chapter 7.
64. Treaty of Amsterdam, new Title on Employment to be inserted after Title VI of the Treaty of Rome.

concept of 'lifelong learning' which blurs the distinction between education and vocational training.

The Treaty of Maastricht also affected areas of European social policy more central to the regulatory activities of the EC, concerned with creating and sustaining the internal market. The most notable of these changes was the establishment of citizenship of the European Union.[65] Every person holding the nationality of a Member State is a 'citizen of the Union' (EUC), and is entitled to enjoy the citizenship rights conferred by the Treaty. These rights mainly take the form of consolidation of existing rights, such as rights of free movement and residence,[66] along with new rights to participate (to an extent) in the democratic process in the Member State of residence.[67] Significantly, there are no 'social citizenship' rights, and no suggestion that the EU might have duties of social protection to its citizens in the way that its Member States do. However, it is conceivable that social citizenship rights might be developed in the future on the basis of citizenship of the EU.

As for redistributive policies, the Structural Funds were modified[68] in the wake of the TEU amendments to promote more transparency, establish simpler and more flexible procedures and exercise more rigorous financial control.[69] A Cohesion Fund has been established as a counterpart to economic and monetary union (EMU),[70] with the remit of investment in infrastructure, with specific Member States of the EU (those most likely to fail to achieve the convergence targets set by the TEU provisions on EMU) targeted. A further amendment and reorganisation of the Structural Funds, due in 1999, with a view to enlargement of the EU to include Central and Eastern European states, is heralded in 'Agenda 2000', the Commission's medium term strategy for the EU.[71]

It appears to be generally agreed among the Member States and the institutions of the EU that the most pressing social problem for the Union of the 1990s and beyond is unemployment. It seems to be accepted that the main activities of the EU in the task of dealing with unemployment should be focused on combating economic and social exclusion, and tackling structural unemployment.[72] But there is as yet no clear agreement on how to tackle these problems,

---

65. Article 8 EC.   66. Article 8a EC.
67. Article 8b EC. The right to participate does not extend to general elections.
68. Article 130d EC.   69. Kenner, *supra* n 1, pp 26–30.   70. Article 130d EC.
71. Commission Communication Doc 97/6, 15 July 1997. See Chapter 9.
72. *White Paper, European Social Policy: A Way Forward for the Union* COM(94) 333 final; Carter *supra* n 34, p 247.

nor is there likely to be as long as the tensions created by the various different models of social policy remain. Perhaps in a deliberate attempt to forge agreement where there is none, the dichotomy between flexibility and social protection has been increasingly obfuscated in Commission and Council documents. The White Paper on Social Policy takes account of both 'competitiveness' and 'solidarity',[73] with paradoxical (at least from the point of view of some models) statements such as 'high social standards are a key element in the competitive formula'.[74] At the Essen Summit in November 1994, the European Council launched its action plan on combating unemployment,[75] which contains both concepts of flexibility and deregulation, and concepts of the social market. The Delors White Paper on Growth, Competitiveness and Employment[76] further obscures the distinction between social policy and creating a European Union which can compete in world markets. This obfuscation will be enshrined in the Treaty with the Amsterdam amendments to Article 117 and the new title on employment, on which Heads of State and Government, Jospin, Kohl and Blair could agree, even though their approaches to the problem of unemployment differ substantially.

The Commission's White Paper on Social Policy sets out the main lines of current social action at EU level, providing the basis for a definitive work programme subsequently established in 1995. The content of the Social Action Programme 1995–97 has been strongly influenced by the principle of subsidiarity introduced by the Treaty of Maastricht.[77] According to the principle, legislation is to be enacted only where necessary, and non-binding methods of regulation are to be preferred where possible. Hence the Commission put forward only a very small legislative programme in the area of social policy, with a strong emphasis on 'cooperation and common action', the introduction of minimum standards where absolutely necessary, and otherwise convergence of national policies respecting their diversity. There are four broad themes to the SAP: the creation of jobs (with proposals for the adaptation of the Structural Funds to combat unemployment, a focus on education and training, and a proposed directive on transfer of pension rights in occupational and supplementary schemes); equal opportunities (measures on the reconciliation of family and professional life); social protection (the Commission will consider ways to

73. P 9. 74. P 10; see Deakin, *supra* n 5. 75. COM(94) 529.
76. COM(93) 700 final. 77. Article B TEU; Article 3b EC.

28

enhance the coordination of national social security systems, and will simplify and ensure more effective implementation of existing legislation); and social policy analysis and research. This fairly unambitious programme is likely to be continued in the next SAP, and probably reflects the impossibility of agreement on a more wide-ranging programme in view of the unresolved conflicts and tensions in conceptualisations of European social policy.

The consequences of economic and monetary union (EMU) for European social policy have yet to be worked through, and are likely to become increasingly central to the debate. Begg and Nectoux claim that, 'as Europe moves towards economic and monetary union, the shortcomings in the development of European social policy will become more apparent'.[78] EMU will inevitably involve a decrease in the discretion of Member States in macroeconomic management, which will impact on national social policies.[79] The 'economic convergence' criteria involve reducing government deficit to 3% and public debt to 60% of GDP, which will require national austerity measures in virtually all (if not all) Member States. Austerity measures are likely to include both a raising of taxation, and reductions in public spending. A large proportion of public expenditure is represented by redistributive provisions of social policy, so any reductions are bound to have an impact on national welfare state spending. One obvious way to reduce expenditure would be to reduce public spending and at the same time to encourage private provision of social protection. As mentioned above, this approach appears to be supported by the EU institutions. The convergence criteria on inflation are likely to have the tendency of depressing economic activity, and therefore might increase pressure on social protection budgets. Added to this is the fact that the fiscal policy and public sector borrowing requirement rules set out in the Treaty preclude pursuance of objectives other than monetary stability. There are no rules in the convergence criteria about levels of unemployment or levels of social protection – they can be as high as 'necessary'.[80]

78. Begg and Nectoux, 'Social Protection and Economic Union' (1995) 4 JESP 285–302, p 285; see also Nielsen and Szyszczak, *supra* n 1, p 63.
79. Begg and Nectoux, *supra* n 78, p 286.
80. Begg and Nectoux, *supra* n 78, pp 290–1; Streek, *supra* n 14, p 56; Deakin, *supra* n 5, pp 82–3; Room, 'European Social Policy: competition, conflict and integration' (1994) 6 Social Policy Rev 17–35, pp 22–3; Miller, *The Future of Social Security in Europe in the context of EMU* (Report to the European Commission, Observatoire Social Européen, 1993).

The alternative, positive (but only long-term) scenario is that EMU will produce additional growth from the efficiency gains it will introduce. If this were to happen, the total resources available for social protection in all the Member States would increase. However, it seems likely that, whatever the long-term prognosis, in the short and medium term 'there is a real risk that a mismanaged transition to EMU could put severe strain on social systems by simultaneously increasing demands on them and limiting their funding'.[81]

The EU institutions appear to be alive to these problems. An initiative from the German Council presidency led to the resolution of Social Affairs Council, in December 1994 (under the auspices of the SPA) on 'a contribution to economic and social convergence in the Union'. This is encapsulated in six principles: improving the competitiveness of the Union and increasing opportunities for job-creating growth; protecting employees' rights by minimum standards; respect for subsidiarity and proportionality; convergence not unification of systems; strengthening the social dialogue; and meshing economic and social measures. The more recent Commission Communication[82] 'Agenda 2000' refers to the imperative of 'modernisation' of the Member States' employment systems, by making social protection systems 'more employment friendly', concentrating on lifelong education and training, and reforming pensions and health care systems. How these kinds of initiatives might translate into concrete policy measures remains to be seen.

---

81. Begg and Nectoux, *supra* n 78, p 299.
82. Doc 97/6, 15 July 1997.

CHAPTER THREE

Contexts: legal structures and mechanisms

The social law and policy of the EC and EU have been developed and continue to develop within a particular structural context. European social policy owes much of its peculiar character to the legal and institutional framework for its formation, implementation, interpretation and effect. This chapter and the next are therefore concerned with outlining the principal legal structures and institutional framework within which EC social law is enacted, implemented and enforced.

Legal structures

The institutions of the EU are legally empowered by the Treaties to take various types of action in the social policy field, or which may affect national social policies. It will be remembered that 'European social policy' does not operate simply at the European level, but is constituted in interactions between national, sub-national and European Union institutions.[1] Basically, action by the European Union institutions can take one of four main types: deregulation, re-regulation, coordination and financial support. The legal competence of the EU institutions to act on a particular matter governs not only the issue of whether the EU may lawfully enact measures in a particular sub-field of social policy (for example, to promote education for children of migrant workers), but also the issue of what type, or level of intensity, of action (for instance, requiring all national education systems to provide extra linguistic schooling for children of migrant workers, or supporting projects

---

[1.] See Chapter 1.

which give such extra schooling from EC funds) is permitted or mandated by the Treaty.

All four types of action (and combinations of each) may promote 'harmonisation', in the sense of the attempt to create an integrated, unified, or at least coordinated EU-wide policy. However, in legal texts, the term 'harmonisation' normally relates to deregulation and re-regulation only.[2]

Deregulation

The Treaty provisions concerned with creating the internal market combine a policy of deregulation, in the sense of removing nationally imposed regulatory standards, with the legal basis for re-regulation at EU-level.[3] The 'deregulatory' measures prohibit quantitative restrictions on movement between the Member States of goods, persons, services and capital, and 'measures having equivalent effect', rendering their application null and void within the Member States. The principle of 'non-discrimination on grounds of nationality' requires for instance that goods or persons moving between Member States of the EU are granted equal treatment with nationally produced goods or nationals of the host state. Thus, the free movement of the 'factors of production' is guaranteed by legally enforceable measures throughout the internal market. This type of legal provision is often termed 'negative law'[4] and the process 'negative integration'.

Negative integration may jeopardise national social policy provision. The creation of a larger integrated market may have adverse social effects on people in some geographical areas of the market (for instance, those on the periphery where infrastructures are not developed sufficiently to ensure benefit from a wider market), and some groups in society (for instance those employed in enterprises which are subsumed in the operation of economies of scale implicit in a larger market). Moreover, the application of the principle of non-discrimination may operate to constrain national

---

2. Slot, 'Harmonisation' (1996) 21 ELRev 378–397.
3. See Joerges, 'European Economic Law, the Nation-State and the Maastricht Treaty in Dehousse (ed), *Europe After Maastricht: An Ever Closer Union?* (Beck, 1994) p 39.
4. Weatherill, *Law and Integration in the European Union* (Clarendon, 1995) pp 225, 282; Deakin, 'Labour Law as Market Regulation', in Davies et al. (eds), *European Community Labour Law: Principles and Perspectives* (Clarendon, 1996) p 71.

policy options, by affecting the legality and the financial or political viability of certain policy measures. Social benefits may no longer be lawfully withheld from non-national migrant EUC workers and their families, so national social policies, which would only be feasible if they were exclusively for the benefit of nationals, may no longer be lawfully pursued.[5] So, for instance, a 'guest worker' state pension policy, which required host workers to return home on retirement is not permitted for migrant EUCs, in accordance with the rules on free movement of persons.[6]

More seriously, an absolute policy of negative integration could significantly undermine legitimate measures of national social policy, leaving a regulatory void or 'gap' if no EU-level social policy measures were enacted to replace national measures. The relative strength of the deregulatory impulse of EC law, as opposed to the weaker competence of the EC to enact EU-level measures replacing national regulation, is a potentially disruptive feature of EC law.[7] 'Measures having equivalent effect' to quantitative restrictions on the movement of goods and provision of services across national boundaries within the EU can take the form of 'product-related measures', such as consumer protection standards. These have been dealt with in the context of EC law by the principle of mutual recognition of standards, which operates on the assumption that so long as consumer protection provisions across the EU meet the minimum standards set out in EC legislation, consumer protection is best guaranteed within the internal market simply by giving product information. However, 'measures having equivalent effect' may also be 'process-related' or welfare-related national regulation.[8] These national measures are not concerned with the safety of the product or service itself, but with matters such as whether the product has been produced in a manner harmful to the environment, or by workers who are not guaranteed sick pay or retirement pensions. Strictly speaking, these national rules, if applied to

---

5. Streek, 'Neo-Voluntarism: A New European Social Policy Regime?' (1995) 1 ELJ 31–59, pp 53–4.

6. See further Chapter 5.

7. Scharpf, *A New Social Contract? Negative and Positive Integration in the Political Economy of European Welfare States* (EUI Working Paper RSC 96/44, 1996); Dehousse, 'Integration v. Regulation? On the Dynamics of Regulation in the European Community' (1992) 30 JCMS 383–402; Majone, 'The European Community between Social Policy and Social Regulation' (1993) 31 JCMS 153–170.

8. Scharpf, *supra* n 7; Deakin, *supra* n 4, pp 71–2.

goods and services originating outside of the regulating state, would contravene the free movement provisions of the Treaty as it is possible that they would have an adverse effect on free movement of goods or services.[9] However, these national rules are obviously socially desirable.

For this reason, deregulation in EC law has never been absolute. Exemptions are provided in the Treaties[10] and have been developed by the Court[11] to protect national measures which may, or in fact do, affect the establishment of the internal market, but are justified on good policy grounds; for instance 'public policy, public security and public health'[12] or 'public morality ... the protection of health and life of humans ...'[13] These justifications are often grounded in national social policy provision. So, for instance, in the *Delattre* case,[14] the Court held that national rules prohibiting the sale of certain medical products in retail outlets other than authorised dispensing pharmacies were justified on grounds of protection of public health. Moreover, the Treaty envisages EU-level regulation, to ensure the proper functioning of the internal market[15] – 'an area ... in which the free movement of goods, persons, services and capital is ensured *in accordance with the provisions of this Treaty*'.[16] At least arguably, 'the provisions of this Treaty' include those provisions concerned with ensuring protection of social interests within the operation of the internal market, a policy aim which would by definition require re-regulation at EU-level, as explained below.

Re-regulation

'Regulation' or 're-regulation' does not enjoy a precise definition. The 'central meaning' of regulation may be understood as 'sustained and focused control exercised by a public agency over activities that are valued by a community'.[17] This definition is based on

---

9. Case 8/74 *Procureur du Roi v Dassonville* [1974] ECR 837.
10. Article 36 EC; Article 48 (3) EC; Article 56 EC.
11. See in particular Case 120/78 *Cassis de Dijon* [1979] ECR 649.
12. Article 48(3) EC. 13. Article 36 EC.
14. Case C-369/88 [1991] ECR I-1487; see Chapter 7.
15. Article 100a EC. 16. Article 7a EC, italics added.
17. Selznick, 'Focusing Organizational Research on Regulation' in Noll (ed), *Regulatory Policy and the Social Sciences* (University of California Press, 1985) p 363, cited in Ogus, *Regulation: Legal Form and Economic Theory* (Clarendon Press, 1994) p 1 and Majone, 'A European regulatory state?', in Richardson (ed), *European Union: Power and Policy-making* (Routledge, 1996) p 264.

the assumption that market processes are generally of value in promoting the economic and social good of society. However, certain 'market failures', such as inadequate communication of information, monopoly power and 'negative externalities' (that is, the effects of market transactions on third parties to those transactions), need to be corrected by regulatory action. Moreover, regulation is also necessary to deliver 'public goods', such as a healthy environment, which would not otherwise be provided through market processes.[18] For these reasons, as Majone[19] points out, systems of government do not in practice observe policies of total deregulation. Regulatory intervention to protect various social goals, such as protection of the environment or health and safety, is seldom challenged. What is practised is a mix of deregulation and regulation.

In the EU context, therefore, the internal market needs to be regulated to guard against 'market failures'. Such regulation could, in theory, take place at either national or EU level. However, national regulatory measures which adversely affect the establishment of the internal market may be denied application through the operation of EC law and the process of 'negative integration'. EU-level re-regulatory measures or legislation harmonising the matter concerned[20] will therefore be necessary, in order to ensure the integration process is continued on an efficient basis. These measures of EU-level regulation are known as 'positive law'[21] and the process as 'positive integration'.

EU-level re-regulation may also be justified by the need to correct 'market failures' in the competition between the different regulatory regimes of the Member States.[22] If governments of the Member States are prevented by the directly effective provisions of EC law from hindering the free movement of capital within the EU, then the tendency will be for capital to be invested wherever is judged to be the most 'efficient' regulatory regime within its internal market. However, just as regulation *within* a particular regime is necessary to correct market failures, so may regulation *between* regimes also be necessary. Regulation at the EU-level may there-

---

[18.] Ogus, *supra* n 17, pp 4–5; Majone, *supra* n 17, p 263.
[19.] Majone, *Deregulation or Reregulation? Regulatory Reform in Europe and the United States* (Pinter, 1990) p 3.
[20.] Dehousse, *supra* n 7.
[21.] Weatherill, *supra* n 4, pp 226, 282.
[22.] Joerges, *supra* n 3, pp 42–7.

fore operate to correct 'international regulatory failures',[23] arising from imperfect knowledge and information concerning the extra-national effects of national policies, and the tendency of national governments to try to provide public goods for their citizens simply by maintaining policies which aim to advance the competitiveness of their regime as against others.[24] So for instance, public goods such as social welfare protection may be jeopardised in a 'free market' regime competition within the EU. Member States may be tempted to enter a 'regulatory race to the bottom', whereby regulation, for instance requiring employers to contribute to social security schemes, is progressively relaxed, in order to increase the competitiveness of each regime as against others. In order to prevent such a race to the bottom, and to ensure that Member States can trust each other to maintain appropriate standards of protection, EU-level regulation of social welfare provision may therefore be justified. This position is closely connected with the 'social dumping' ideas inherent in social cohesion models of European social policy.[25]

In the EU context, regulation denotes not simply law-making functions, but 'the whole realm of legislation, governance and social control', from enactment of laws to their implementation and enforcement.[26] Regulation is therefore a matter not only for the EU institutions, but also for national (and sub-national) ministries, agencies and other public bodies who are charged with implementation of regulatory norms enacted at European level. There are problems with this style of regulation in contrast to the US style of regulation through specialist agencies with the expert knowledge of the field necessary for enforcement.[27] Implementation at national level may be incomplete, especially if formal compliance with EC regulatory norms is seen as more important than implementation in practice.[28] The EU institutions themselves have very few mechanisms to compel compliance.

There are also problems arising from the 'asymmetry'[29] in the EU between deregulation and re-regulation. Negative integration

23. Majone, in Richardson *supra* n 17, p 268.
24. Majone, in Richardson, *supra* n 17, p 274; Deakin, *supra* n 4, pp 86–8.
25. See Chapter 1; Deakin, *supra* n 4, pp 85–6.
26. Majone, *supra* n 19, pp 1–2; Majone in Richardson *supra* n 17, p 264.
27. Majone, *supra* n 19; Dehousse, *supra* n 7, pp 391–2.
28. Dehousse, *supra* n 7, pp 391–2.
29. Scharpf, *supra* n 7; see also Dehousse, *supra* n 7, pp 386–7, pp 394–5.

proceeds on the basis of directly applicable and directly effective Treaty provisions, enforced either by the Commission through the Article 169 EC procedure, or by individuals bringing claims before national courts (which may be referred to the European Court of Justice) based on the direct effect of the internal market provisions. Positive integration, on the other hand, requires competence of the EU institutions to act, and the political will in Council to do so. Positive integration is therefore more difficult to effect than negative integration. If the EU fails to re-regulate, a 'regulatory gap' may emerge, as the relevant social interest will be the subject of neither national nor European-level regulation.[30]

Regulatory activity, including European-level re-regulation, especially social regulation, is often characterised as burdensome on business and capital. However, businesses, especially large multinationals, may in fact welcome European level re-regulation, as this ensures a consistent 'level playing field' of competition, making longer-term planning and investment easier, may prevent some national legislatures from introducing *higher* regulatory standards and removes the need to mount expensive legal challenges to national laws which are technically breaching EC law, but continue to be applied by national administrations.[31] Those who oppose European-level regulation may more often be doing so because such regulation constitutes homogenisation of cultural differences, not for market-related reasons.

Coordination

Deregulation and re-regulation at European level have the effect of rendering national laws inapplicable and, in the case of re-regulation, replacing them with European standards. Coordination, on the other hand, leaves national measures in place, but aims to promote the integration process by ensuring or encouraging coordination

---

30. This danger may be overstated, see Scott, 'The GATT and Community Law: Rethinking the "regulatory gap" ' in Shaw and More (eds), *New Legal Dynamics of European Union* (OUP, 1995) pp 154-5.
31. Cram, *Policy-making in the EU: conceptual lenses and the integration process* (Routledge, 1997) p 121; Weatherill, *supra* n 4, p 283; Majone, 'Cross-National Sources of Regulatory Policymaking in the European Community and the United States' (1991) 11 JPP 79–106, pp 96–7; Cochrane, 'Comparative Approaches in Social Policy' and 'Looking for a European Welfare State' in Cochrane and Clarke, *Comparing Welfare States: Britain in International Context* (Open University Press, 1993); Majone, in Richardson, *supra* n 17, p 267.

between national regulatory regimes. European-level coordination of national policies is effected either by binding measures ('hard' or regulatory coordination) or by soft law (soft or persuasive coordination). An example of hard coordination is Regulation 1408/71, which requires coordination of national social security benefits for migrant EUC workers.[32] Regulatory coordination of social security systems is therefore limited to the very small number of migrant EUCs.[33] The 'new approach' directives are also an example of regulatory coordination, combined with re-regulation. These directives work on the basis of a minimum floor of standards set at European level – 're-regulation' – coupled with a duty of mutual acceptance of national regulatory regimes between the Member States – 'coordination'. Each national regime remains largely unaffected, but the regulatory regimes of the Member States are coordinated sufficiently to ensure effective functioning of the internal market. This approach, often termed 'minimum harmonisation',[34] has been used by the EU in its social policy, for instance to coordinate recognition of educational diplomas.[35] The measures for the ERASMUS programme provide an example of persuasive or soft co-ordination.[36] Persuasive coordination is often accompanied by financing measures, for instance the ERASMUS education programme which does not require national universities to participate, but supports those which do by ensuring coordination of movement of students between European universities, and providing financial support for their movement.[37]

Financial support

The European Union provides some financial support for various specific social policy measures in the fields of education, health and welfare or the alleviation of poverty.[38] Often these are targeted at particularly vulnerable groups, such as the elderly or the disabled. In addition, the EU operates relatively modest programmes

---

[32.] See further Chapter 5.
[33.] 1.5% of the workforce; Cochrane, in Cochrane and Clarke, *supra* n 31, p 259.
[34.] Weatherill, 'Beyond Preemption? Shared Competence and Constitutional Change in the European Community' in O'Keeffe and Twomey (eds), *Legal Issues of the Maastricht Treaty* (Wiley, 1994) pp 23–5.
[35.] See Chapter 6.
[36.] See further Chapter 6.
[37.] Ibid.
[38.] See further Chapters 6, 7 and 8.

which redistribute resources to certain groups, especially those living in certain geographical areas, in the form of the structural funds: the ERDF, ESF and EAGGF (Guidance Section).[39] The EU's financial support goes beyond that of other international organisations, as (at least in theory) it affects individuals and groups within the Member States directly, without being mediated through national administrators and subsumed into national policies.[40] However, in practice, application of the principles of partnership and subsidiarity mean that practical management of EC funds is devolved to national (or regional) levels.

Where the EC simply provides financial support for certain social policy activities, the relevant EC legal measures obviously do not regulate social policy matters in the sense of prohibiting or mandating certain action. However, EC finance encourages certain sorts of activities over others by granting them extra support, above that granted at national or sub-national level – often action with a European or cross-frontier dimension – and thus can promote the process of integration. This is 'harmonisation by carrots rather than sticks'.

It may be easier for the Member States to reach the necessary consensus for action in the form of financial support, as it does not involve the 'imposition' of 'foreign' legal provisions, and is seen as 'enabling and facilitative' rather than 'restrictive and regulatory'.[41] Be that as it may, the legality of action of the EU institutions is as significant for measures granting financial support as it is for regulatory harmonisation. Financial propriety, legitimacy and accountability in the allocation of funds to these policies must be safeguarded. So for instance, the UK has challenged the 'Poverty 4' programme on the grounds that the Commission had no competence to enact the relevant provisions.[42]

A number of commentators have pointed out that the EU institutions are more likely to take (de)regulatory action than to provide significant financial support. The EU's limited finances and competence prevent any wide-ranging policies of taxation and spending. Regulatory intervention is politically easier to achieve

39. See further Chapter 9.
40. Peters, 'Bureaucratic Politics and the Institutions of the European Community' in Sbragia (ed), *Euro-Politics: Institutions and Policymaking in the 'New' EC* (Brookings, 1992) p 96.
41. Shaw, 'Twin-track Social Europe – The Inside Track' in O'Keeffe and Twomey (eds), *Legal Issues of the Maastricht Treaty* (Wiley, 1994) p 305.
42. Case C-106/96 *UK v Commission* OJ 1996 C 145/7.

than redistributive policies, as it is more difficult to identify 'winners and losers' in policy, costs are borne by national actors, for instance employers, and the EU institutions do not have the burden of collecting taxation (increasingly unpopular among European electorates).[43] The strength of the EC's legal order, and the various mechanisms for enforcement of EC regulatory norms, enhance the viability of (de)regulation.[44]

Sources of EC social law

The principal sources of EC social law comprise Treaty sources, secondary legislation, and measures of 'soft law'. The main Treaty sources are the Treaty of Rome (including various protocols annexed thereto), the Treaty of Maastricht, and (if ratified) the Treaty of Amsterdam. Secondary legislation comprises the various regulations, directives and decisions which are relevant to social policy as broadly defined. In addition, provisions of non-binding 'soft law', both acts of the EU institutions (for instance, Commission recommendations and opinions) and acts of the Member States (for example, the Community Charter) form part of an emerging European social policy.

Treaty sources

Articles 2 and 3 of the Treaty of Rome refer to a number of 'tasks' and 'activities' of the European Community and Union which have a social dimension. These provisions were altered by the Treaty of Maastricht and will be by the Treaty of Amsterdam, to reflect current political and economic reality and, to a certain extent, to establish an increased social agenda for the EC. For example, the original Article 2 EEC referred to economic 'expansion' and the 'raising of living standards'. New Article 2 EC, as amended by the Treaty of Amsterdam, will refer to 'a high level of employment

---

43. Cram, *supra* n 31, pp 107–9; Peters, *supra* n 40, p 77; 93; Cram, 'Calling the Tune without Paying the Piper? Social Policy Regulation: the Role of the Commission in European Social Policy' (1993) 21 Policy and Politics 135-146, p 136; Cochrane, in Cochrane and Clarke, *supra* n 31, p 258; Majone, 'The European Community: Between Social Policy and Social Regulation' (1993) 31 JCMS pp 153–69, 161; see further Chapter 4.
44. Wincott, 'Political Theory, Law and the European Union' in Shaw and More (eds), *New Legal Dynamics of European Union* (OUP, 1995) p 303.

and social protection, sustainable ... growth respecting the environment, ... the raising of the standard of living and quality of life, and economic and social cohesion among Member States'.

Article 3 lists the 'activities' of the Community as including the following:

(c)   an internal market characterised by the abolition ... of obstacles to the free movement of ... persons;

(d)   measures concerning the entry and movement of persons in the internal market as provided for in Article 100c (common visa policy);

(ha)[45] the promotion of coordination between employment policies of the Member States with a view to enhancing their effectiveness in developing a coordinated strategy for employment;

(i)   a policy in the social sphere comprising a European Social Fund;

(j)   the strengthening of economic and social cohesion;

(k)   a policy in the sphere of the environment;

(o)   a contribution to the attainment of a high level of health protection;

(p)   a contribution to education and training of quality and to the flowering of the cultures of the Member States.

Title VIII of the Treaty is entitled 'Social policy, education, vocational training and youth'. The original Treaty of Rome contained Title III, entitled simply 'Social policy', which set out a number of socio-economic provisions based broadly on labour market participation.[46] The new Title, with the new 'Social Chapter' added at Amsterdam, is considerably expanded in scope, with the inclusion of the 'flanking policies' on education and vocational training.[47] However, the focus on the labour market remains central to these provisions. In addition, there is a separate title on public health.[48]

New Article 117 EC sets out in more detail the objectives of the EC in the field of social policy. Like the pre-Amsterdam Article 117,[49] the new provision is not a legal basis for action by the EU

---

45. Added by the Treaty of Amsterdam.
46. Szyszczak, 'Social Rights as General Principles of Community Law' in Neuwahl and Rosas (eds), *The European Union and Human Rights* (Martinus Nijhoff, 1995) p 208.
47. Articles 126 and 127 EC. See further Chapter 6.
48. Article 129 EC. See further Chapter 7.
49. Case 126/86 *Zaera* [1987] ECR 3697; Case 149/77 *Defrenne* [1978] ECR 1365; Case 170/84 *Bilka Kaufhaus* [1986] ECR 1607.

institutions, but an affirmation of aims and objectives, which may be relevant in the construction of other Treaty provisions and measures of secondary legislation. The social objectives of the Community and the Member States, according to Article 117 EC, are to be 'promotion of employment, improved living and working conditions ... proper social protection, dialogue between management and labour, the development of human resources ... and the combatting of exclusion'. In pursuing these objectives, the Community is to bear in mind 'fundamental social rights', such as those in the Community Charter 1989. The wording of Article 117 EC reflects a compromise between various quite different conceptions of the economic significance of social protection. A convergence model is suggested in paragraph 3, which affirms that 'the functioning of the common market will favour the harmonisation of social systems'. 'Levelled up' harmonisation, guarding against a regulatory 'race to the bottom' in social standards, is suggested in paragraph 1 which calls for 'improved living and working conditions so as to make possible their harmonisation while improvement is being maintained'. Neo-liberal thinking is reflected in paragraph 2, which requires that the Community is to take account of 'the need to maintain the competitiveness of the Community economy' in implementing its social policy.

Title VIII also contains provisions on one of the structural funds, the European Social Fund. The structural funds provide the mechanism for the EC's (fairly limited) distributive policies. The European Social Fund[50] is aimed at facilitating employment and re-employment of workers, their mobility and their adaptation to industrial change. Title XIV on 'economic and social cohesion'[51] sets out as an objective of the European Community 'the strengthening of economic and social cohesion, in particular ... [reduction] of disparities between the levels of development of less favoured regions'.[52] To this end, the EC is to support Member States' activities by means of the structural funds and the Social Cohesion Fund.[53] The structural funds are the European Social Fund, the European Regional Development Fund[54] which is intended to redress imbalances in development of regions within the EU, and the European Agricultural Guidance and Guarantee Fund (Guidance Section).[55] The EC is also required to take into account the aims of Article 130a

50. Articles 123–5 EC. 51. Article 130a–e EC.
52. Article 130a EC. 53. Article 130d EC. 54. Articles 130c–e EC.
55. Article 40(4) EC.

EC in the formulation and implementation of all its policies, and actions taken for the creation and maintenance of the internal market.

There are various other provisions in the Treaty which have a social dimension or particular relevance in the social field. For instance, the free movement of goods provisions[56] include provision justifying restrictions on imports or exports for reasons of public policy and the protection of human health. Measures enacted in order to achieve the establishment of the single internal market[57] must take as a base a high level of protection in proposals concerning health, safety, environmental protection and consumer protection.[58] The common agricultural policy has a social dimension,[59] as does the EC's environmental policy.[60]

Very few Treaty provisions on the social dimension are directly enforceable sources of EC social law. The most notable exceptions are Article 119 EC on equal pay for men and women, and Article 48 EC on free movement of workers. However, provisions which are not directly enforceable are not necessarily totally lacking in legal effect.[61] They may, for instance, be taken into account by the Court when interpreting EC legislation.[62]

Several Treaty provisions are also important sources of EC social law not in themselves, but as legal bases for further action of the EU institutions, which may include binding EC law.

Secondary legislation

The second main source of EC social law is found in the provisions of many legally binding acts of the EU institutions – regulations, directives and decisions – with a social content. The EC does not have general competence to enact legislation; a specific competence (or *legal basis* for the act) must be given by the Treaty. Article 190 EC requires that a statement of reasons must be given by the EU institutions for each piece of secondary legislation enacted. This statement includes a reference to the relevant legal basis provision

---

56. Articles 12–36 EC. 57. Article 7a EC.
58. Article 100a EC.
59. Article 39 EC – objectives include a fair standard of living for the agricultural community.
60. Article 130r EC. 61. Case 126/86 *Zaera*, para 14.
62. Case 126/87 *Zaera*; Case C-72/91 *Sloman Neptun* [1993] ECR I-887, para 26.

in the Treaty. Acts of the EU institutions without a legal basis or based on the wrong Treaty provision are unlawful, and may be subject to judicial review before the European Court of Justice.[63]

Traditional legal analysis[64] of the question of competence of the EU institutions divides areas of activity into those where the EC enjoys 'exclusive competence',[65] those where the Member States retain competence, and those areas falling somewhere in between, which are known as areas of 'concurrent competence'. The doctrine of subsidiarity must be applied to determine the extent of the EC's competence. In areas of 'concurrent competence', Member States retain competence to act until the EC does so, thereby 'preempting' national action, either wholly or (more often) partially, as in the case of 'minimum harmonisation'.[66] The question of the general competence of the EC to act in the social policy field is still contentious; the answer depends upon the particular perspective of the person or body answering it.[67] According to the Court,[68] the EC 'enjoys an internal legislative competence in the area of social policy'. The general consensus[69] appears to be that this competence is concurrent, not exclusive.

The Treaty of Rome contains various general and specific legal basis provisions. The European Court of Justice has held that the EU institutions are required to proceed on more specific legal basis provisions, if they are available.[70] The main specific legal basis provisions in the Treaty of Rome of relevance to social policy are as follows:

63. Article 173 EC.
64. See eg Bieber, 'On the Mutual Completion of Overlapping Systems' (1988) 13 ELRev 147-158; Weatherill, *supra* n 4, pp 13–33.
65. Eg common commercial policy; see Opinion 1/75 [1975] ECR 1355.
66. See Cross, 'Pre-emption of Member States' Law in the EEC: A Framework for Analysis' (1992) 29 CMLRev 447–472, and above.
67. See Chapter 1 for models of European social policy, and Watson, 'The Community Social Charter' (1991) 28 CMLRev 37–68, pp 40–1 for a summary of positions.
68. Opinion 2/91 [1993] ECR I-1061.
69. See Barnard, 'A European Litigation Strategy: The Case of the Equal Opportunities Commission' in Shaw and More (eds), *New Legal Dynamics of European Union* (OUP, 1995) pp 24–5; Watson, *supra* n 67, pp 40–43. See also the text of Article 117 EC, which refers to competence of the Member States and the Community, and Cases 281, 283, 285/85 and 287/85 *Germany and others v Commission* [1987] ECR 3203.
70. Case C-300/89 *Titanium Dioxide* [1991] ECR I-2867; Case C-155/91 *Waste Directive* [1993] ECR I-939; Case C-84/94 *Working Time* [1996] ECR 5755.

- new Article 6a (basic procedure, unanimity) within the limits of the powers conferred by the Treaty, Council may take appropriate action to combat discrimination based on sex, racial or ethnic origin, religion or belief, disability, age or sexual orientation;
- Article 49 (Article 189b procedure) enables Council to issue directives or make regulations setting out measures required to bring about, by progressive stages, freedom of movement for workers;
- Article 51 (basic procedure, unanimity) enables Council to adopt measures in field of social security as necessary to provide freedom of movement for workers;
- new Article 118(1) and (2) (Article 189b procedure) Council may adopt directives setting out minimum requirements for gradual implementation with a view to achieving the objectives of Article 117 EC. The EC is empowered to 'support and complement' activities of the Member States in the fields of improvement of the working environment, health and safety of workers, working conditions, information and consultation of workers, integration of persons excluded from the labour market and sex equality in the labour market. Council is to encourage cooperation between Member States in combatting social exclusion;
- new Article 118(3) (basic procedure, unanimity) unanimity is required for acts in the areas of social security and social protection of workers, protection of workers on the termination of their employment contract, collective labour law, employment conditions for third country nationals (TCNs) and financial contributions for promotion of employment and job creation;
- new Article 119(3) (Article 189b procedure) Council to adopt measures to ensure sex equality in employment;
- Article 126 (Article 189b procedure) Council to adopt 'incentive measures excluding harmonisation of laws' in the sphere of eduction;
- Article 127 (Article 189c procedure) Council to adopt 'incentive measures excluding harmonisation of laws' in the sphere of vocational training;
- Article 130d (basic procedure, unanimity) Council to define tasks, priority objectives and organisation of the structural funds;

- Article 130e (Article 189c procedure) for implementation of decisions relating to ERDF. For EAGGF and ESF Articles 43 and 125 apply.

General legal basis provisions are as follows:

- Article 100 (basic procedure, unanimity) enables Council to issue directives for the approximation of laws, regulations or administrative provisions of the Member States 'as directly affect the establishment or functioning of the common market';
- Article 100a (Article 189b procedure) for achievement of objectives in Article 7a (establishing the internal market) enables Council to adopt 'measures for the approximation of the provisions laid down by law, regulation or administrative action in Member States which have as their object the establishment and functioning of the internal market'. The Commission is to take a high level of protection as a base in proposals concerning health, safety, environmental protection and consumer protection; and
- Article 235 (basic procedure, unanimity) action by the Community necessary to attain one of the objectives of the Treaty, and Treaty does not otherwise provide powers.

There are a small number of specific legal basis provisions in the Treaty of Rome which permit action in the social sphere. These include Article 49 EC (measures required to bring about free movement for persons), Article 51 EC (measures in the field of social security as necessary to provide free movement for workers), and Article 118 EC (mainly employment, but also social protection). The legal basis for acts required to run the structural funds is found in Articles 130d and 130e EC.

Most existing secondary social legislation is enacted under one of the general legal basis provisions in the Treaty, either Article 100, Article 100a, or Article 235 EC. The new Article 118 EC, perhaps in combination with new Article 6a EC, is likely to be the basis for more secondary legislation in the future. Article 235 EC provides that if action by the Community proves necessary to attain one of the Community's objectives, and if no other Treaty provision gives the necessary powers, then Council shall take the appropriate measures. This 'catch-all' competence provision depends for its use in the social field on a definition of the Community's objectives as including social matters. Its successful use in practice also depends upon unanimous agreement in Council. In fact, Article 235 EC is the legal basis for many provisions of EC social law. Article 100 EC enables Council to issue directives for the approximation of laws, regulations or administrative provisions of the Member States as directly affect the establishment or functioning of the common market. The utilisation of Article 100 EC as a legal basis for provisions in the social field depends therefore upon the establishment of a direct and positive nexus between the common market and the social provision envisaged. The problem here may be the difficulty of showing, for many social policy provisions, such a 'direct' link. For instance, in the area of social security, disparities in social security provisions would have only a negative and indirect effect on the common market. However, such judgments are likely to prove arbitrary: the admission that disparities in social security provisions may disturb the free movement of workers, or indeed distort competition and the free movement of capital, sits uneasily with the denial that such provisions have a 'direct' effect on the functioning of the common market.[71]

In theory by way of derogation from Article 100 EC, but in practice instead of Article 100 EC, Article 100a EC (added to the Treaty by the Single European Act) provides a legal basis for the achievement of the objectives in Article 7a EC, that is the establishment of the 'internal market'. The amendments of Article 100a and Article 7a were made to the Treaty in order to establish the basis for the 1992 programme – the completion of the single market in goods, persons, services and capital by 31 December 1992. Article 100a permits measures for the approximation of national law, regulation or administrative action 'which have as their object the establishment and functioning of the internal market'.

The legal basis for a particular EC act determines the legislative procedure by which that act is adopted. Two issues are of particular importance here: the increased role of Parliament in the procedures under Article 189b and 189c EC (codecision and cooperation procedures) and the question of whether decision in the Council of Ministers is to be taken by unanimous vote, or by a qualified majority. Crucially, while Article 100 EC requires the basic legislative procedure and unanimity in Council, Article 100a EC refers to the Article 189b procedure, and qualified majority in

---

71. Holloway, *Social Policy Harmonisation in the European Community* (Gower, 1981) p 25.

Council. Given the difficulty of procuring unanimous agreement in Council over social proposals (and especially the infamous position of UK Conservative governments), the successful enactment of a proposal often depended on whether a qualified majority basis, such as Article 100a EC,[72] was its correct legal basis. These difficulties are likely to be alleviated by the enactment of the new 'Social Chapter' with the specific social policy legal basis provision in new Article 118 EC. Although new Article 118 EC provides a qualified majority basis for social policy provisions, it also reserves the requirement of unanimity for various 'sensitive' issues expressly enumerated in paragraph 3. There is likely to be disagreement over what exactly falls within these paragraph 3 areas, and therefore there will still be scope for judicial review of social policy measures, by means of Article 173 EC, at least at the behest of the 'privileged applicants' of the Member States, and the institutions.[73]

If one were to list provisions of EC secondary legislation – regulations, directives and decisions – in the social sphere, the list would exemplify the lack of coherence of European social policy. Many provisions of EC secondary legislation have some social dimension, in the sense of affecting individuals as social beings, rather than as economic units of production or consumption. The main provisions of secondary legislation to be discussed in this book are: Regulation 1612/68/EEC, Regulation 1408/71/EEC, Directive 79/7/EEC, Directive 86/378/EEC, Directive 92/85/EEC;[74] Directives 89/48/EEC and 92/51/EEC, Directive 77/486/EEC;[75] Regulation 2309/93/EC[76] and Regulations 2081- 2085/93/EC,[77] although many other provisions are mentioned and many more could have been included. The list itself does not reveal much beyond the point, already established, that there does not exist one, unitary, guiding idea of what social policy is or should be at EU level.

The only other general conclusion that it might be possible to draw from a list of provisions of EC social law is that 'hard' secondary legislation in the social sphere tends to be enacted as directives, rather than as regulations. With the exception of measures

---

72. Or the old Article 118a EC.
73. It is more difficult for non-privileged applicants (natural and legal persons) to establish *locus standi* under Article 173 EC. See eg Case 25/62 *Plaumann* [1963] ECR 95; Cases 41-44/70 *International Fruit Co* [1971] ECR 411; Case C-309/89 *Cordoniu* [1994] ECR I-1853.
74. See Chapter 5. 75. See Chapter 6. 76. See Chapter 7. 77. See Chapter 9.

relating to free movement of persons, which is regulated by regulation, this is particularly so for the EU's labour market legislation.[78] Directives leave to the Member States the choice of form and method for their implementation. Directives – especially those which set out only minimum requirements – are therefore seen as being the most appropriate form for harmonisation by regulation or coordination in the social policy area.

Where there are relevant regulations, they tend to be in areas regarded as central to the EU endeavour both in terms of the Treaty, and in terms of political debates about the proper role for the EU institutions in social affairs, given the principle of subsidiarity. In addition, regulations also tend to predate the 1980s watershed from which point the drive to deregulation and flexibility dates. The new approaches of flexibility and deregulation fitted with the 1992 programme, concerned to remove national regulatory barriers which were hindering the creation of the internal market. European-level intervention in social affairs (as in other areas) tended to be in a less detailed regulatory form, hence the rejection of the regulation, in favour of the directive, as the favoured format for EC law.

More recently the doctrine of subsidiarity has led to a trend for even less detail in regulation, and also less regulation in general,[79] and a consequent preference for 'soft law'. Also, action in new areas of competence is likely to be more vulnerable to challenge on grounds of breach of the subsidiarity principle,[80] and therefore the EU institutions are likely to proceed by non-binding acts, rather than regulations or directives.

Soft Law

The role of 'soft' or non-binding measures taken by the EU institutions in the social sphere should not be underestimated. Soft law measures do not place legally enforceable obligations on Member

---

78. Eg Directives 75/117/EEC OJ 1975 L 45/19 (equal pay), 76/207/EEC OJ 1976 L 39/40 (equal treatment), 89/391/EEC OJ 1989 L 183/1 (health and safety at work), 75/129/EEC OJ 11975 L 48/29 (collective redundancies), 77/187/EEC OJ 1977 L 61/27 (transfer of undertakings), 80/987/EEC OJ 1980 L 283/23 (insolvency), 94/45/EC OJ 1994 L 254/64 (works councils), 94/33/EC OJ 1994 L 216/12 (young people), 93/104/EC OJ 1993 L 307/18 (working time).
79. Maher, 'Legislative Review by the EC Commission: Revision without Radicalism' in Shaw and More (eds), *New Legal Dynamics of European Union* (OUP, 1995).
80. Shaw *supra* n 41, pp 299–300.

States or on individuals, and consequently do not grant rights to individuals. However, they are significant in providing a reference point for interpretation of hard law measures, in constituting a statement of 'best practice' and in carving out areas of EC competence or at least concern, thus 'paving the way' for future EC action of a binding nature.

Community Charter of Fundamental Social Rights of Workers 1989

Probably the most significant provision of soft law in the social sphere is the Community Charter of Fundamental Social Rights of Workers adopted at the Strasbourg Summit in 1989 by eleven of the then twelve Member States. The Community Charter is not an amendment to the Treaty of Rome, nor does it extend the EC's competences under the Treaty. It is 'merely' a political statement, with no formal legal effect, that is to say, it is a form of EC 'soft law'. Nevertheless, the Community Charter is significant, not least in that it provided the basis for the subsequently enacted SPA, now incorporated (as amended) in the Treaty at Amsterdam.

Delors described the Community Charter thus:

> The Charter is intended to form a keystone of the social dimension in the construction of Europe in the spirit of the Treaty of Rome supplemented by the Single European Act. It is a solemn declaration and lays down the broad principles underlying our European model of labour law and, more generally, the place of work in our societies. (Delors 1989)

The Community Charter is firmly based around the issue of employment, rather than a more general conception of social policy. Nevertheless, it is significant in contributing to the construction of 'European social policy' in a broad sense.

The objectives of the Community Charter are to promote social improvements regarding, *inter alia*, the free movement of persons; living and working conditions; health and safety at work; social protection; education and training; and equal treatment, including equal treatment of migrant workers and nationals of third countries. Title I of the Charter sets out twelve heads of basic social rights for workers:

1 freedom of movement
2 employment and remuneration

3 improvement of living and working conditions
4 right to social protection
5 right to freedom of association and collective bargaining
6 right to vocational training
7 right of men and women to equal treatment
8 right of workers to information, consultation and participation
9 right to health and safety at the workplace
10 protection of children and adolescents
11 protection of elderly persons
12 protection of disabled persons.

Many of these are also reflected in Treaty provisions, for instance Articles 48-51 EC, new Article 117 EC, new Article 118 EC and Article 119 EC. However, many also (at least apparently) reflect a desire on the part of the signatories to extend EC competence in the social sphere, for instance to cover the matter of equitable wages, extension of employment protection to those in atypical work, and protections for the 'excluded' categories of children and adolescents, elderly persons and disabled persons. Most of these aspirational statements were not repeated in the hard law legal basis provisions of the SPA, or in the Treaty of Amsterdam. In so far as they were, unanimity in Council is required for further binding EC action.

Implementation of the Community Charter is principally the responsibility of the Member States, by means of legislation or collective agreements. However, a role is also envisaged for the Commission, in the submission of initiatives to Council. The Commission took action in the form of the SAP of 1989 to fulfil this obligation, but the effect of the Community Charter was limited by the need to identify suitable legal bases in the Treaty on which to ground legislative proposals. Nevertheless, many of the themes of the SAP were carried through to Commission action under the SPA, and will continue in future under the new Amsterdam 'Social Chapter'. The Community Charter was a catalyst in the development of European social policy first among the eleven, and now, with the Treaty of Amsterdam, among all fifteen Member States.

Recommendations, opinions

Where there is no legal basis for the enactment of harmonisation provisions, the Commission may use recommendations to prompt voluntary convergence of national laws, regulations or administrative practices by Member States. One such area is that of social assistance, where the legal basis for harmonisation provisions is very limited indeed.[81] For instance Recommendations 92/441/EEC[82] and 92/442/EEC[82] adopt various principles upon which Member States are recommended to base their social protection and social assistance policies.

'Soft law' may be used by the EU institutions, especially the Commission, to create a precedent for EC action in a particular area. Soft law is particularly useful where Member States would not have consented to EC action of a more substantial or regulatory nature. By enacting a measure as soft law, the Commission establishes a 'Community interest' in the field, without affecting the formal position of lack of EC competence to act. By this gradual accretion of bureaucratic activity, soft law measures may prove significant in that they prepare the ground for regulation in the future.[83]

Programmes, research

As with soft law, the EU institutions may use (small-scale) direct expenditure programmes in various areas to justify Commission activities.[84] EC action to 'support and complement' actions of Member States in areas of health and employment policies[85] are good examples. Programmes are used as a means of claiming that the Commission now has some interest in the particular field, even if it has no formal competence. For example, the Commission has managed to justify its interest in the area of social welfare by establishing the Poverty Programme, thereby creating itself a role in that field.[86] The history of the activities of the European Com-

---

[81.] Luckhaus, 'European Social Security Law' in Ogus and Wikeley (eds), *The Law of Social Security* (Butterworths, 1995) p 697.

[82.] OJ 1992 L 245/46; OJ 1992 L 245/49. See further Chapter 8.

[83.] Cram, 'The European Commission as a Multi-Organization: Social Policy and IT Policy in the EU' (1994) 1 JEPP 195–217, pp 209–10; Cram, *supra* n 43, pp 143–4; Wellens and Borchardt, 'Soft Law in European Community Law' (1989) 14 ELRev 267-321, p 302.

[84.] Cram, *supra* n 83, pp 209–10.

[85.] To be added by the Treaty of Amsterdam.

[86.] See COM(91) 511 final. Cram, *supra* n 83, p 211.

munity in the field of education (as opposed to vocational training, not covered by the original Treaty of Rome) is another example of the institutions supporting action in an area in which the EC had no competence eventually feeding into Treaty amendment leading to the position where the EC can act in the sphere of education.

Chalmers points out the potentially paradoxical nature of these 'flanking policies' in which the EC supports and supplements action of the Member States, terming this the 'Frankenstein effect'.[87] Flanking policies prove necessary to ensure that the internal market functions effectively, and more importantly, to ensure that its consequences are socially acceptable. However, the policies themselves run counter to the principles of the internal market, and may eventually subsume it. The principles of policies such as regional, educational, cultural and even environmental policy have a 'spatial constituent, to the extent that their development requires different rules to be applied to the local environment than those applied to the Community environment'. For instance, educational policies may favour people speaking a local language, protection of cultural artifacts may require that they remain in the region, a policy of waste disposal on the principle that waste be disposed as close to source as possible creates a local, not a Community, market in waste. The development of the flanking policies may thus turn out to prompt a fundamental change in the relationship of the social dimension of the European Community to the single internal market endeavour.

The sponsoring of EU-wide research programmes has also been a significant development in the social dimension of the EU. These research programmes establish the EU as an important forum for debate. The cross-national data made available from these research programmes enables the Commission to 'identify common problems' and therefore areas which might lend themselves to future regulation and harmonisation.[88] For example, the Commission sponsored research in the area of biomedicine and bio-ethics is likely to inform current and potential future efforts at regulation of the industry.[89]

---

87. Chalmers, 'The Single Market: From Prima Donna to Journeyman' in Shaw and More (eds), *New Legal Dynamics of European Union* (OUP, 1995) p 67.
88. Cram, *supra* n 43, p 144; Cram, *supra* n 83, p 211.
89. See Chapter 7.

Mechanisms for enforcement

The final section of this chapter gives a very brief overview of the mechanisms for the implementation and enforcement of provisions of EC social law in the Member States. Generally speaking, European social policy is implemented and takes effect in the Member States by means of administrative and legislative action taken at the national level. In some circumstances, provisions of EC social law will take effect directly in the national legal orders of the Member States. If Member States fail to comply with EC (social) law, the Commission may bring an action before the Court based on Articles 169–171 EC.

Where measures of EC social law are found in the Treaty or enacted in regulations,[90] these have the legal status of 'direct applicability' and 'direct effect' in the Member States, and, if sufficiently precise to do so, confer rights directly on individuals in the Member States, which become part of their 'legal heritage'.[91] National courts are obliged to give effect to directly effective provisions of EC law as if they were measures of national law.[92] Where the content of the rights meets the preconditions of enforceability, the EC law rights may be relied on as a cause of action, or as a defence, in legal proceedings before national courts. Very few Treaty provisions concerned with social law are directly effective.[93]

Provisions enacted in directives are also 'directly effective' in certain circumstances, in particular after the deadline for implementation of the directive by the Member States has passed.[94] However, provisions in directives are enforceable only against an 'emanation of the state'.[95] As most social (as opposed to employment) legislation provides for rights against the state, rather than private bodies, the distinction is not likely to have great significance in the field of European social law. However, it is conceivable that the trend toward privatisation of social benefits may result, in the future, in the exclusion of recipients of benefits or services from private sources from protections granted by EC law.

90. Eg Regulation 1612/68; Regulation 1408/71.
91. Case 26/62 *Van Gend en Loos* [1963] ECR 1, para 11.
92. Case 26/62 *Van Gend en Loos* [1963] ECR 1; Case 6/64 *Costa v ENEL* [1964] ECR 585.
93. The main ones being Article 48 EC and Article 119 EC.
94. Case 9/70 *Grad* [1970] ECR 825; Case 41/71 *Van Duyn v Home Office* [1974] ECR 1337; Case 148/78 *Ratti* [1979] ECR 1629.
95. Case 152/84 *Marshall I* [1986] ECR 723; Case C-188/89 *Foster v British Gas* [1990] ECR I-3313.

National courts are obliged, in accordance with Article 5 EC, to take account of provisions of EC law in interpreting provisions of national law, both those which implement EC provisions, and others.[96] This duty has particular significance for the effect of measures of soft law on national legal orders.[97] All remedies available in national law for similar rights are available to enforce EC rights.[98] In addition, national courts are under a duty to guarantee 'effective protection' of EC rights.[99] In certain limited circumstances, damages may be available against the state for losses arising from the state's failure to comply with a duty in EC law.[100]

Where the competence of the EU institutions to enact a measure of EC law is contested, the legal mechanism for challenge is judicial review of Commission action, or of action of the national authorities in implementing the policies.[101] It is notoriously difficult for private individuals to meet the stringent *locus standi* requirements of Article 173 and 175 EC, in order to bring a review action. One potential ground of review is that the act of the institution infringes general principles of EC law, or the 'fundamental rights' which form an integral part of the EC's legal order.[102] Although definitions of fundamental rights encompassing economic rights, procedural rights and traditional civil and political rights have been successfully relied upon to challenge acts of the EU institutions, social rights are not generally[103] treated in this way by the Court.[104]

96. Case C-106/89 *Marleasing* [1990] ECR I-4135.
97. Case C-322/88 *Grimaldi* [1989] ECR 4407.
98. Case 33/76 *Rewe-Zentralfinanz v Saarland* [1976] ECR 1989.
99. Case 45/76 *Comet* [1976] ECR 203; Case 158/80 *Rewe Handesgesellschaft* [1981] ECR 1805; Case 79/83 *Harz v Deutsche Tradax* [1984] ECR 1891; Case C-271/91 *Marshall II* [1993] ECR I-4367.
100. Cases C-6 & 9/90 *Francovich I* [1991] ECR I-5357; Cases C-46 & 48/93 *Brasserie du Pêcheur/Factortame III* [1996] ECR I-1029; Case C-392/93 *British Telecommunications* [1996] ECR I-1631; Case C-5/94 *Hedley Lomas* [1996] ECR I-2553.
101. See Temple Lang, 'The Sphere in which Member States are obliged to comply with General Principles of Community Law' (1991) LIEI 23-35.
102. Case 11/70 *Internationale Handelsgesellschaft* [1970] ECR 1125; Case 4/73 *Nold v Commission* [1974] ECR 491; Article F TEU.
103. With the exception of the right to equal treatment on grounds of sex.
104. See de Búrca, 'The Language of Rights and European Integration' in Shaw and More (eds), *New Legal Dynamics of European Union* (OUP, 1995) pp 31–39; Shaw *supra* n 4, pp 301–2; but cf Szyszczak, *supra* n 46, pp 207–20, whose definition of 'social rights' is somewhat broader than that adopted here.

CHAPTER FOUR

Contexts: institutional structures

The legal context for the formation of European social law and policy and the harmonisation process was set out in Chapter 3. This chapter aims to set out the context for interactions and processes both within the EU institutions and between EU and national institutions. These contexts are important for policy formation. The staff of the EU institutions, after all, come from the Member States and have a background in their own national social policies, which may inform their views on appropriate solutions to social policy problems. The legislative institutions (especially the Council of Ministers) are influenced by pressures from national political, social, civil and other groups, in addition to those organised on a European level. Institutional contexts are also important for the implementation and enforcement of EC social law and policy, as this is carried out largely by national agencies and courts at national level, and takes place within existing social policy structures in each Member State.

National social policies

The EU institutions take action in the social policy field in the context of widely differing types of national social and welfare policies in the different Member States. Member States' social policies fall into quite distinct 'regime types'. They are built on diverse institutional structures and do not share common policy traditions. These differences beg the question of whether harmonisation in the social sphere is viable; whether legal norms can really be imposed by the EU on systems into whose structure they do not readily fit;[1]

1. Kahn-Freund, 'On Uses and Misuses of Comparative Law' (1974) 37 MLRev 1–27.

and whether (to return to the 'models of European social policy' set out in Chapter 1) a convergence model, according to which the social policies of the Member States will converge 'naturally' from the 'bottom up' without regulatory intervention, is a realistic model for European social policy.[2]

As space does not permit an examination of all fifteen Member States, the following section will identify 'families' or 'typologies' of welfare regimes, to give an idea of the breadth of approaches to social policy present within the territory of the EU.

Typologies of welfare regimes

These typologies have been developed using aggregated data, as a tool for comparative social policy research. The relevant data used to identify regime types include historical influences, levels of social or welfare spending, financial and institutional structure of welfare support, patterns of income distribution, class structure, and political parties or groups enjoying power.[3] The aggregated data produce four clusters of regime types present within the European Union: 'Scandinavian', 'Bismarckian', 'Anglo-Saxon' and 'Latin Rim'.[4] Of course, no Member State represents one regime type perfectly; rather, each Member State's social policy includes a mix of regime types, with stronger elements of a certain type or types.[5] There is a certain (partial) correlation between types of welfare

2. Begg and Nectoux, 'Social Protection and Economic Union' (1995) 4 JESP 285–302, pp 287–8 point to some convergence; but see Scharpf, *A New Social Contract? Negative and Positive Integration in the Political Economy of European Welfare States* (EUI Working Paper RSC 96/44, 1996) p 11; Leibfried, 'Towards a European Welfare State?' in Jones (ed), *New Perspectives on the Welfare State in Europe* (Routledge, 1993) pp 142–3; Pierson and Leibfried, 'Multitiered Institutions and the Making of Social Policy' in Leibfried and Pierson (eds), *European Social Policy: Between Fragmentation and Integration* (Brookings, 1995) p 32; Majone, 'The European Community: Between Social Policy and Social Regulation' (1993) 31 JCMS 153–169, p 161; Mosley, 'The social dimension of European integration' (1990) 129 International Labour Rev 147–163, p 162; Shanks, 'The Social Policy of the European Communities' (1977) 14 CMLRev 375–383, p 376.
3. Gomà, 'The Social Dimension of the European Union: a new type of welfare system?' (1996) 3 JEPP 209–230, p 212; Cochrane, 'Comparative Approaches in Social Policy' and 'Looking for a European Welfare State' in Cochrane and Clarke, *Comparing Welfare States: Britain in International Context* (Open University Press, 1993) pp 6–7; Esping-Andersen, *The Three Worlds of Welfare Capitalism* (Polity, 1990) p 3; Ginsburg, *Divisions of Welfare* (Sage, 1992) p 22.
4. Leibfried, *supra* n 2.
5. Cochrane, *supra* n 2, p 9, p 239; Esping-Andersen, *supra* n 3, p 28; Ginsburg, *supra* n 3, p 23.

regime and the 'models of European social policy' as set out in Chapter 1. The particular regime type forming the background for particular actors in the political (or academic) debate concerning European social policy may help explain their position on the appropriate 'model' for European social policy.

'Scandinavian' welfare regimes

'Scandinavian' regime types are also termed 'social democratic', 'socialist', 'universalist' or 'modern' welfare regimes. These regimes are based on the 'right to work' for all, rather than on income redistribution through compulsory insurance. The welfare state subsidises labour market entry and operates as an institutional 'employer of first resort' (especially for women). The institution of 'social citizenship' ensures universal welfare protection on an equal basis for all nationals. High standards of benefits and services are provided to both middle and working classes. The state takes on many of the social roles of the family (and especially women), such as providing support for children, the elderly and the disabled. Individual independence, through participation in the labour market, is thereby encouraged.[6]

According to Esping-Andersen:[7] 'This model crowds out the market, and consequently constructs an essentially universal solidarity in favour of the welfare state. All benefit; all are dependent; and all will presumably feel obliged to pay.' 'Scandinavian' welfare regimes rely on full employment as the central element of policy. This is for both ideological and practical reasons. The welfare of individuals is to be protected primarily through their participation in the labour market. High levels of participation, along with high taxation rates, ensure sufficient revenue to maintain the high costs of a universalist welfare system.[8] Reliance on high levels of employment may make this type of regime difficult to sustain during times of economic difficulties.[9] Within the EU, Sweden,[10] Denmark and Finland have strongly 'Scandinavian' welfare regimes.

[6.] Gomà, *supra* n 3, p 213–15; Leibfried *supra* n 2, p 140; Cochrane, in Cochrane and Clarke, *supra* n 2, p 9; Ginsburg, *supra* n 3, p 22; Esping-Andersen, *supra* n 3, pp 27–8; Titmuss *Social Policy* (eds Abel-Smith and Titmuss) (Allen and Unwin, 1974) p 31.

[7.] *Supra* n 3, p 28.

[8.] Cochrane, *supra* n 3, p 9; Esping-Andersen, *supra* n 3, pp 27–8.

[9.] Cochrane, *supra* n 3, p 15.

[10.] See further Esping-Anderson, *supra* n 3; Ginsburg, *supra* n 3, pp 30–66.

'Bismarckian' welfare regimes

'Bismarckian' welfare regimes are also termed 'conservative' or 'corporatist' welfare regimes. These regimes aim to guarantee a 'right to social security', rather than a 'right to work'. State institutions take the place of the market in providing welfare through a system of social insurance, with both means-tested and private occupational benefits playing only a marginal role. However, social security entitlements are not granted on an 'equal' or 'universal' basis, but are earned in accordance with 'merit, productivity and work performance', in other words, in accordance with status. The welfare regime therefore reinforces existing class structures and has little effect on the redistribution of income. These regimes are highly influenced by the Roman Catholic church, and so also tend to reinforce traditional family institutions, which tend to assume women will undertake caring roles within the family. The principle of 'subsidiarity' (in its original 'non-EU' form) prohibits state intervention in the family unless the family has failed to provide for the welfare of its members.[11]

Within the EU, Germany and Austria, have strongly 'Bismarckian' welfare regimes; Italy and France have less strong versions.[12] Ireland also has strong elements of Bismarckian regimes, but with lower levels of income support, and more elements of Anglo-Saxon regimes than, say, Germany.[13]

'Anglo-Saxon' welfare regimes

'Anglo-Saxon' welfare regimes are also termed 'liberal' or 'residual' welfare regimes. These regimes characterise social policy as a mechanism for ensuing employment 'by force' (as high levels of benefit are assumed to reduce work incentives) rather than by subsidisation or by education or training policies. The welfare state is a 'compensator of last resort'. The market and the family are regarded as the main institutions to guarantee welfare; with the state intervening only to provide a minimum 'safety net' of benefits, often with high levels of stigmatisation attached. Welfare is

---

11. Gomà, *supra* n 3, p 213; Leibfried, *supra* n 2, p 140; Cochrane, *supra* n 3, p 8; Esping-Andersen, *supra* n 3, p 27; Ginsburg, *supra* n 3, p 22; Titmuss, *supra* n 6, p 31.
12. Cochrane, in Cochrane and Clarke, *supra* n 3, pp 14–15; Ginsburg, *supra* n 3, pp 67–97.
13. Cochrane, *supra* n 3, p 15.

provided on a stratified and differentiated basis, with private provision for the majority being encouraged and in some cases actively
subsidised by the state, and concentration of means-tested welfare
benefits on a class or even an underclass of 'poor' dependent on
the state. Political regimes have neither the high mobilisation of
the working class present in the 'Scandinavian' regimes, nor the
strong presence of the Roman Catholic church present in the
'Bismarckian' regimes.[14]

The 'classic' 'Anglo-Saxon' regimes are the USA, Canada and
Australia. Within the EU, the UK is the regime closest to an 'Anglo-
Saxon' regime, although the UK enjoys a significant measure of
universalism.[15]

'Latin Rim' welfare regimes

'Latin Rim' or 'rudimentary' welfare regimes are the fourth family
of welfare regime represented in the EU. In these welfare regimes,
no 'right to welfare' is given. Some elements of 'Anglo-Saxon'
regimes are present, such as residualism, but within the context of
historically-based institutional structures of welfare support based
on the family and local community. Structures of labour markets
are very different from those in 'Anglo-Saxon', 'Bismarckian' or
'Scandinavian' welfare regimes, with a strong emphasis on a 'subsistence' economy, often with an agricultural basis. There is no
tradition of full (paid) employment; especially for women. The administrations in these regimes have recently made promises of
state-supported welfare, and some social security measures (for instance pensions) have taken on the function of providing income
support. Spain, Portugal and Greece all fall into the 'Latin Rim'
category. To some extent southern Italy shares its characteristics,
as does France, although even less so.[16]

It should be noted that this particular typology is only one
possible way of categorising welfare regimes, and may in particular
be criticised for paying insufficient attention to gender and race.[17]

14. Gomà, *supra* n 3, p 213; Cochrane, *supra* n 3, p 9; Ginsburg, *supra* n 3, p 22;
Esping-Andersen, *supra* n 3, pp 26–272; Leibfried, *supra* n 2, p 141; Titmuss,
supra n 6, pp 30–1.
15. Cochrane, *supra* n 3, p 13; Ginsburg, *supra* n 3, p 23; Leibfried *supra* n 2, p 141.
16. Gomà, *supra* n 3, p 215; Leibfried, *supra* n 2, pp 141–2.
17. Lewis, 'Gender and the Development of Welfare Regimes' (1992) 2 JESP
159–173; Lewis, *Women and Social Policies in Europe* (Edward Elgar, 1996);
Cochrane, *supra* n 3, pp 243–4.

For our purposes, however, this four-way typology serves simply to underline the radically different institutional structures of social policy represented within the Member States of the EU.

Convergence?

Given those highly divergent institutional structures, is it realistic to expect convergence of national social policies within the EU, in the context of the integration of the internal market? A number of trends towards convergence may be identified, but overall the differences seem to be so great as to preclude 'automatic' convergence without some sort of harmonisation activity (be that regulation, coordination, or even simply financial support) from the EU institutions.[18]

Global trends in social policy may prompt a certain degree of convergence in Member States' social policies. At the present time, at least a 'profound realignment', if not a revolution, is taking place in economic and social orders of western democracies, characterised by labels such as 'post-modernism', 'post-industrialism', and 'post-Fordism'.[19] The 1950s and 1960s settlement of 'welfare capitalism' cannot be expected to withstand world-wide pressures of increased competition, reduced levels of government expenditure as governments seek to take austerity measures aimed at improved economic efficiency, and the influence of 'new right' thinking on welfare.[20] The 1980s saw either stationary or falling levels of social expenditure as a proportion of GDP in almost all Member States of the EU. The end of 'full' employment, and the increase in 'atypical' work patterns have upset the balance necessary for the effective functioning of existing social insurance systems. Demographic trends such as women's greater activity in the paid labour market (as opposed to the provision of welfare within the family), the ageing population, and increased demands on social policy systems[21] have also affected their equilibrium. Neo-liberal political models have provided an alternative to socialist or corporate models, with increased interest in 'privatisation' of

18. Leibfried, *supra* n 2.
19. Gomà, *supra* n 3, p 215; Esping-Andersen, *supra* n 3, p 222; for an explanation of Fordism, see Cochrane, *supra* n 3, p 2 and pp 241–2.
20. Cochrane, *supra* n 3, pp 246–7.
21. For example, the costs and expectations of health care systems have expanded immensely due to technological, professional, demographic and consumer pressure; Ginsburg, *supra* n 3, p 193.

welfare provision (for instance, granting of direct cash benefits to be spent in the 'market' of social service providers), or the contracting out of service provision to private enterprises in competition for government social service contracts. The Commission's interest in privatisation models is made clear in the White Paper on Growth, Competitiveness and Employment:

> certain services for which the State has been responsible hitherto and which are subject to increasingly tight budget restrictions could be transferred permanently to the market. There are many examples of such new services related to communication and social relations: education and training, culture, security, etc. They cannot be developed free of charge and be funded implicitly by the taxpayer. They call for the introduction of new methods of payment ...[22]

However, 'new right' thinking has not replaced socialist or corporate models totally in any Member State, not even in the UK.[23]

Certain similarities are shared by all the welfare regimes represented in the EU. For instance, all make assumptions (although different ones) concerning the 'proper' role of women. Some of these assumptions are carried through to the EC's regulation of sex equality in social policy, although in some cases the EC's legal rules operate to upset assumptions about the role of women in national contexts.[24] More crucially, all the welfare regimes discussed above provide welfare only for 'citizens', those who 'belong' to the relevant nation, who are 'insiders', to whom duties of solidarity are owed. The historical basis for national welfare regimes is closely bound up with notions of nationhood and 'social citizenship'. The group of 'social citizens' within a nation is not the group of all those who are living (or even living lawfully) in the territory. 'Outsiders' have differentiated rights and access to social benefits, invariably with much lower levels of social and welfare

---

22. White Paper, Part B, Chapter 5. As Kuper points out in his critique of the White Papers, this tendency towards privatisation of European social policy makes the UK appear a 'model Member State', not a Member State which had 'opted out' of European social policy. Kuper, 'The Green and White Papers of the European Union: The Apparent Goal of Reduced Social Benefits' (1994) 4 JESP 129–37; Carter,'The European Union Social Policy Debate' in Barbour (ed), *The European Union Handbook* (Fitzroy Dearborn, 1996) p 247.

23. Esping-Andersen (*supra* n 3, Chapter 9) argues that the US influenced liberal model is becoming dominant across European welfare states. However, other commentators (Cochrane, *supra* n 3, p 16; Leibfried, *supra* n 2) conclude with more ambivalence, stressing the difficulties in predicting future developments.

24. See further Chapter 5.

protection.[25] The intervention of EC law has widened the category of 'insiders' to a certain extent, to ensure that migrant EUC workers enjoy equal protection with nationals. But migrant 'third country' national (TCN) workers continue to be excluded from various social benefits, and, may, depending upon national race relations and immigration laws, run the risk of losing even the right to remain once they lose their jobs. Moreover, identification of some groups of *citizens* with TCN migrants (on the basis of race) may help to legitimise their inferior treatment under national social policies. People in these groups are often (paradoxically) those in fact in most need of social welfare protection.[26] The extent to which these similarities are carried through to the EU level will be considered in Chapter 10.

However, these similarities or trends do not provide sufficient grounds on which to base the conclusion that there is a 'European' model of social welfare[27] towards which social policies of the Member States are converging. Austerity measures (especially in the light of the convergence criteria of EMU) and pressures towards privatisation and 'Anglo-Saxon' regimes may be countered by pressures from within other regimes resisting residualisation of social policies. The very great socio-economic differences between the relatively rich northern and central Member States and the relatively poor southern and periphery Member States stand in the way of convergence around a 'norm' for an acceptable 'European' standard of welfare, let alone a welfare regime type.[28] It is within this context that the formation of social policy measures at EU level, and the enactment of social law by the EU institutions, takes place.

EU institutions

The framework of welfare regimes within the Member States forms an important context for the creation of European social

25. Pierson, *Beyond the Welfare State? the new political economy of welfare* (Polity, 1992) p 80, cited in Cochrane, *supra* n 3, p 245.
26. See Williams, 'Gender, Race and Class in British Welfare Policy' in Cochrane and Clarke (eds), *supra* n 3, pp 77–102; Wilson, 'The German Welfare state: A Conservative Regime in Crisis' in Cochrane and Clarke, *supra* n 3, pp 141–69; Cochrane, *supra* n 3, 245.
27. No matter what the Commission may assert!
28. Begg and Nectoux, *supra* n 2, pp 286–7; Leibfried, *supra* n 2, pp 139, 143; Cochrane, *supra* n 3, p 17, pp 250–2; Ginsburg, *supra* n 3, p 195.

law and policy. A second important context is provided by the EU's unique institutional framework. 'Institutions matter': they influence not only the conditions and procedure under which European law and policy is made, but also the substance of that policy. To understand policy outcomes, it is useful to understand the role of institutions in shaping the decision-making process, the operation and interrelations of the institutions, and the legal and political framework within which the institutions carry out their work.[29] If, following Leibfried and Pierson, the European Union is conceptualised as 'the central level – albeit a weak one – of an emergent multi-tiered system of governance',[30] the nature of the European Union's institutional framework means that European social policy will be made simultaneously at two levels 'with complex interactions between them, and among the national systems operating in the international order and situated in the integrated economy that underlies it'.[31] The scope for social policy made at the 'central' (European) level is limited, although it is expanding as Europe's economic and political integration increases.[32] The powers of Member States may be preserved by principles such as subsidiarity, but the powers under the general legal basis provisions, such as Articles 100, 100a and 235 EC, are potentially sweeping.

Leibfried and Pierson point to four characteristics of the EU which suggest that the 'central tier' of the EU system of governance should not simply be characterised as firmly under the control of national governments. These are the relatively autonomous activity of the EU institutions; the dynamic of policy commitments entered into by Member States in the past, from which they cannot escape although they might now wish to do so; the phenomenon of 'issue density', that is the tendency for EC competences to spill over into

---

29. Cram, *Policy-making in the EU: conceptual lenses and the integration process* (Routledge, 1997); Armstrong, 'Regulating the Free Movement of Goods: institutions and institutional change' in Shaw and More (eds), *New Legal Dynamics of European Union* (OUP, 1995) p 167; C. Scott, 'Changing Patterns of European Community Utilities Law and Policy: An Institutional Hypothesis' in Shaw and More (eds), *New Legal Dynamics of European Union* (OUP, 1995) p 193; Bulmer, 'The Governance of the EU: A New Institutionalist Approach' (1994) 13 Journal of Public Policy 351–380; Cf Moravcsik, 'Liberal Intergovernmentalism and Integration: a rejoinder' (1995) 33 JCMS 611–620; Moravcsik, 'Preferences and Power in the EC: A Liberal Intergovernmentalist Approach' (1993) 31 JCMS 473–524.

30. Pierson and Leibfried, *supra* n 2, pp 3, 15–19.

31. Streek, 'Neo-Voluntarism: A New European Social Policy Regime?' (1995) 1 ELJ 31–59, p 32.

32. Pierson and Leibfried, *supra* n 2, p 4.

new issues, whereby EC action on one issue has unforeseen consequences in related areas; and the role of independent non-state actors, organising at the European, rather than the national level.[33]
An 'intergovernmentalist' perspective, which, broadly speaking,
seeks to explain policy developments as arising essentially from the
autonomous will of the national governments of the Member
States, does not do justice to these characteristics. A more nuanced
perspective, combining intergovernmentalist and institutionalist
insights, will be necessary.[34]

With this institutional perspective in mind, simplistic or formulaic
characterisations of the formation of European social policy are
rejected. For instance, the assumption that the Commission
favours social policy, but Member States exercise their national
vetoes and oppose on national economic grounds, is too simplistic
to form a useful framework to understand the process of policy
formation. In fact a much more complex interplay between various
actors, both at EU level and at the level of Member States, takes
place. For example, in setting up a common transport policy, the
Commission favoured a free competition model, but some within
Member States, responding to pressures at national level, were
concerned about the social implications of an essentially deregulatory policy. As the fundamental philosophy behind the legal basis
provisions for a common transport policy was not clear,[35] this left
room for political manoeuvre. The Commission responded with
detailed harmonisation measures, many of which were blocked in
Council. Eventually, the European Parliament brought an action
before the European Court of Justice,[36] holding Council to account
for failure to enact common transport policy provisions, in which
Parliament enjoyed some success.[37]

Another assumption which should be treated carefully is the
assumption that some actors (such as multinational companies, or,
historically, the UK Conservative government) are always in oppo-

---

33. Ibid.
34. See Cram, *supra* n 29, pp 170–1 for a discussion of the *rapprochement* of these
    fundamentally different positions of integration theory. See also Armstrong,
    'New Institutionalism and EU Legal Studies' in Craig and Harlow (eds),
    Law-Making in the European Union (Kluwer, 1997).
35. With a basic commitment to a free market in transport, but with many
    exceptions to take account of the social aspects of transport and infrastructure.
36. Case 13/83 *European Parliament v Council (Re Transport Policy)* [1985] ECR
    1513.
37. See Wise and Gibb, *Single Market to Social Europe: The European Community
    in the 1990s* (Longman, 1993) pp 135–7.

sition to social policy initiatives, whereas others always support them. It may be the case that opposition simply enables actors to engage in 'cheap talk' about the social dimension.[38] Such an environment of 'cheap talk' may mask the real positions of governments and interest groups at the national level within the other Member States, and make it difficult to predict future positions.[39] For example, the ability to engage in 'cheap talk', behind the security of UK opposition, may help explain support for the Community Charter (1989) of the governments of some Member States such as Spain, which had much to lose economically by the impact of higher standards imposed at European level, and also Germany, whose conservative government could (safely) take the opportunity to appeal to its more socialist national supporters, employees and trade unions.[40]

Interactions within and between institutions at European and national level, in the formation of European social policy display various features.[41] Governments of the Member States may attempt to extract as much (financially, and in terms of sovereignty) from the EU as possible, while relinquishing as little as possible. Institutions may seek to gain more power from other institutions; sub-sections within institutions may attempt to gain more power as against other sub-sections. Actors other than the formal institutions, such as interest and pressure groups, political parties, and others, may seek to use the EU as an arena for their political agendas.

The first feature may help to explain many disputes in the social policy arena, with the insight that, often, such disputes are not actually concerned with social policy itself, but reflect a more fundamental debate about national sovereignty in the EU. For those who espouse a neo-liberal market model,[42] such as the former UK Conservative government, competence to implement what are conceived as harmful national regulatory social policies is (paradoxi-

---

38. Cram, *supra* n 29, p 59; Whiteford, 'W(h)ither Social Policy?' in Shaw and More (eds), *New Legal Dynamics of European Union* (OUP, 1995); Lange, 'The Politics of the Social Dimension' in Sbragia (ed), *Euro-Politics: Institutions and Policy-Making in the 'New' EC* (Brookings, 1992) p 242.

39. Lange, *supra* n 38, p 242. 40. Ibid.

41. These are described by Peters 'Bureaucratic Politics and the Institutions of the European Community' in Sbragia (ed) *Euro-Politics: Institutions and Policy-making in the 'New' EC* (Brookings, 1992) pp 106–7) using a model of four 'large games'.

42. See Chapter 1.

cally) not linked to national sovereignty.[43] It will be interesting to see whether the accession of the Scandinavian states of Sweden and Finland, whose governments, like that of Denmark, are not 'federalist' in the sovereignty debate, but are committed to generous welfare policies,[44] changes the dynamic on sovereignty and the implementation of European social policy in the medium term.

Council of Ministers and European Council

The Council of Ministers is the principal legislature of the European Community, and as such has a significant impact in terms of creating European social policy. The agreement of Council is necessary for all measures of binding and non-binding Community law. As described above, the enactment (or non-enactment) of provisions of social law is often determined by the 'legal basis' of the proposed measure, and especially the issue of whether unanimity or qualified majority support for the measure is required in Council.

Obviously, the most important Council for the purposes of social policy is the Social Affairs Council. Ministers in Social Affairs Council may act essentially to preserve national interests. As Streek[45] points out, even proposed legislation which appears to be concerned with integration of European social affairs may be essentially concerned with protecting the national sovereignty of hegemonic Member States. For example, the posted workers directive[46] essentially has the effect of protecting German employers, who, under the German social security system, make significant contributions to social funds, from competition from foreign employers who do not make such large social contributions.

The main characteristics of meetings of the Social Affairs Council are the failure to agree, resulting in lack of action, and a tendency to 'water down' proposals to the 'lowest-common-denominator' acceptable to all members, in order to gain agreement.[47] The dynamic of Council meetings, especially the requirement for at least a qualified majority of members to be in favour of a proposal, makes non-action easier than action. It is far more difficult to

---

43. Hagen, 'The Social Dimension: A Quest for a European Welfare State', in Ferge and Eivind (eds), *Social Policy in a Changing Europe* (Westview, 1992) p 297.
44. See Hagen, *supra* n 43, p 299.
45. Streek, *supra* n 31, pp 41–2.
46. Directive 96/71/EC OJ 1997 L 18/1.
47. Pierson and Leibfried, *supra* n 2, p 8. For instance, the provisions on maternity leave in Directive 92/85/EEC; see Chapter 5.

initiate new policies than to make 'non-decisions'. In the sphere of social policy, this makes it easier for those opposing change, for instance those espousing a neo-liberal model of non-intervention at European level, to succeed.[48]

However, it is important to beware of the tendency to characterise Council members as simply seeking to safeguard national interests. Ministers in the Social Affairs Council may also be considering the policy interests represented by their ministries, as against other national ministries or departments. These concerns do not necessarily divide ministers along national lines. Since Council meetings are held in private,[49] it is difficult ascertain their dynamics, and the relative weight of different interests represented.

Although the Social Affairs Council is the most significant in terms of the formation of European social policy, other Councils, for instance the Economic and Financial Affairs Council (Ecofin), also play an important role. Ecofin is one of most important councils[50] generally speaking, as it is responsible for coordinating and harmonising monetary and fiscal policies among Member States. Decisions made in Ecofin have an impact on all European policy areas, and are especially important in the social policy area for two reasons. The first is that social policy regulation has to take place against the drive to deregulation and flexibility which Ecofin ministers tend to support. The second is that the distributive elements of European social policies have a direct relationship to monetary and fiscal affairs.

An example of the influence of Ecofin in social affairs may be seen in the action plan concerned with combating unemployment[51] which relies heavily on a report by the Economic Policy Committee presented to Ecofin Council. The action plan stresses three pressing problems of the labour market: first, the lack of 'work incentives', arising from 'inappropriate' levels of social security benefits and high rates of marginal taxation, which create disincentives to work; second, the costs of work, that is high indirect costs and minimum wages create disincentives to employers to recruit labour; and third, the 'institutional, social and general

48. Lange, *supra* n 38, p 232.
49. The Code of Practice on Transparency in Council agreed after the Edinburgh Summit in 1992 has not improved this situation, see Wallace and Wallace, *Policy-Making in the European Union* (Oxford University Press, 1996) p 59. See also Council and Commission Code of Conduct 1995 (Bull EU 10/95); Shaw, *Law of the European Union* (Macmillan, 1996) pp 118–19.
50. Peters, *supra* n 41, p 80. 51. COM(94) 529.

background against which labour markets operate'. The conceptualisation of the problem in this way leads (unsurprisingly) to the conclusion that greater flexibility, not social regulation, is required.

Sometimes the lack of consensus in the Council of Ministers can only be overcome by agreement at European Council (summit) level. This is the '*haute politique*' of European Union governance. At summit meetings, a 'package deal' can often be agreed, which links agreement in various different policy areas so that all Member States derive some benefit and Community policy can move forward. Social policy formation may therefore be dependent on other, totally unconnected policy areas. Decision-making in the European Council relies heavily on coalition building. The historical account in Chapter 2 shows examples of coalitions of shared perspectives among national governments of the Members States, which enabled the development of European social policy.

European Commission

In addition to Council, the European Commission also plays a key role in policy formation and enactment of legislation in the European Union. The day-to-day work of Commission bureaucrats has a significant influence upon the environment in which the Council and European Council take policy decisions.[52] The European Commission has gradually increased its power through a bureaucratic process of promoting common policies and standards, at European level and through its contacts with national bureaucracies and with national and transnational interest groups.[53] The Commission may often be engaged in attempting to increase its competence, by means of a strategy of 'purposeful opportunism'.[54] The Commission is therefore likely to pursue only those goals judged to be attainable, in order to keep integration moving and to enhance its own status.[55]

The Commission acts as both legislature and executive for the

---

[52] Cram, 'The European Commission as a Multi-Organization: Social Policy and IT Policy in the EU' (1994) 1 JEPP 195–217, p 196.

[53] Cram, *supra* n 29; Peters, *supra* n 41, p 76.

[54] Cram, *supra* n 29; Cram, *supra* n 52, p 197.

[55] Cram, *supra* n 29, p 5; Lange, *supra* n 38, p 255. This is a clear theme in Ross, *Jacques Delors* (Polity, 1995) which describes Delors' efforts to revitalise European social policy.

European Union. Too strong a focus on the Commission's efforts to increase its competence as against other institutions, especially Council, might lead to a conceptualisation of Commission and Council as adversaries. This would be misleading.[56] As the members of Council (the governments and administrations in Member States) also play both legislative and executive roles, in order for policy to be implemented effectively (or indeed at all), it is essential that national interests are fed into European policies. In practice, the Commission and Council are in a complex relationship of interdependence.

Nowhere is this interdependence more evident than in links between the Commission and Councils in the 'comitology' of the EU. These committees, comprising ministers from national executives and chaired by Commission officials, link national bureaucracies to the EU institutions. The committees are extremely important as they work out details of policy – for instance, by taking decisions on who will benefit from EU finance – and mechanisms for enforcement of legislation. For instance, decisions on the Commission's 'own initiative' structural funding are taken by management committee.[57] The Committee for Proprietary Medical Products grants authorisations for the marketing of new medical products in the EU.[58] The comitology system is characterised by extreme privacy and an almost total lack of openness.[59]

As Cram notes,[60] it is important to avoid a view of the Commission as a 'monolithic unit', but to see it as an organisation within which separate parts may have different priorities and agendas. Various 'sub-sections' within the European Commission – for instance, individual Commissioners, the President, the separate Directorates General – may play particular roles in the formation of European social policy, or have differing aims, aspirations and agendas for European social policy.

---

56. Ludlow 'The European Commission' in Keohane and Hoffmann (eds), *The New European Community: Decisionmaking and Institutional Change* (Westview, 1991) p 87.
57. See Chapter 9. 58. See Chapter 7.
59. As Weiler notes ('The EU Belongs to its Citizens: Three Immodest Proposals' (1997) 22 ELRev 150–6, p 151) it is not even possible to determine the *number* of committees, much less their precise remit, membership and so on. See further Vos, 'The Rise of Committees' (1997) 3 ELJ, 210–29; Bradley, 'The European Parliament and Comitology: On the Road to Nowhere' 3 ELJ (1997), 230–54.
60. Cram, *supra* n 29, pp 157–8, 160–6; Cram, *supra* n 52, p 196.

The Commission (in the sense of the Commissioners) as a whole is, theoretically speaking, a collegiate system, according to which any individual Commissioner can speak with authority on almost any business. Therefore, the portfolio held by a particular Commissioner, and the Directorates General (DGs) within that portfolio, might not be regarded as particularly significant. However, in reality, the position of particular Commissioners who seek to impose their position on a policy issue is likely to be stronger or weaker, depending on whether the proposal is within the area of their portfolio.[61] The influence of the Commissioner responsible for social affairs (at present Pádraig Flynn) on social policy is likely to be greater than that of other Commissioners.

As the Commission as a whole may seek to increase its competence, so may the individual Directorates General (DGs) within the Commission. DGs may attempt to increase their competence by getting their preferred issues onto the legislative agenda.[62] In addition to promoting 'hard law' proposals, DG V (Social Affairs) has made judicious use of 'soft law' and small-scale direct expenditure programmes in order to advance its 'competence' or at least its areas of interest.[63] DGs may also seek to define policy issues so as to fall within their remit. For instance, DG XXII might seek to define vocational training as an education issue, whereas DG V might seek to define it as part of labour market policy.[64] Different DGs also have their own cultures in terms of organisation and policy emphasis,[65] which they may also seek to advance. All of these differences may influence the formation and content of social policy. For instance, the White Paper on Social Policy and White Paper on Growth, Competitiveness and Employment were prepared by different DGs. This may explain the contradictions between the two documents and the differences in their focus.[66]

The main DG relevant for the formation of European social policy is DG V, which deals with employment, industrial relations and social affairs. The activities of other DGs, such as DG XVI, (regional policies), DG XXII (education, vocational training, youth policy, and the European Foundation for the Improvement of

---

61. Ludlow, *supra* n 56, p 90.
62. Cram, *supra* n 29, pp 157–8, pp 160–6; Cram, *supra* n 52, p 197.
63. See above. 64. Peters, *supra* n 41, p 107; see Chapter 6.
65. Wallace and Wallace, *supra* n 49, p 48.
66. See Kuper, 'The Green and White Papers of the European Union: The Apparent Goal of Reduced Social Benefits' (1994) 4 JESP 129–137.

Living and Working Conditions), and DG XII, (science, research and development, which includes some aspects of European health policy) may also have direct effects on some core aspects of national social policies. However, as most European policy developments are likely to have a social dimension of some sort, other DGs, such as DG II (economic and financial affairs), DG III (industry), DG IV (competition, including state aids to industry), DG VI (agriculture), and DG VII (transport) may also have some influence.

The relative autonomy of the EU institutions may help to explain why there are any measures of EC social policy at all, given the opposition of governments of Member States, and the need for agreement in Council. The desire of the Commission to increase its sphere of competence is one factor in the development of European social policy. In particular, the role of DG V has proved significant in this area. The other factor is the relatively costless nature of regulatory policy making.[67] Council may give support for Commission proposals in the social area because the costs inherent in proposed new policies will fall on private actors, such as employees, not national governments. So, for instance, policies on vocational training, traditionally the responsibility of employers, have enjoyed much more success at European level than education policies, which are a state-financed activity.[68]

European Parliament

The role of the European Parliament in the formation of EC law and policy is, as is well known, limited to consultation, and, in certain circumstances, negative assent.[69] The Treaty of Amsterdam amendments, extending the codecision procedure to most areas of policy making, may enhance the European Parliament's status as co-legislator. The European Parliament may attempt to increase its influence on European policies in general, by asserting its own powers and prerogatives against those of the other institutions.[70] In the particular area of the social dimension, the European Parliament may seek to advance its own powers by direct reference to its

---

67. See further Chapter 3. Cram, *supra* n 29; Majone *supra* n 2; Cram, 'Calling the Tune without Paying the Piper? Social Policy and IT Policy in the EU' 21 *Policy and Politics* (1993) 135–146, pp 135–7.
68. Cram, *supra* n 67, p 142.
69. Article 189a EC, Article 189b EC, Article 189c EC.
70. Peters, *supra* n 41, p 92.

democratic mandate and its direct relationship with the 'peoples of Europe'.[71] As the only EU institution directly elected by the EU electorate, the European Parliament may seek to claim that its democratic mandate should give it an increased power to determine social affairs.

The European Parliament also seeks to enforce its prerogatives, especially as against the Commission, in a legal context, by means of actions under Article 173[72] or 175 EC[73] brought before the European Court of Justice. An example of this institutional interplay was given above, concerning transport policy. Another example may be found in the European Parliament's challenge to Directive 90/366/EEC,[74] on rights of residence for students, on the grounds that the correct legal basis for that directive required the cooperation procedure, not the basic procedure.[75] Directive 90/366/EEC was subsequently replaced – with greater influence for the European Parliament – by the virtually identical Directive 93/96/EEC.[76]

As with the Commission, it is important to differentiate subsections within the European Parliament. The current left/green bias among MEPs taken as a whole tends to lead to a conceptualisation of the European Parliament as an advocate of a social justice model of European social policy. However, this view may mask differences in approaches to social policy between parties within the European Parliament.[77] Also, the influence of different committees, whose remit includes social policy issues, such as the Social Affairs Committee, and others, should be taken into account.

The social partners

The 'social partners' – representatives of management and labour[78] – play a role both in the implementation of social policy measures

71. Lange, *supra* n 38, p 255.
72. Judicial review of Commission action.
73. Requiring Commission to act, where it has failed to do so.
74. OJ 1990 L 180/30.
75. Case C-295/90 *European Parliament v Council* [1992] ECR I-4193.
76. OJ L 1993 L 317/59. See Chapter 6.
77. For further details, see Hix, 'Parties at the European Level and the Legitimacy of EU Socio-Economic Policy' (1995) 33 JCMS 527–554, p 539.
78. See COM(93) 600 for the criteria to determine which bodies are included; Barnard, *EC Employment Law* (Wiley, 1996), p 71; Nielsen and Szyszczak, *The Social Dimension of the European Union* (Handelshojskolens Forlag, 1997), p 48. There is some disagreement concerning who the social partners should be, see Case T-135/96 OJ 1996 C 318/21 UEAPME action for annulment of the parental leave agreement.

and in their formation. Article 3 SPA requires the Commission to consult the social partners before submitting 'proposals in the social policy field', a phrase which presumably refers at least to the matters set out in Article 2(1) and (3) SPA.[79] These matters are mainly concerned with labour law, but include 'the integration of persons excluded from the labour market' (Article 2(1) SPA) and 'social security and social protection of workers' (Article 2(3) SPA). The social partners are therefore involved in EU-level social policy development not only in the area of labour law, but also in social law more generally, in the sense used in this book.

According to Article 4 SPA, the social partners, may if they wish, initiate a process of dialogue between them, which may lead to 'an agreement'. The agreement may be implemented by national measures, or by a Council decision on a proposal from the Commission (Article 4(2) SPA). Thus, the social partners may play a key role in the formation of European social legislation. The Treaty of Amsterdam will, if ratified, incorporate the SPA provisions within a new 'Social Chapter'. New Articles 118–118b EC will incorporate the provisions of Articles 2–4 SPA with very few changes.

The power of the social partners to agree measures of European social legislation without reference to the European Parliament has been questioned by the Parliament, which is, in effect, excluded from the legislative process.[80] If the appropriateness of the social partners' role in development of European *labour* law is in question, then their role in the development of social security and social protection legislation must be even more so, as the interests at stake in such legislation are wider than those represented by management and labour. Moreover, even ostensibly 'labour' legislation may often include social security or social protection provisions. For instance, the proposed Council directive based on the agreement on part-time work extends (on a pro rata basis) equality of treatment in working conditions to atypical workers. 'Working conditions' may include for instance the right to sick pay, maternity (and paternity) leave, and pension rights, all of which are concerned with social security or social protection more generally.

[79.] But see Bercusson, *European Labour Law* (Butterworths, 1996), p 547.

[80.] See COM(96) 448 final Commission Communication on the Development of Social Dialogue at Community level, concerning the negotiation of the parental leave agreement; Nielsen and Szyszczak, *supra* n 78, p 49; Barnard, 'The United Kingdom, the "Social Chapter" and the Amsterdam Treaty' (1997) 26 ILJ 275–282, p 279.

Consultative institutions and the 'civil dialogue'

Other consultative bodies, such as the Economic and Social Committee (ECOSOC) and Committee of the Regions, also play a role in the formation of European social policy. ECOSOC is a long-standing institution, mainly concerned with labour policy, which gives it a particular perspective on more general social affairs. The Committee of the Regions, established by the TEU, plays a role in the implementation of the EC's structural funds, especially the ERDF.

A network of non-governmental organisations (NGOs) and other bodies active in the social field has also developed, with whom the Commission consults in preparing its social policy initiatives and measures. This network was placed on a more formal basis in 1996 with the creation of the 'civil dialogue', bringing together around 1,000 representatives of NGOs and other bodies in a 'Forum on Social Policy'. The idea of the civil dialogue is to promote collaboration between various social actors in the Member States, such as churches, voluntary organisations, pressure groups, charities and other voluntary providers of social services, and regional and local governments, and the EU institutions.

The Forum's remit was to discuss a report of the Comité des Sages entitled 'For a Europe of Civil and Social Rights'.[81] The report stresses social citizenship entitlements and the need for representative and participatory democracy. Grassroots involvement in the discussion of the report was promoted through a series of Commission-funded meetings in the Member States. The establishment of a formalised process of civil dialogue is likely to have a significant influence on the future directions of European social policy. Consultation of such a broad range of groups concerned with social matters by the EU institutions may give the interests they represent an enhanced status within the EU policy-making process, and may give a voice to groups of actors which hitherto have been too disorganised and diverse to be effectively heard at the EU level.[82]

---

81. Brussels, October 1995–February 1996; the Comité des Sages was set up in line with the Commission's medium term social action programme 1995–97.
82. The author is grateful to Fiona Williams for early sight of her paper 'Contestations of Gender 'Race'/Ethnicity and Citizenship in EU Social Policy', presented to the European Sociological Association on 28 August 1997, in which these ideas are elaborated.

European regulatory agencies

The Maastricht Treaty established various new European regulatory agencies. These are institutions staffed by specialised policy experts in specific policy areas. They have delegated authority to take decisions on the regulation of their areas of expertise. For instance, the European Medicines Evaluation Authority grants EU-wide authorisation for the marketing of new biotechnology and high-technology products, once it is satisfied that the products meet consumer safety standards. These new regulatory agencies are likely to have an influence on EC policy making, especially regulation, in the areas for which they will develop expertise. Their actions may increase 'regulation by bureaucrats', as opposed to regulation by politicians, thus raising questions of legitimacy.[83] However, a more positive view is that delegating regulatory responsibility to independent regulatory agencies may actually *increase* accountability. Such agencies are insulated from political pressures, and so, provided that mechanisms for controlling these agencies – such as 'clearly defined statutory objectives, procedural constraints, judicial review, professional standards, monitoring by interest groups [and] even inter-agency rivalry' – are put in place, these are likely to be more effective than partial and limited accountability to an elected parliament (either at national or at EU level).[84]

The European Court of Justice

The European Court of Justice also plays a significant role as a policy-making institution of the EU. The 'activist' stance of the Court is well documented elsewhere. The judges of the Court are often seen as advancing a 'mission' or 'idea of Europe', based on integration through law.[85] The Court's method has had various effects on the formation of EC social law and policy. Generally speaking, the main contribution of the Court is the extensive inter-

---

[83.] Majone, *supra* n 2, p 166; Majone, 'A European regulatory state?', in Richardson (ed), *European Union: Power and Policy-making* (Routledge, 1996), pp 273–5.

[84.] Majone, *supra* n 83, p 274.

[85.] See, seminally, Rasmussen, *On Law and Policy in the European Court of Justice* (Martinus Nijhoff, 1986); more recently Neill, *The European Court of Justice: A Case Study in Judicial Activism* (Conference paper, 1995); Pierson and Leibfried, *supra* n 2, pp 11–12.

pretation of provisions of Community law beyond their essentially economic aims.[86] An extreme example is Case 186/87 *Cowan v Trésor Public*,[87] in which the Court extended the entitlement in Community law of freedom to provide services to include a right to compensation for injury resulting from criminal acts for non-nationals from other Member States visiting a Member State as a tourist, on the same terms as nationals.

A second, and significant, contribution of the Court to the formation of European social policy is the Court's development, through its interpretative rulings, of legal principles which are subsequently reflected in Treaty amendments or other provisions of hard law. For instance, in the sphere of education and vocational training, the Court held in Case 293/83 *Gravier*[88] and Case 24/86 *Blaizot*[89] that university students with the nationality of another Member State should be entitled to equal treatment with nationals. The spectre of uncoordinated movement of students relying on this case law prompted the Council to adopt the ERASMUS programme.[90] Subsequently, Article 127 EC, restricting EC policy in education to a 'flanking policy', was inserted in the Treaty at Maastricht.[91]

The Court has occasionally contributed to the development of EC social law by promoting a retreat of EC action in a social policy matter. The Court may have acted to preserve its own powers, and the cohesion of the European Community as a whole, in the face of the intransigent opposition of other powerful actors, especially Member States. A good example of this, in the area of health policy, is the Court's ruling in Case C-159/90 *Grogan*,[92] in which the Court did not take advantage of the opportunity to extend the principle of freedom to provide services to cover the right of students unions to advertise the services of abortion clinics in Ireland. More recently, this type of contribution from the Court is becoming more common, as more imaginative (and therefore potentially more disruptive to national social policies) interpretations of EC law are brought before the Court. For instance, in the

---

86. Moxton-Browne, 'Social Europe', in Lodge (ed), *The European Community and the Challenge of the Future* (Pinter, 1993) pp 161–2.
87. [1989] ECR 195. 88. [1985] ECR 593. 89. [1988] ECR 379.
90. Shaw, 'Twin-track Social Europe – The Inside Track', in O'Keeffe and Twomey (eds), *Legal Issues of the Maastricht Treaty* (Wiley, 1994) pp 295–311, 307.
91. For another example, see the transport policy case referred to above.
92. [1991] ECR I-4685.

recent case of *Sodemare*[93] the Court was faced with a claim by a Luxembourg (profit-making) company, which set up subsidiaries in Italy to run old people's homes there. Italian law entitled only non-profit-making operation of such homes to be reimbursed from public funds for providing social welfare services of a 'healthcare nature', such as provided by Sodemare's homes. Sodemare claimed that the relevant Italian law was contrary to EC law, *inter alia*, concerning freedom of establishment. Unlike its Advocate General (whose opinion was that the Italian law was indirectly discriminatory, and considered the possibility of justification), the Court held[94] that Community law does not detract from the power of Member States to organise their social welfare provisions, and that the rule excluding profit-making operations was an essential part of Italy's social welfare system.

The Court may play a role in mediating interactions between the other institutions and the Member States through the legal process, which may affect social policy formation. This is particularly the case with judicial review procedures, especially those concerned with competence and legal basis issues. For instance, the UK government has challenged the Commission's decisions under the 'Poverty 4' programme, on the grounds that the Commission had no legal competence to allocate finances to 'Poverty 4' without authority from the Council.[95]

Interest groups

The final group of institutional actors considered here, as contributing to the formation of European social policy, are non-governmental interest groups. These fall into two broad types – 'Eurogroups' (that is, those groups officially recognised by European institutions)[96] and lobbying organisations. The influence of interest groups is particularly relevant in Council and in the Commission. Council ministers are particularly sensitive to pressure from national interest groups on social issues. Where regulatory social policy is proposed, the short-term consequences of new policies are widely debated in the public domain. The dynamics of the formation of

---

93. Case C-70/95 Sodemare [1997] ECR I-3395.
94. Following Cases C159/91 and C-160/91 *Poucet* and *Pistre* [1993] ECR I-637, and Case 238/82 *Duphar* [1984] ECR 523.
95. Case C–106/96 OJ 1996 C 145/7; see further Chapter 8.
96. Such as ETUC and UNICE; see also above re 'civil dialogue'.

distributive policies, on the other hand, are much less transparent, and so the influence of interest groups is likely to be less significant.[97]

In addition to seeking to influence national actors in Council, an increasing number of interest groups are organising on a European level, often with Commission support, and bringing their lobbying efforts directly to the institutions in Brussels.[98] 'Euro-lobbying' has traditionally been dominated by commercial interests, but, as European Union social policy develops, interest groups concerned with social affairs are likely to continue to proliferate.[99] Barnard describes the relationship between interest groups and the Commission as 'symbiotic'.[100] From the point of view of interest groups, relations with the Commission provide an invaluable opportunity to seek to influence future policies and proposals. The Commission can provide interest groups with information about its policies and plans, and the legitimating status which being consulted brings. From the Commission's point of view, interest groups can provide information independent from official data collected and interpreted by national governments. They also give the Commission direct access to interests of various individuals and groups at a sub-national level, thus serving (at least to an extent) to increase the legitimacy of Commission action.[101]

Effect of institutional structure on social policy

The structure of policy making in the EU is highly decentralised and disparate, with actors at both European and national levels shaping both the policy process and outcomes. One consequence of this is the importance of coalitions, and loosely organised 'policy networks' in the formation of policy. Bargaining takes place, and coalitions are formed, enabling decisions to be taken between those who share policy interests, for instance national ministries, specialist agencies, national interest groups, European-wide interest

---

97. Lange, *supra* n 38, p 238.
98. Cram, *supra* n 29, pp 125–132; Pierson and Leibfried, *supra* n 2, pp 13–14.
99. Barnard, 'A European Litigation Strategy: the Case of the Equal Opportunities Commission', in Shaw and More (eds), *New Legal Dynamics of European Union* (OUP, 1995) p 253.
100. Barnard, *supra* n 99, p 267. See also Commission *White Paper, European Social Policy: A Way Forward for the Union* encouraging involvement of voluntary groups COM(94) 333, p 57.
101. Cram, *supra* n 29, pp 137–9; Barnard, *supra* n 99, p 267.

groups, the relevant DGs in Brussels, and committees of the European Parliament.[102]

Policy making under these conditions is likely to result in a relative lack of coherence and uniformity in policy outcomes. The predominance of interest politics, coalitions, and bargaining between those seeking to protect special interests, is likely to produce European social policies which are fragmented, partial, piecemeal and poorly coordinated. Social policy development is likely to be especially prone to lowest-common-denominator agreements and to policy packages.[103] Actors involved in social policy making are likely to attempt to escape the gridlock created by the need for support in Council which is not present. One such method of escape is to rely on social policy developments brought about by the European Court of Justice. The Court's apparently expansive view of its own role and that of the European Union in social affairs has, at least in the past, lent itself to this type of policy making.[104]

It is highly unlikely that a European social policy based on broad principles, developed by stable political and social coalitions,[105] will emerge under the current institutional structure. This raises serious questions about the legitimacy of European social policies, and whether the current situation represents the most appropriate trade-off between 'making decisions that are European' and 'making the best possible decisions in the name of Europe'.[106] Court-led policy development cannot provide the solutions here, as it is dependent in practice upon the actions brought before the Court, and it does not take sufficient account of political interests not represented in Court hearings. As Leibfried and Pierson[107] point out, multi-tiered systems make centralised policy making difficult for a good reason, that is, to protect national and local interests. If those protections are circumvented, it is likely to create resentment. Formation of a coherent, principled European social policy would have to arise from a reformed EU in which the current democratic deficit had been effectively addressed.

Having set the scene in terms of the historical, legal and institutional contexts for the formation of European social policy, and the enactment of EC social law, the remainder of the book is

102. Peters, *supra* n 41, p 117.   103. Pierson and Leibfried *supra* n 2, p 35.
104. Pierson and Leibfried, *supra* n 2, pp 36–7.
105. Lange, *supra* n 38, pp 228–9.   106. Peters, *supra* n 41, p 120.
107. Pierson and Liebfried, *supra* n 2, p 38.

concerned with its substance. The discussion introduces the main areas of regulatory EC social law and policy – social security, education, health and social assistance or welfare – and the EC's redistributive policies in the form of the structural funds. The issue of legitimacy is reconsidered in the concluding chapter.

CHAPTER FIVE

Social security

Introduction

For the purposes of this chapter, social security is defined in accordance with the traditional categories of risk against which social security provides insurance: illness, invalidity, industrial accidents, old age, death (social security provided for survivors), maternity and family needs.[1] Social security is traditionally understood to provide insurance for employed and self-employed people (and, by extension, for their families) who are no longer available to work for one of the above reasons. Social security is to be contrasted with general measures of 'social assistance', which provide a minimum level of protection (for instance, a minimum income) to ensure that individuals' basic human living requirements are met.[2]

EC law in the arena of social security is not concerned with 'positive' regulatory harmonisation of national social security laws. Neither top-down regulation of national social security regimes nor their replacement with a European-level social security regime is on the EC policy agenda. Rather, most EC social security law is concerned with coordination of national social security schemes, as part of the free movement of persons provisions. Free movement of persons is one of the 'four freedoms' which the Treaty accords central status for the purposes of formation of the internal market. Some coordination of national social security provision is necessary to prevent persons who move from one Member State to another (for the purposes of employment, or connected purposes)

[1.] ILO Convention No 102, 1956.
[2.] Holloway, *Social Policy Harmonisation in the European Community* (Gower, 1981) p 6; for further discussion of social assistance see Chapter 8.

suffering detriment in respect of social security entitlements as a consequence of having exercised their free movement rights. The principal coordination instrument is Regulation 1408/71/EEC,[3] which is supplemented by Regulation 574/72/ EEC,[4] providing for its detailed implementation in the Member States.[5]

Regulatory measures of EC law which have a bearing on national social security law do exist. However, their aim is not to put in place European-level social security rules. One of the most important of these is the provision in Regulation 1612/68/EEC,[6] Article 7(2), which entitles EU citizen (EUC) migrant workers and members of their families to 'the same social and tax advantages as national workers'. This provision, guaranteeing non-discrimination on grounds of nationality, has proved significant in extending protection of national social security systems to EUC migrant workers, especially since the concept of 'social advantage' has been held by the European Court of Justice to cover provisions of social assistance, in addition to social security.

Social security regimes of the Member States are also affected by European-level provisions on non-discrimination on grounds of sex. Directives 79/7/EEC[7] and 86/378/EEC,[8] imposing sex equality in state social security and occupational social security schemes respectively, have affected national social security systems by rendering unlawful measures within them which discriminate on grounds of sex. The European Court of Justice has held that Article 119 EC (equal pay for men and women) requires sex equality in most aspects of occupational pension schemes. The pregnancy and maternity Directive 92/85/EEC[9] makes specific provision for entitlements to maternity leave and maternity benefits.

However, it must be stressed that these provisions do not add up to a European Community policy on social security. It seems absolutely clear that any wide-spread harmonisation in this area will only come about by means of voluntary *convergence* of national schemes, if Member States adapt their own regimes

3. OJ 1971 L 149/2; OJ Sp Ed 1971 II p 416.
4. OJ 1972 L 74/1.
5. For criticism of the coordination approach, see Laske, 'The Impact of the Single European Market on Social Protection for Migrant Workers' (1993) 30 CMLRev 515–539.
6. OJ Sp Ed 1968 II p 475.   7. OJ 1979 L 6/24.
8. OJ 1986 L 225/40, as amended by Directive 96/97 EC OJ 1997 L 46/20.
9. OJ 1992 L 348/1.

towards a European Community 'average standard'. The EU institutions have issued various non-binding instruments to assist this possible convergence, and to ensure that it is along the lines to which EC social policy aspires.[10] Whether these convergence-type instruments will lead to the formation of a 'levelled up' common policy in the future is a matter for conjecture and debate.[11] The Commission's proposals to Council, although affirming commitment in broad terms to a high level of social protection in the Member States, actually reveal in the detail a general tendency towards cost containment, and privatisation of social security provision.[12]

The relevant legislation: context and objectives

Regulations 1408/71[13] and 574/72[14] (which contains detailed implementing provisions) were adopted to replace the early Regulations 3 and 4 (which were actually a product of intergovernmental agreement, and were subsequently adopted as Community law) in the wake of a series of innovative rulings of the European Court of Justice. The legal basis of Regulations 1408/71 and 574/72 is Article 51 EC, which empowers Council to adopt 'such measures in the field of social security as are necessary to provide freedom of movement for workers'. As regulations, they are directly applicable in the Member States, and may be enforced by individuals before national courts and tribunals. They may also apply, in certain circumstances, to EEA nationals, and to nationals of states with which the EU has entered into Association or Co-operation Agreements.[15]

The Regulations, still in force today, have undergone many

10. Eg the Council has issued recommendations on the common elements of a scheme of social protection for the Member States (OJ 1992 L 245/48) and on common criteria for social assistance and guaranteed minimum income schemes (OJ 1992 L 245/46). See further Chapter 8.
11. Barnard, 'A European Litigation Strategy: The Case of the Equal Opportunities Commission' in Shaw and More (eds), *New Legal Dynamics of European Union* (OUP, 1995) pp 155–7; Luckhaus, 'European Social Security Law' in Ogus and Wikeley (eds), *The Law of Social Security* (Butterworths, 1995) pp 696–8.
12. See eg COM(95) 457 final, esp 57–80.
13. OJ 1971 L 149/2.   14. OJ 1972 L 74/1.
15. Turkey, Morocco, Algeria, Tunisia. Nielsen and Szyszczak, *The Social Dimension of the European Union* (Handelshojskolens Forlag, 1997) p 130; Burrows, 'Non-Discrimination and Social Security in Co-operation Agreements'

amendments.[16] Together they form a complex and intricate set of legal rules, which is further complicated by a large number of interpretative rulings from the European Court of Justice.[17] The application of the EC regulations within the Member States takes place in the context of the different rules on entitlement in each Member State, the different types of benefit available in national legal systems, and the different economic and social circumstances under which Member States decide to make benefits available.[18] For example, most Member States have an unemployment benefit scheme for the whole workforce, whereas Greece and Spain exclude some sectors, and Denmark and France rely on an unemployment insurance system.[19] The different national social security systems of the Member States are so embedded in national practices that reforms often take little account of EC measures.[20] However, the imperatives of EC law may make policy options which avoid the application of EC law more appealing to national policy makers.[21]

For the purposes of this book, treatment of the coordination rules of the regulations cannot be at a level of close detail, but will be concerned with broad principles and objectives. There are four over-arching principles which find expression in Regulation 1408/71. These are the prohibition of discrimination on grounds of nationality; the principle of aggregation and apportionment (or

(1997) 22 ELRev 166–169; Luckhaus, *supra* n 11, p 698; Storey, 'United Kingdom Social Security Law: European and International Dimensions' (1994) 1 Journal of Social Security Law 110–132 and 142–154, pp 113 and 118.

16. For the latest codified version see Regulation 118/97/EC OJ 1997 L 28/1.

17. See Peers, '"Social Advantages" and Discrimination in Employment: Case Law Clarified and Confirmed' (1997) 22 ELRev 157–165; Eichenhofer, 'Coordination of social security and equal treatment of men and women in employment: recent social security judgments of the Court of Justice' (1993) 30 CMLRev 1021–1042; Munroe, 'A Review of the Case Law of the Court of Justice on Migrant Workers and Social Security' (1990) 27 CMLRev 547–571; Morgan, 'A Review of the Case Law of the Court of Justice on Migrant Workers and Social Security' (1987) 24 CMLRev 483–507. On the importance of the role of the Court, see Pierson and Leibfried, 'Multitiered Institutions and the Making of Social Policy' in Leibfried and Pierson (eds), *European Social Policy: Between Fragmentation and Integration* (Brookings, 1995) pp 43–65.

18. Pieters (ed), *Introduction into the Social Security Law of the Member States of the European Community* (Bruylant, 1990); see Chapter 4 for a typology of welfare regimes represented within the Member States.

19. Pieters (ed), *supra* n 18, pp 37, 49–50, 76, 86–8; Wikeley, 'Migrant Workers and Unemployment Benefit in the European Community' (1988) Journal of Social Welfare Law 300–315, p 305.

20. Laske, *supra* n 5, p 517.

21. Pierson and Liebfried, *supra* n 17.

proraterisation) of benefit rights; the exportability of benefits from Member State to Member State; and the 'single state' rule in terms of affiliation, liability to contribute, and benefit entitlement (which incorporates the principle of non-duplication of benefits).[22]

Luckhaus[23] identifies two competing views of the broad objectives of Regulation 1408/71. According to one view, the purpose of the Regulation is to remove disadvantage from migrant workers, and thereby promote free movement. The focus on disadvantage is a 'constant feature'[24] of the Court's jurisprudence, and as a consequence migrant workers may actually *benefit* from the application of the EC rules. The other view maintains that the regulation's objective is to remove the territorial character of national social security systems of the Member States, which is regarded as being the main obstacle to the free movement of workers.[25] Entitlement to social security is to be placed on an individual, rather than a territorial basis. Individuals should be *neither disadvantaged nor advantaged* as a result of the application of the EC's coordinating rules, which should merely provide a 'logically coherent, technically faultless system'.[26]

Regulation 1612/68 has the objective of securing freedom of movement for workers within the European Union. Enacted on the basis of Article 49 EC, Regulation 1612/68 operates by means of the specific application of the principle of non-discrimination on grounds of nationality, expressed in Article 6 EC. Under the regulation, national rules preventing or hindering employment of EUCs in Member States of which they are not nationals are rendered inapplicable. In addition, EUC migrant workers may not be treated differently from national workers. The extension of equality of treatment to 'social and tax advantages'[27] is particularly

---

22. Article 3; Article 18(1), Article 38, Article 45, Article 64, Article 67, Article 72; Article 10(1); Article 12(1) and 46(3). Nielsen and Szyszczak, *supra* n 15, pp 130–1; Barnard, *EC Employment Law* (Wiley, 1996) pp 140–5; Luckhaus, *supra* n 11, pp 706–13; Storey, *supra* n 15, p 112; Wyatt and Dashwood, *European Community Law* (Sweet and Maxwell, 1993) pp 314–15; Steiner, 'Social Security for EC Migrants' (1992) JSWFL 33–47, pp 34, 38–45.
23. *Supra* n 11, pp 699–701. See also Nielsen and Szyszczak, *supra* n 15, pp 131–2.
24. Luckhaus, *supra* n 11, p 699.
25. See Cornelissen, 'The Principle of Territoriality and the Community Regulations on Social Security (Regulations 1408/71 and 574/72)' (1996) 33 CMLRev 439–471.
26. Luckhaus, *supra* n 11, p 700.
27. Regulation 1612/68, Article 7(2).

significant for the purposes of this chapter. Migrant EUC workers are entitled to the same treatment as nationals under the national social security scheme of the Member State in which they work.

The requirements of the principle of non-discrimination on grounds of nationality in this context have been the subject of many interpretative rulings from the European Court of Justice. The Court has adopted a broad interpretation of the concept of 'social advantage'. On the concept of discrimination, the Court's jurisprudence has been constant in respect of 'reverse discrimination' – that is, the less favourable treatment of nationals than EUC migrants by national law. The objective of the EC's free movement of labour provisions is to create a single European market in labour. Therefore, these rules apply only where a worker has exercised his or her right to migrate under EC law. Workers cannot benefit from the application of EC law unless they are migrant workers. Thus, EC law does not prevent 'reverse discrimination'. Because it may operate to give migrant workers greater legal protection than other workers, this position echoes the Court's 'disadvantage' approach to interpretation of Regulation 1408/71.

Benefits which may be claimed as social advantages under Regulation 1612/68 are not exportable, but may be enjoyed only in the Member State of employment and residence. Therefore, migrant workers who return to their Member State of nationality can no longer claim benefits under that regulation. In addition, although Regulation 1612/68 requires that migrant EUCs be given *the same level* of social protection as nationals of the Member State in which they work, it does not require *any particular level* of social protection. Therefore, Member States are free to be as generous or as restrained in their social security policies as they wish, subject only to the requirement that EUCs be treated the same as national workers under those policies.

The sex equality in social security directives (Directive 79/7 and Directive 86/378) is based on Article 235 EC and Articles 100 and 235 EC respectively. The original intention of the Commission was to enact the content of Directive 79/7 in what eventually became Directive 76/207 on equal treatment of men and women in employment.[28] However, lack of consensus in Council made it politically expedient to separate out the employment provisions from

28. COM(75) 36 final.

the social security provisions.[29] Directives 79/7 and 86/378 envisage a *progressive* move towards sex equality in social security, and each provide for various areas in which full sex equality may be deferred by the Member States. However, relying on Article 119 EC and the 'general principle' of equality, the European Court of Justice has significantly eroded these exclusions through a series of rulings. Directive 96/97, amending Directive 86/378, consolidates the directive in the light of this jurisprudence.[30]

The pregnancy and maternity Directive 92/85/EEC has as its legal basis Article 118a EC, and is mainly concerned with protection of pregnant women, and women who have recently given birth, from health and safety hazards in the workplace. However, the directive does include a measure on entitlement to maternity leave,[31] and provision of maternity benefit for the woman during that time.[32] What was originally intended to be a fairly generous provision for maternity leave was eventually watered down, in the interests of gaining support in Council. During the period of maternity leave, the directive requires either maintenance of pay or entitlement to an adequate living allowance, or both, in accordance with national law and practice.[33]

The relevant legislation – personal and material scope

Regulation 1408/71[34]

Personal scope

Article 2(1) lists the persons covered by Regulation 1408/71: these are employed or self-employed persons (defined by reference to affiliation to and insurance under a national social security scheme), who are EUCs, or stateless persons or refugees resident in a Member State, and their families[35] and survivors. Non-employed

29. COM(76) 650 final; Hoskyns and Luckhaus 'The European Community Directive on Equal Treatment in Social Security' (1989) 17 Policy and Politics 321–355, pp 323–4; Wyatt and Dashwood, *supra* n 22, p 631.
30. OJ 1997 L 46/20. See COM(95) 186 final.
31. Article 8.   32. Article 11(2).   33. Article 11(2)(b) and 11(3).
34. Nielsen and Szyszczak, *supra* n 15, pp 127–133; Luckhaus, *supra* n 11, pp 701–6; Wyatt and Dashwood, *supra* n 22, pp 316–23, Steiner, *supra* n 22, pp 35–8, Barnard, *supra* n 22, pp 145–55.
35. Though see Case 94/84 *Deak* [1985] ECR 1873.

(or rather non-insured) persons, students[36] and third country nationals (TCNs)[37] are excluded from the scope of the Regulation.
Article 2(1) refers to persons 'subject to the legislation of one or
more Member State'. Thus, there is no need for a person to have
exercised their free movement rights under the Treaty of Rome in
order to be covered by the Regulation.[38] For instance, if an EUC
insured in their home Member State requires medical benefits during a holiday visit to another Member State, that person will be
covered under the Regulation.

Material scope

Article 4 lists the types of national social security benefits covered
by Regulation 1408/71. The list comprises sickness and maternity
benefits, invalidity benefits, old-age benefits, survivors' benefits,
benefits in respect of accidents at work and industrial diseases,
death grants, unemployment benefits, and family benefits. All social
security schemes, whether general or special, contributory or non-
contributory, are covered. 'Special non-contributory benefits'[39] which
supplement, substitute for or provide ancillary cover against the
risks listed above are also covered.

Article 4 (4) of Regulation 1408/71 expressly excludes application
of the regulation to social and medical assistance. The concept of
'social assistance' is not defined in the regulation, and its interpretation has been a matter for the European Court of Justice. The
Court considers whether the benefit accrues as of right, after a
period of employment or affiliation to a social insurance scheme,
on the occurrence of a specific risk, or whether there is an element
of discretion or means-testing.[40] Discretionary or means-tested
benefits for those in need are 'social assistance' and do not fall
within the scope of Regulation 1408/71. Article 4(4) also excludes

---

36. Case 66/77 *Kuyken* [1977] ECR 2311.
37. Save those who are members of EUC workers' families; Case C-308/93
   Cabanis-Issarte [1996] ECR I-2097, overturning Case 40/76 *Kermaschek*
   [1976] ECR 1669. See Moore, 'Case C–308/93 *Cabanis-Issarte*' [1997] 34
   CMLR 727–739.
38. Case 75/63 *Hoekstra (Unger)* [1964] ECR 177; Case 44/65 *Maison Singer*
   [1965] ECR 965; Case C-2/89 *Kits Van Heyningen* [1990] ECR I-1795.
   Cornelissen, *supra* n 25, p 444.
39. A new category of benefit added to the scope of the Regulation by Regulation
   1247/92, OJ 1992 L 136/1.
40. Case 139/82 *Piscitello v INPS* [1983] ECR 1427; Barnard, *supra* n 22, p 147.

benefit schemes for victims of war, and special schemes for civil servants.[41]

Occupational social security schemes are implicitly excluded from the scope of Regulation 1408/71 – benefits falling within the regulation must be conferred by 'legislation', which presumably excludes benefits conferred contractually, or as a result of collective agreements between management and labour, even though in practice some of these are heavily regulated by national legislatures. The Commission has identified the lack of coordination of occupational social security schemes, especially pension schemes, as a barrier to free movement for workers, particularly those in skilled and professional groups. Although finding techniques for coordinating aspects of occupational schemes has been on the Commission's agenda for some time,[42] the Social Affairs Council has not been able to reach agreement on the issues.[43]

Regulation 1612/68[44]

Personal scope

Regulation 1612/68 applies to migrant EUC workers. For the purposes of this book, the significant provision of Regulation 1612/68 is Article 7(2), granting workers entitlement to 'enjoy the same social and tax advantages as national workers'. Unlike in the case of Regulation 1408/71, where 'worker' is determined by the concept of an insured person, defined by reference to the national system, 'worker' in the context of Regulation 1612/68 is a European Community concept.[45] The European Court of Justice has given this concept a very generous interpretation, reflecting the centrality of

---

41. Case C-443/93 *Vougioukas* [1995] ECR I-4033. In its judgment, the Court expressed the opinion that, in maintaining the exclusion for the civil service sector, Council had not yet discharged its duty (in Article 51 EC) to introduce coordinating rules in the sector. This ruling may increase pressure on Council to adopt the Commission's proposal (OJ 1992 C 46) to bring special civil service insurance schemes within the scope of Regulation 1408/71.

42. At least since the SAP of 1989. See in particular Communication SEC/91/1332 final.

43. Agence Europe No 7003, 26 June 1997; Barnard, *supra* n 22, pp 154–5; Luckhaus, *supra* n 11, p 706; Laske, *supra* n 5, p 521–7.

44. Barnard, *supra* n 11; Wyatt and Dashwood *supra* n 22; O'Keeffe, 'Equal Rights for Migrants: the Concept of Social Advantages in Article 7(2), Regulation 1612/68' (1985) 5 YEL 93–123.

45. Wyatt and Dashwood, *supra* n 22, p 318, Steiner, *supra* n 22, p 35.

free movement of workers to the system of EC law. Generally speaking, to be a worker in this EC sense, a person must be engaged in performing services for remuneration as part of a 'genuine and effective economic activity'. Part-time work, on-call work and work remunerated at levels lower than subsistence may all constitute work for these purposes. The test is whether the activities carried out are 'genuine and effective' economic activity, and not on such a small scale as to be 'marginal and ancillary'.[46] The Court's broad interpretation of the personal scope of Regulation 1612/68 is well illustrated by Case 139/85 *Kempf*.[47] There the Court held that Mr Kempf was a 'worker' for the purposes of the regulation, even though he was reliant on supplementary social security benefits for subsistence, as he was employed part-time as a music teacher.

The Court has held that freedom of movement for workers cannot be guaranteed without guaranteeing movement and residence rights for members of workers' families. The EU institutions' (especially the Court's) conception of migrant labour is not one of 'guest workers', whose families are expected to remain at home, but one of a genuinely single market in labour in the EU, with migrant workers and their families becoming integrated in the host state. This conception is reflected in provisions of secondary legislation, including Regulation 1612/68. The preamble of that regulation states that 'freedom of movement constitutes a fundamental right of workers and their families'. Regulation 1612/68, Article 10 (granting family members the right to install themselves with the worker) defines the worker's family as 'his spouse and their descendants who are under the age of 21 years or are dependants, and dependent relatives in the ascending line of the worker and his spouse'. 'Spouse' in this context denotes married partner, as defined by national law.[48]

A textual analysis of Regulation 1612/68, Article 7(2) (which is found in Title II of the regulation dealing with employment and equality of treatment, and not in Title III, which deals with rights of family members) would tend to lead to the conclusion that

---

46. Case 53/81 *Levin* [1982] ECR 1035; Case 66/85 *Lawrie-Blum v Land Baden-Württemburg* [1986] ECR 2121; Case 139/85 *Kempf v Staatsecretaris van Justitie* [1986] ECR 1035; Case 196/87 *Steymann v Staatsecretaris van Justitie* [1988] ECR 6159; Case C-357/89 *Raulin* [1992] ECR I-1027.
47. [1986] ECR 1035.
48. Case 59/85 *Netherlands v Reed* [1986] ECR 1283.

social advantages are to be granted on a non-discriminatory basis to workers themselves, but not to members of their families. However, in keeping with its conception of migrant labour, the Court has adopted a much more general (and generous) approach to the application of Article 7(2) to family members.[49] So, for instance, in Case 32/75 *Christini*,[50] an Italian widow of an Italian worker on the French national railways was entitled to reduced rail fares for her large family, under the same conditions as families of French railway workers.

Material scope

Consistent with its purposive interpretation of the regulation, and its model of migrant labour in the EU, the Court has interpreted the concept of 'social advantage' broadly. 'Social advantage' has been defined by the Court as including all advantages 'which whether or not linked to a contract of employment, are generally granted to national workers primarily because of their objective status as workers, or by virtue of the mere fact of their residence on the national territory and the extension of which to workers who are nationals of other Member States therefore seems suitable to facilitate their mobility within the Community'.[51] The crucial factor in terms of entitlement to social advantages appears to be lawful residence in the host Member State. 'Social advantage' includes all social security benefits and social assistance benefits. In addition to benefits granted as of right, it also includes discretionary benefits.

The application of Article 7(2) of Regulation 1612/68 has been extended to benefits paid to members of a worker's family.[52] The Court refers to two inter-connected reasons for this: the need to encourage workers to migrate (without their family, workers would be less inclined to do so) and the need to integrate the family in the host Member State. Of course, the issue of whether granting or refusing benefits to family members will in itself necessarily affect movement of workers to a particular Member State is a matter of conjecture. Various other factors, in particular the state of job

49. O'Keeffe, *supra* n 44, p 95.   50. [1975] ECR 1085.
51. Case 207/78 *Ministère Public v Even* [1979] ECR 2019. See Peers, *supra* n 17, pp 162–5.
52. Case 32/75 *Christini v SNCF* [1975] ECR 1085; Case 261/83 *Castelli v ONPTS* [1984] ECR 3199; Case 63/76 *Inzirillo* [1976] ECR 2057.

markets, linguistic skills, previous links with a particular Member State (for instance, through being educated there) and availability of housing, may prove more significant than provision of social security. The Court's approach of regarding social advantages as a crucial factor which may affect mobility may therefore be seen as a means of expanding the personal and material scope of Regulation 1612/68, Article 7(2).

Article 119 EC; Directives 79/7 and 86/378[53]

Personal scope

Directive 79/7 on the progressive implementation of sex equality in social security and social protection applies to 'the working population'. 'The working population' includes all workers in the EU, migrant or non-migrant, EUCs and TCNs. The Directive applies to workers and the self-employed, those who are no longer able to work due to 'illness, accident, or involuntary employment', those seeking work, and retired workers.[54] The interruption of work need not be due to the risk covered by the directive befalling the worker her- or himself. In Case 150/85 *Drake*[55] the Court held that a woman whose work was interrupted by the invalidity of her mother would fall within the scope of the directive. The crucial factor is whether the person concerned is (or was) a member of the working population whose work was interrupted or ceased due to one of the risks covered by the Directive.[56] Part-time workers also fall within the scope of the Directive.[57]

Article 3 of Directive 86/378 on the progressive implementation of sex equality in occupational pension schemes repeats the wording of Article 2 Directive 79/7 concerning its personal scope. The relevance of Directive 86/378 has been significantly reduced by the Court's jurisprudence to the effect that Article 119 EC applies to

---

53. Nielsen and Szyszczak, *supra* n 15, pp 187–203; Hoskyns *Integrating Gender* (Verso, 1996); Sohrab, *Sexing the Benefit: Women, Social Security and Financial Independence in EC Sex Equality Law* (Dartmouth, 1996); Hoskyns and Luckhaus, *supra* n 29; Steiner, 'The principle of equal treatment for men and women in social security' in Hervey and O'Keeffe (eds), *Sex Equality Law in the European Union* (Wiley, 1996).
54. Article 2. 55. [1986] ECR 1995.
56. Case 48/88 *Achterberg-te Riele* [1989] ECR 1905; Case C–31/90 *Johnson v Chief Adjudication Officer* [1991] ECR I-3723; Case C-77/95 *Züchner* [1996] ECR I-5689.
57. Case 102/88 *Ruzuis Wilbrink* [1989] ECR 4311.

occupational pension schemes. Article 119 EC applies to all those in an employment relationship. Directive 86/378 has been amended to reflect this jurisprudence.[58]

Material scope

Directive 79/7 applies to statutory social security schemes protecting against the risks of sickness, invalidity, old age, accidents at work and occupational diseases, unemployment, and 'social assistance, in so far as it is intended to supplement or replace' those schemes.[59] Survivors' benefits and family benefits (except those granted by means of increases to benefits for the risks aforementioned) are explicitly excluded.[60]

The issue of whether provisions of social assistance schemes fall within the scope of the Directive has been before the Court on several occasions. The Court's original approach was to apply a purposive, and therefore expansive, test: benefits which either provided protection against one of the enumerated risks as part of a statutory scheme, or which were 'a form of social assistance having the same objective' fell within the scope of the Directive.[61] However, the Court's current legal test is more restrictive: the Court asks whether the benefit is 'directly and effectively linked' to one of the enumerated risks.[62] General social assistance benefits designed to provide resources for those whose basic subsistence needs are not otherwise met, for instance housing benefit or income support, do not fall within the scope of the Directive. The 'directly and effectively linked' test is phrased in open-textured language, and its application in an individual case is not readily discernible in advance of a ruling from the Court. The Court's more restrictive approach to the scope of the Directive may be contrasted with its approach to Regulation 1612/68, Article 7(2). The difference may be explained by the relative centrality of the free movement of persons to the Court's scheme of EC law, and, by contrast, the relatively peripheral nature of sex equality. Sex equality is not as clearly a central requisite of the internal market as mobility of labour. Directive 79/7 also explicitly permits Mem-

---

58. Directive 96/97/EC. 59. Article 3. 60. Article 3(2).
61. Case 150/85 *Drake v Chief Adjudication Officer* [1986] ECR 1995.
62. Case C-243/90 *Smithson* [1992] ECR I-467; Cases C-63–4/91 *Jackson and Cresswell v Chief Adjudication Officer* [1992] ECR I-4737; Case C-137/94 *Richardson* [1995] ECR I-3407; Case C-228/94 *Atkins* [1996] ECR I-3633.

ber States to make various further exclusions from its scope, the most significant of which relates to the determination of state pensionable age.[63]

Provisions of occupational pension schemes which are considered to be 'pay' in the meaning of Article 119 EC must be granted equally to men and women in accordance with that directly effective treaty provision.[64] Article 119 EC applies to most aspects of occupational pension schemes, including receipt of benefits under schemes, access to schemes,[65] and payment of employee[66] and employer[67] contributions. Directive 86/378 thus has only a residual role, as reflected in its amended form, and is mostly relevant for self-employed persons.

Directive 92/85/EEC[68]

Personal scope

Directive 92/85/EEC applies to 'pregnant workers' and 'workers who have recently given birth or who are breastfeeding'.[69] These terms are defined in Article 2 of the directive, which requires that a woman must *notify* her employer of her pregnancy in accordance with national law and practice, in order to fall within the terms of the directive.

Material scope

The main thrust of Directive 92/85 is to ensure health and safety within the workplace of pregnant workers and workers who have recently given birth, by requiring employers to undertake risk assessments, if necessary adjusting pregnant workers' working conditions and protecting pregnant workers from specified hazardous substances and environments within the workplace.

---

63. Article 7.
64. Case C-262/88 *Barber v Guardian Royal Exchange* [1990] ECR I-1889. Whiteford, 'W(h)ither Social Policy?' in Shaw and More (eds), *New Legal Dynamics of European Union* (OUP, 1995); Barnard, *supra* n 22, pp 226–40.
65. Case 170/84 *Bilka* [1986] ECR 1607; Case C–57/93 *Vroege* [1994] ECR I–4541; Case C-128/93 *Fisscher* [1994] ECR I-4583.
66. Case C-200/91 *Coloroll* [1994] ECR I-4389.
67. Case 192/85 *Newstead* [1987] ECR 4753.
68. Barnard, *supra* n 22, pp 204–8; Burrows and Mair, *European Social Law* (Wiley, 1996) pp 159–72.
69. Article 1.

In terms of social security, the directive requires that pregnant workers be given a period of at least 14 weeks' maternity leave.[70] During that time, a worker's employment rights, with the exception of pay, are to be guaranteed.[71] Article 11(2)(b) requires that, during the period of maternity leave, a worker is to be entitled to either 'maintenance of a payment' or 'an adequate allowance' or both. Allowances are 'adequate' if they are at least equivalent to statutory sick pay.[72]

Protected risks

Binding provisions of European Community law thus have a limited impact on national social security systems providing benefits protecting against the 'traditional risks' of social security, and an even more limited impact on provisions of social assistance.[73] As shown above, the material scope of each relevant provision of EC law, and the persons covered, varies. This section provides an overview of applicable EC law on each main type of social security benefit.

The broad distinction between long-term benefits (such as old-age pensions) and short- and medium-term benefits (such as sickness benefits, and (at least traditionally) unemployment benefit) has been adopted. The discussion begins with benefits which are clearly in the category of long-term social security benefits, and moves through medium- and short-term social security, to benefits which are more in the nature of social assistance. For some benefits provided in national schemes, the 'fit' between the benefit and the 'social security'/'social assistance' dichotomy may not be straightforward. Moreover, with changing patterns of unemployment, the distinction between long- and short-term benefits may no longer be appropriate.

Within national social security systems of the Member States, there is an increased interest in, if not tendency towards, private protection against the traditional risks of social security. Private insurance schemes and occupational schemes are becoming increasingly appealing to policy makers who wish to reduce

---

70. Article 8.
71. Article 11(2); Case C-342/93 *Gillespie* [1996] ECR I-475; Case C-400/95 *Larsson* [1997] ECR I-2757.
72. Article 11(3).   73. See further Chapter 8.

national spending budgets and national taxation.[74] EC law has so far had a very limited impact indeed on the harmonisation (by regulation or coordination) of private social security schemes.[75] The only developed area of legislation or jurisprudence appears to be the requirements of sex equality in occupational pension schemes.

Old-age pensions and death benefits

Migrant EUC workers, irrespective of the Member State in which they reside on retirement, are entitled to have all periods of insurance within a Member State of the EU taken into account for the purposes of calculating entitlement to old-age and death benefits. If a person moves around the EU during his or her working life, all periods of employment are counted towards the final pension payable. The coordination of national schemes providing old-age pensions and death benefits is governed by Title III, Chapter 3 of Regulation 1408/71.[76]

The key principle is that the cost of pensions should be borne proportionately by the Member States which received contributions during an individual's working life. Therefore, provision is made for the application of the principles of aggregation and apportionment to old-age and death benefits. Detailed rules govern the calculation of the amount of old-age pension payable by each relevant Member State, by means of a system of proraterisation, that is, calculation of actual benefit due as a proportion of a total (theoretical) amount which would have been due had the individual spent an entire working life in one Member State.[77]

However, the simple process of aggregation and apportionment might lead to an individual being entitled to greater pension rights than they would have been if they had been employed in only one Member State. This might arise if, for instance, Member States give a proportion of the old-age pension as a flat rate, irrespective of contributions paid, or number of years worked. Therefore,

74. Luckhaus, 'Privatisation and Pensions: Some Pitfalls for Women?' (1997) 3 ELJ 83–100.
75. See eg the provisions in the first life insurance Directive 79/267/EEC OJ 1979 L 63 as amended by Directives 90/169/EEC OJ 1990 L 330 and 92/96/EEC OJ 1992 L 360.
76. Articles 44–51; Barnard, *supra* n 22, pp 153–4; Wyatt and Dashwood, *supra* n 22, pp 342–5.
77. Article 46.

Article 46a permits Member States to enforce rules preventing the overlapping of such benefits.

Occupational pensions are not at present covered by any coordinating measures of EC law. The Commission's Communication on transferability of occupational pensions between Member States[78] was annulled by the European Court of Justice.[79] The more recent Green Paper on supplementary pensions in the single market[80] stresses the potential financial benefits of coordination of supplementary pension schemes and the removal of restrictive rules governing their operation. The report of the High Level Group on Free Movement of Persons to the Commission[81] calls for 'modernisation' of Regulation 1408/71, *inter alia*, to allow people to preserve their acquired rights to private supplementary pensions when working in different Member States.

Migrant EUC workers who remain in the host Member State will be entitled to receive old-age pensions and death benefits granted by that state to its own nationals in accordance with the principle of non-discrimination on grounds of nationality, and its specific application in Regulation 1612/68, Article 7(2). The European Court of Justice originally held the position that if an old-age benefit was covered by Regulation 3 (the precursor to Regulation 1408/71), there was no need to consider entitlement under Regulation 1612/68.[82] However, the Court now appears to hold the position that benefits may fall within the scope of both regulations. Regulation 1612/68, Article 7(2) may be particularly significant where a benefit is held to fall outside Regulation 1408/71 on the grounds that it is in the nature of social assistance. The Court has held that Regulation 1612/68, Article 7(2) entitles migrant EUC workers to old-age benefits for those who have no national social security pension[83] and to a guaranteed minimum income for old persons[84] on the same terms as national workers.

All workers in the EU are entitled to equal treatment with workers of the opposite sex in the provision of state and occupational pensions. However, in the area of state pensions, Directive 79/7, Article 7 permits derogations, the most significant of which is the

78. 94/C 360/08 OJ 1994 C 360/7; Barnard, *supra* n 22, p 155.
79. Case C-57/95 *France v Commission* [1997] ECR I-1627.
80. http://europa.eu.int/comm/dg15/en/finances/pensions/507.htm.
81. http://europa.eu.int/comm/dg15/en/people/hlp/summ.htm.
82. Case 1/72 *Frilli* [1972] ECR 457.
83. Case 157/84 *Frascogna* [1985] ECR 1739.
84. Case 261/83 *Castelli* [1984] ECR 3199.

maintenance of differential state pensionable ages for men and women, and 'the possible consequences thereof for other benefits'. The Court has held that, in order to fall within the derogation, a difference in treatment must be 'objectively and necessarily linked' to different state pensionable ages.[85] Originally, Directive 86/378 provided a similar exclusion for occupational pension schemes. However, the Court's jurisprudence based on Article 119 EC has removed this exclusion. Even where these reflect state pensionable ages, occupational pension schemes may not set different *retirement* ages for men and women.[86] Likewise, entitlement to benefits under occupational pension schemes may not accrue at different ages for men and women.[87] However, provisions concerning the level of benefits payable by bridging pensions (generally, a pension paid to men between the ages of 60 and 65 to compensate for the unavailability of state pensions) payable under occupational schemes which take account of different state pensionable ages may be consistent with Article 119, where the effect is to make total pension provision for men and women under the scheme more equal.[88]

Sickness and invalidity benefits; accidents at work and occupational diseases; maternity benefits[89]

Migrant EUC workers who reside and work in a host Member State, and become ill in that state, are entitled to the same sickness and invalidity benefits as nationals. Title III, Chapter 1 of Regulation 1408/71[90] covers the provisions concerning coordination of sickness benefits. The principle of aggregation applies.

Generally speaking, the Member State in which an individual is *resident* is to provide for health and welfare services for that

---

85. Case C-9/91 *R v Secretary of State for Social Security, ex parte EOC* [1992] ECR I-4297; Case C–328/91 *Secretary of State for Social Security v Thomas* [1993] ECR I-1247; Case C–92/94 *Secretary of State for Social Security v Graham* [1995] ECR I-2521; Case C–137/94 *Richardson* [1995] ECR I-3407; Case C–139/95 *Balestra* [1997] ECR I-549.
86. Case 152/84 *Marshall No 1* [1986] ECR 723.
87. Case C-262/88 *Barber* [1990] ECR I-1889; Case C–110/91 *Moroni* [1993] ECR I-6591; Case C-173/91 *Commission v Belgium* [1991] ECR I-673.
88. Case C-132/92 *Birds Eye Walls v Roberts* [1993] ECR I-5579; Whiteford, 'Occupational Pensions and European Law: Clarity at Last?' in Hervey and O'Keeffe (eds), *Sex Equality Law in the European Union* (Wiley, 1996).
89. For EC law concerning health policy, see further Chapter 7.
90. Articles 18–36.

individual. In some circumstances, the most common of which is where an individual is employed in a different Member State from the Member State of residence, an individual will be affiliated to the social security system in another Member State. In that case, the Member State of affiliation (the competent Member State) will be responsible for the cost of benefits provided to an individual, even where those benefits are provided by another Member State. Moreover, entitlement is determined by the rules of the competent Member State, not (necessarily) the providing Member State. Regulation 1408/71 makes a distinction between benefits in kind, which are provided by the Member State of residence, and cash benefits, which are provided by the competent Member State. (However, the two Member States concerned may agree that the Member State of residence provides cash benefits on behalf of the Member State of affiliation.) In this context, benefits in kind have been defined by the Court as including health care, medical treatment and welfare services, and also benefits which reimburse the individual for benefits in kind paid for by the individual. Cash benefits are defined as benefits to compensate for loss of earnings due to absence from work because of ill-health.[91]

EUCs who fall within the scope of Regulation 1408/71 are covered by Regulation 1408/71, even where their presence in a Member State other than the competent Member State is due to reasons unconnected with work. For instance, where an EUC visits another Member State for a holiday, Regulation 1408/71 still applies.[92] Where the person's condition requires immediate benefits, they are to be given in accordance with Article 22(1). A system of forms, such as the E-111 form, showing entitlement to health benefits in other Member States provides the administrative framework for these entitlements.[93]

An example of the Court's interpretation of the concept of 'social security' (as opposed to social assistance) for the purposes of determining the scope of application of Regulation 1408/71 may be found in respect of invalidity benefits. The Court has held that invalidity benefits in the form of allowances for disabled

---

91. Case 65/61 *Vaassen* [1966] ECR 261; Wyatt and Dashwood, *supra* n 22, pp 336–339; Barnard, *supra* n 11, pp 149–51.
92. Article 22.
93. Though, in practice, problems remain; eg the Commission has commenced Article 169 proceedings against Belgium, concerning *inter alia*, its administration of the E-111 scheme.

adults and children (including the UK mobility allowance), which are not linked to contributions to a national social security scheme, may fall within the scope of Regulation 1408/71.[94] The relevant national legislation must provide for a 'legally protected right' and must not be discretionary.[95]

Sickness and invalidity benefits (including maternity benefits) may also constitute social advantages in the sense of Regulation 1612/68, Article 7(2), if they are generally granted to national workers by reason of their objective status as workers, or by virtue of their residence in the Member State. Migrant EUC workers are thus entitled to whatever medical benefits the host Member State makes available to its own nationals, on the same terms as those nationals.[96]

Directive 79/7 applies to sickness and invalidity benefits. However, the exclusion provision in Article 7, concerning the maintenance of differential state pensionable ages and the consequences for 'other benefits' may have consequences for sickness and invalidity benefits. The Court has considered such benefits in several recent cases. In Case C-328/91 *Secretary of State for Social Security v Thomas*,[97] the Court held that there was no necessary and objective link between state pensionable ages and the payment of severe disablement and invalid care allowance, because the benefits were non-contributory and therefore equalisation would not disrupt the financial equilibrium of the state social security system. The Court gave a judgment in similar terms in Case C-137/94 *Richardson*[98] on the subject of differential charges for men and women for medical prescriptions provided under the state social security system. However, in Case C-92/94 *Secretary of State for Social Security v Graham*[99] the Court found that there *was* an objective and necessary link between state pensionable age and entitlement to invalidity pensions and invalidity allowances, apparently on the grounds that, otherwise, Member States would no longer be able to effectively set different pensionable ages for men and women, and the consistency of the national social security scheme would be undermined. This decision has been criticised for being sparsely reasoned.[100]

94. Case 187/73 *Callemeyn* [1974] ECR 553; Case 39/74 *Costa* [1974] ECR 1251; Case 7/75 *Mr and Mrs F* [1975] ECR 679; Case 63/76 *Inzirillo* [1976] ECR 2057; Case C-356/89 *Newton* [1991] ECR I-3017.
95. Luckhaus, *supra* n 11, p 704. 96. Case 207/78 *Even* [1979] ECR 2019.
97. [1993] ECR I-1247. 98. [1995] ECR I-3407. 99. [1995] ECR I-2521.
100. Steiner, *supra* n 53.

Entitlement to maternity benefits is also governed by Directive 92/85 on the protection of pregnant workers and workers who have recently given birth. The Court of Justice has recently confirmed that the provisions of EC law on equal pay (Article 119 and Directive 75/117) and equal treatment in employment (Directive 76/207) on grounds of sex do not require that women receive full pay during maternity leave, nor that any particular criteria be applied to determine the level of maternity pay or benefits.[101]

Unemployment benefits

The relevant coordination provisions for unemployment benefits are found in Title III, Chapter 6 of Regulation 1408/71.[102] The principle of aggregation applies: all periods of employment in the Member States are to be taken into account in determining entitlement of a migrant EUC worker to unemployment benefit, and in calculating the amount of unemployment benefit due. If the amount of benefit is calculated with respect to previous earnings, the last employment in the competent Member State (that is the Member State responsible for paying the benefit) is the relevant employment.[103]

The Member State responsible for payment of unemployment benefits is, generally speaking, the Member State in which the individual was last employed. The exception is where an individual 'frontier worker' has been resident in another Member State during their last period of employment; however, this exception is to be interpreted strictly, requiring the individual to show habitual residence and close ties with the Member State of residence.[104]

The coordinating provisions also grant a limited entitlement to job-seekers to receive unemployment benefit in another Member State to which the job-seeker has gone to look for employment.[105] In order to fall within the provision, an individual must already have been employed.[106] Registration provisions must be complied with. Benefit is payable only for three months, after which time the job-seeker must return to the original (responsible) Member State, failing which all entitlement to benefit may be lost.

101. Case C-342/93 *Gillespie*; Case C-400/95 *Larsson*.
102. Articles 67–71; Barnard, *supra* n 22, pp 150–2; Cornelissen, *supra* n 25, pp 457–60; Wyatt and Dashwood, *supra* n 22, pp 346–50; Wikeley, *supra* n 19.
103. Article 68; Case 145/84 *Cochet* [1985] ECR 801.
104. Article 71; Case C-131/95 *Huijbrechts* [1997] ECR I-1409.   105. Article 69.
106. Case 66/77 *Kuyken* [1977] ECR 2311; Case 238/83 *Meade* [1984] ECR 2631.

However, the European Court of Justice has mitigated the stringency of this rule in certain (exceptional) circumstances by application of the principle that Regulation 1408/71 may not operate to diminish rights acquired under national law, independently of EC-level rules. Thus, where a job-seeker would still be entitled to receive unemployment benefit under national law, even after being in another Member State seeking work for more than three months, the national authorities may not apply Regulation 1408/71 to deprive the individual of that entitlement.[107]

The three-month rule in Regulation 1408/71, Article 69, has affected the Court's interpretation of the free movement of workers provisions of EC law. In the past, the Court stressed that Article 48 EC does not expressly grant an unqualified right to free movement for work-seekers, as opposed to workers.[108] However, such a right might certainly be said to be within the spirit of the Treaty, and in particular the aims of the creation of a truly European labour force.[109] The Court confirmed that Article 48 EC does allow for the free movement of work-seekers in Case C-292/88 *Antonissen*,[110] in which the Court held that, in the absence of EC regulatory harmonisation of the matter, a national rule requiring job-seekers to leave the host state if they had been unable to find work after a period of six months would be compatible with Community law.

Nevertheless, although free movement is guaranteed to work seekers under EC law, Regulation 1612/68, Article 7(2) does not apply to work-seekers, but only workers.[111] Therefore, work-seekers may not claim unemployment benefits in the host state on the grounds that those benefits constitute a social advantage to which they are entitled in the same way as national work-seekers.

The Court has upheld the application of Regulation 1612/68, Article 7(2) to unemployment benefit where entitlement to the benefit derives from a migrant EUC worker family member. In Case 94/84 *Deak*,[112] the Court held that an unemployed TCN national whose mother was an EUC migrant worker was entitled to receive a special unemployment benefit for young persons as a social advantage.[113]

107. Cases 41/79, 121/79, 769/79 *Testa* [1980] ECR 1979.
108. Case 20/75 *D'Amico* [1975] ECR 891.   109. Wikeley, *supra* n 19, p 311.
110. [1992] ECR I-745.   111. Case 316/85 *Lebon* [1987] ECR 2811.
112. [1985] ECR 1873.
113. O'Keeffe, *supra* n 44, pp 116–18; but see Case C-278/94 *Commission v Belgium* [1996] ECR I-4307 concerning Belgium's system for encouraging the hiring of young unemployed people; Peers, *supra* n 17.

Family benefits

For the purposes of the coordination provisions in Regulation 1408/71, the concept of 'family' is to be defined by national law. The only qualification to this is the provision in Article 1(f) that where 'members of the family' is defined in national law by residence under the same roof, this is to be regarded as satisfied if the family member is mainly dependent on the persons concerned.

Application of Regulation 1408/71 to family benefits depends on the benefits concerned being characterised as 'social security' as opposed to 'social assistance'. Where family benefits are supplementary in nature, intended to supplement benefits which are clearly social security, protecting against one of the risks specified in the Regulation, then the Court has been prepared to hold that the family benefits are 'social security' within the Regulation's scope.[114] Various family benefits have been held to constitute 'social advantages' within Regulation 1612/68, Article 7(2): for instance, special discretionary childbirth loans[115] and reductions on rail fares for large families.[116]

Where Regulation 1408/71 applies, family benefits must be granted without direct or indirect discrimination on grounds of nationality, including nationality of the family members. Therefore, for instance, in Case 237/78 *Palermo*[117] it was held that the grant of a special allowance to women over the age of 65 who had brought up at least five children could not be made dependent on the nationality of the woman, or the children.[118] Even if family members are not resident in the relevant Member State, Regulation 1408/71 may still apply.[119]

In an innovative application of the sex equality in employment provisions of EC law (Directive 76/207), the Court has held that EC *employment* law may apply to family benefits designed to assist parents to return to work, that is, concerned with access to employment.[120] Such benefits may not discriminate directly or indirectly on grounds of sex, in particular by not deducting child-care costs in the calculation of income to determine entitlement to benefit, a measure which discriminates indirectly against women,

---

114. Case C-78/91 *Hughes* [1992] ECR I-4839; Luckhaus, *supra* n 11, p 704.
115. Case 65/81 *Reina* [1982] ECR 33.
116. Case 32/75 *Christini v SNCF* [1975] ECR 1085.   117. [1979] ECR 2645.
118. Wyatt and Dashwood, *supra* n 22, p 324.
119. Cases C-4 & 5/95 *Stöber and Pereira* [1997] ECR I-511.
120. Case C-116/94 *Meyers* [1995] ECR I-2131.

as it is more difficult for single parents to arrange unpaid child-care, and more single parents are women than men.

Other measures of social assistance or social advantages[121]

The application of binding EC law to other measures of social assistance or social advantages, for example minimum income benefits, or housing benefit, is very limited indeed. Minimum income benefits and other benefits which are first and foremost needs-based will not constitute 'social security' within Regulation 1408/71, but fall within the category of 'social assistance'.[122] The coordinating provisions of Regulation 1408/71 therefore do not apply.

For migrant EUC workers still in the host Member State, Regulation 1612/68, Article 7(2) may apply. 'Social advantages' include 'the whole range of what may loosely be termed social benefits, pecuniary and otherwise, including discretionary benefits, which are made available by the state, normally at the taxpayer's expense, for a variety of purposes, for certain categories of its nationals'.[123] The Court has held that Article 7(2) applies to minimum subsistence allowances, or guaranteed minimum income benefits.[124]

Conclusions

It is apparent from the above discussion that the provisions of EC law pertaining to social security and social assistance do not constitute a single coherent social security policy, in the traditional sense of a national system providing, if necessary, support for individuals within the state from cradle to grave. Such European-level rules that exist have developed in a piecemeal fashion, mainly from the requirements of the Treaty-enshrined principle of free movement of labour. These affect only a very small number of EUCs; just 1.4% of EU employees are EUC migrant workers.[125] Other

---

121. See further Chapter 8.
122. Case 249/83 *Hoeckx* [1985] ECR 973; Luckhaus *supra* n 11, p 704.
123. Steiner, *supra* n 22, p 38.
124. Case 249/83 *Hoeckx* [1985] ECR 973; Case 261/83 *Castelli* [1984] ECR 3199; Case 122/84 *Scrivner* [1985] ECR 1027.
125. The figure is 1.5% if families are included; Cochrane, 'Comparative Approaches in Social Policy' and 'Looking for a European Welfare State' in Cochrane and Clarke, *Comparing Welfare States: Britain in International Context* (Open University Press, 1993) p 259.

areas of EC employment law, such as sex equality and health and safety law, have had a small impact.

Perhaps less apparent from a discussion of relevant EC law rules are the gaps in their coverage. The rules on personal scope of each provision are particularly relevant in this respect. Examination of EC social security law (such as it is) reveals a hierarchy of entitlement. At the apex of the hierarchy is the migrant EU citizen who is an employee or a self-employed person.[126] Migrant EUC workers are entitled to the benefit of the coordination and regulatory harmonisation provisions, and may in certain circumstances gain greater entitlements than national workers who have not exercised their entitlements to free movement. The migrant EUC worker who has retired or has become involuntarily unemployed shares a similarly elevated position on the hierarchy. Almost as protected are the members of a migrant EUC worker or self-employed person's family. Their nationality is irrelevant: they are protected by virtue of their relationship with the worker. Therefore, their position is not as secure as that of migrant EUC workers; if the relationship breaks down (either by marital breakdown, or by children reaching an age of independence) then the entitlements under EC law may be lost.

Non-migrant EUC workers and self-employed persons are reasonably well-off in the hierarchy of protection. As they gain their social security entitlements from national legal systems, EC measures may not affect them directly at all. Some coordination provisions of EC law may apply to them (for instance in the case of receipt of medical benefits on visits to other Member States). In some circumstances they may fall foul of the principle against reverse discrimination, and find that non-national EUC migrant workers are entitled to greater social security benefits in their host state than they are in that same state. More seriously, in some Member States, non-migrant EUCs may find that their social security entitlements are under pressure from the internal market provisions of EC law, as policy options which discriminate against non-national EUCs, due to their incompatibility with EC law, are no longer available to national governments. National governments may required by financial feasibility to reduce their social security provision, or may do so under the excuse of membership of the EU.

Migrant EUC non-workers are specifically excluded from

---

126. Peers, *supra* n 17, p 165.

entitlement to social advantages. Directives 90/364/EEC[127] and 93/96/EEC,[128] giving residence rights respectively to EUCs not covered by other provisions of EC law and to students, explicitly provide that the right of residence is granted only to those who are self-supporting and will not be a burden on the social security system of the host Member State. So, for instance, the UK's 'habitual residence test', excluding from the benefits 'income support' and 'job-seeker's allowance', those non-workers who are not habitually resident in the UK, although indirectly discriminatory on grounds of nationality, is probably not inconsistent with EC law.

At the bottom of the hierarchy, and conspicuous in their absence from European Community provisions are third country national (TCN) workers, both migrant and non-migrant.[129] This seems anomalous in the context of a single European market in labour. The issue is not the rights of entry of TCNs to the EU – it is the entitlement to equal treatment, *inter alia*, in social security benefits, for TCNs lawfully resident and employed in the Member States. In terms of Marshall's concept of 'social citizenship', these individuals, who are, after all, contributing to the economic and social well-being of the EU, should be entitled to share in the EU's 'social heritage', and enjoy social security protection on an equal basis with EUCs. In spite of various calls for the inclusion of TCN migrant workers in the equal treatment provisions of EC law,[130] and various statements from the institutions concerning their commitment to the fight against racism and xenophobia,[131] the institutions of the EU have so far failed to enact any concrete provisions of entitlement to protection under European social security law for migrant TCN workers. If the concept of citizenship of the EU were to be developed towards a notion of social citizenship,[132] the EU might be able to transcend its current nationality-based conception of EC social security law.

127. OJ 1990 L 180/26. 128. OJ 1993 L 317/59.
129. The numbers of TCN migrant workers within the EU are more than twice those of EUC migrant workers; Cochrane, *supra* n 125, p 259.
130. O'Keeffe, 'The Free Movement of Persons and the Single Market' (1992) 17 ELRev 3–19, p 16–17; Commission 'Social Europe' Supplement 4/96 Progress Report on the Implementation of the Medium Term Social Action Programme 1995–1997; High level panel on the free movement of people http://europa.eu.int/comm/dg15/people/hlp/summ.htm.
131. For instance, the Joint Declaration against Racism and Xenophobia of the European Parliament, Council and Commission OJ 1986 C 158/1.
132. See Shaw, *Citizenship of the European Union: Towards Post-National Membership?* (Academy of European Law, Florence, 1995).

Non-workers, and also TCN workers, form the bulk of the poorest groups in the EU. European Community social security law establishes a hierarchy of entitlement which in effect provides more protection to those in European society who are already relatively well-off. From the point of view of a social justice model, the invisibility of these groups who are the worst off in the European Union may constitute the greatest failing in EC law on social security.

CHAPTER SIX

Education and training

Introduction

Education and training are traditionally viewed as part of national social policies because they are linked, via employment, to the role of the state in providing social protection for those who are unable to provide for their own needs. A well-educated and well-trained population will be better enabled to provide for themselves through employment, thus reducing the drain on public social policy funds. Such a working population will also increase the competitiveness of the nation on world markets. In addition, education plays a 'state-building' function, in the sense of promoting national identity and a sense of civic belonging and hence obligation to the state.

Beyond these similarities, however, approaches to education and training policies vary widely between the Member States of the EU. These variations arise from differences in educational culture, historical roots and political preferences. The involvement of different social, institutional and political actors in the organisation and delivery of education and training also varies considerably between Member States. For instance, the German vocational training apprenticeship system, based on a combination of theoretical education in public colleges and practical training within private companies, with pay at apprentice rates, is firmly rooted in corporatism.[1]

1. Milner, 'Training Policy: Steering between divergent national logics' in Kassim, Meron and Hire (eds), *Beyond the Market: The European Union and National Social, Environmental and Consumer Protection Policy* (Routledge, forth coming); Crouch, 'Organised interests as resources or as constraint: Rival logics of vocational training policy' in Crouch and Traxler (eds), *Organized Industrial Relations in Europe: What Future?* (Avebury, 1995) pp 295–8; Caillods, 'Converging trends amidst diversity in vocational training systems' (1994) 133 International Labour Rev 241-257, pp 245–6.

Within such a system, the social partners have a significant influence over training policy. By contrast, the neo-liberal UK system of vocational training, is (despite changes made in the 1980s and 1990s) largely based on individual training provided on an 'on-the-job' basis.[2] As Milner[3] points out, the EU's approach to vocational training policy appears to vacillate between these irreconcilable conceptions of training policy, and is therefore a typical example of multi-level European social policy.[4]

National education and vocational training policy in the Member States is affected by measures of EC education and training policy, with both economic and social policy objectives. The EU institutions often justify EC education and training policies by reference to the goal of promoting within Europe a highly qualified and well-educated workforce, in order to contribute to European competitiveness. The free movement of workers, especially professionals, mandated by the internal market is to be secured by ensuring that education or training qualifications gained in one Member State are recognised throughout the EU. The EU institutions also seek to rely on education and vocational training policies for explicitly social objectives, for instance to remedy unemployment, particularly in less favoured regions and among 'excluded' groups, which was exacerbated by the creation of the internal market.[5] Finally, the EU's involvement in educational policies is often underpinned by the aim of promoting a sense of belonging to Europe and stressing commonality in European culture or history.

European policy in the sphere of education and training is constrained by the fairly limited competence granted to the EU institutions in that area. Most aspects of education policy (and many of vocational training policy) are firmly located within the sphere of competence of the Member States. Even within the Member States there are significant regional pressures to devolve competence in educational matters to local bodies. These pressures are stronger at the European level.[6] On the other hand, some parallels may be

2. Milner, *supra* n 1; Crouch, *supra* n 1, pp 298–305. 3. *Supra* n 1.
4. See for instance COM(97) 300 final, 'Promoting Apprenticeship Training in Europe' which describes as 'similar objectives' 'getting closer to market needs' and 'promoting job flexibility and mobility', and 'fighting social exclusion' and 'raising the educational level of apprentice diplomas' and 'giving apprentices access to higher education'.
5. Rainbird, 'Vocational education and training' in Gold (ed) *The Social Dimension* (Macmillan, 1993) p 184. See further Chapter 9.
6. Opposition to EU policy in education is strongest in Member States with a

drawn between the actions of national governments and those of the EU institutions in this area.[7] National governments seek to use education policies to enforce overriding policy principles, often concerned with 'constitutional issues'; this may be said of the 'free movement' aspects of EC education law and policy. National governments also seek to use 'the power of the purse' to encourage particular forms of or directions in educational policies; the intervention of the EC in terms of providing funding for particular programmes is a significant aspect of EC educational policy. Provision of such financial support is also an example of the EU institutions attempting to gain some influence over the policy sphere without having the competence to regulate that sphere.

There are both regulatory and coordinating measures of EC law in the policy areas of education and training. The regulatory measures coalesce around the concepts of 'free movement' (the 'uncoordinated and potentially permanent migration of individual workers') and 'mobility' ('coordinated but temporary placements provided through action programmes in the field of education'[8]) of persons, both recipients and providers of education.[9] These measures are mainly measures of 'negative integration', based on the principle of non-discrimination on grounds of nationality,[10] which covers both direct and indirect discrimina-

---

federal or decentralised education structure, eg Germany, where the *Kulturhoheit* (cultural sovereignty) of the Länder gives them competence in the areas of pre-school, school, higher, adult and further education, vocational training, sport, museums, culture and the arts. See Spokkereef, 'Developments in European Community education policy' in Lodge (ed), *The European Community and the Challenge of the Future* (Pinter, 1993) p 345; Hochbaum, in De Witte (ed), *European Community Law of Education* (Nomos, 1989) p 145; Shaw, 'Education and the Law in the European Community' (1992) 21 Journal of Law and Education 415–442, pp 437–8. The new Committee of the Regions, which plays an important role in EU education measures, is supposed to ensure that the constituent entities of the Member States which hold competence for education play a full part in the Community decision- making process. See Lenaerts, 'Education in European Community Law after Maastricht' (1994) 31 CMLRev 7–41, p 34.

7. Lonbay, 'Education and Law: The Community Context' (1989) 14 ELRev 363–387, p 364.

8. Hopkins, 'Education and the children of migrant workers: once a child always a child' (1996) 18 JSWFL 114–118, p 438; Shaw, 'Twin-track Social Europe – The Inside Track', in O'Keeffe and Twomey (eds), *Legal Issues of the Maastricht Treaty* (Wiley, 1994) 295-311, p 307.

9. As European educational policy has developed from a basis of 'free movement' to one of 'mobility', so the numbers of individuals benefitting from European educational policy measure have increased.

10. Article 6 EC.

tion.[11] EC measures of regulatory coordination govern the mutual recognition of educational and training qualifications. Rather than setting European-level standards for professional qualifications, the 'new approach' Directives 89/48/EEC and 92/51/EEC[12] require that qualifications gained in one Member State be recognised in others. Persuasive coordination and financial support underpin the remainder of EC education and training policy, which seeks to pursue the objectives of improving international cooperation, exchange and mobility; improving foreign language learning; introducing a European dimension in national education, promoting changes of attitude to European integration; stimulating relationships between institutions of higher education and industry; improving quality of teaching and introducing new methods of teaching.[13]

The EC's policies in education and training are also linked to the promotion of European integration, and especially the 'human face' of the EC, and its promotion among the peoples of Europe. The focus upon language learning and training, and the inclusion of European dimensions in national education systems, are obvious examples of this aspect of EC educational policy. Here the EC may be said to be adopting a 'badge of statehood', in the sense of seeking to create a European identity through the means of national education systems. Although at present effecting such policy intentions remains extremely limited in practice,[14] it is possible that, in the long term, Europeans of the future may be 'Europeanised' through their education systems.[15]

The relevant Treaty provisions and legislation: context

Measures of EC legislation and Treaty provisions relevant to educational policy are characterised by a marked distinction between

11. Direct discrimination is discrimination which is based on the forbidden ground (here nationality). Indirect discrimination is not on its face based on the forbidden ground, but its *effect* is the detrimental treatment of individuals within the protected group (here, non-nationals).

12. OJ 1989 L 19/16; OJ 1992 L 209/25.   13. Sprokkereef, *supra* n 6, p 342.

14. Ryba, 'Toward a European Dimension in Education: Intention and Reality in EC Policy and Practice' (1992) 36 Comparative Education Rev 10–24.

15. Sprokkereef relates that 'Jean Monnet once told journalists that, given the opportunity to create the EC again, he would take education as a starting point': Sprokkereef, *supra* n 6, p 340.

'education' and 'vocational training'. This distinction is difficult to make in practice, given the conceptual problems in drawing any 'bright line' distinctions between vocational, professional and university training, continuing education and schooling. However, the distinction between education and vocational training was crucial in the pre-Maastricht era of the European Community, because the Treaty provided for a 'common vocational training policy',[16] but made no provision for European Community action in the sphere of education. The Treaty on European Union amended the Treaty of Rome to include a provision on education in Article 126 EC, in addition to amending the provision on vocational training, now found in Article 127 EC. Nevertheless, the distinction between education and vocational training remains significant, not least because Articles 126 and 127 EC provide for different legislative procedures by which the EU institutions may enact policy measures.[17]

The Treaty on European Union inserted a new chapter into the Treaty of Rome on 'Education, vocational training and youth'. This includes Articles 126 and 127 EC. Article 126 gives power to the EU institutions to enact 'incentive measures' in accordance with the 'codecision' procedure,[18] and recommendations by qualified majority in Council on a Commission proposal. 'Incentive measures' are binding measures, which may impose obligations to cooperate on the Member States, adopted in the form of regulations, directives or decisions, or acts *sui generis*. The objectives of the measures which may be supported by the EC in this manner are set out in Article 126, which states that EC action shall be aimed at a number of areas, for instance teaching of languages of the Member States, mobility of students and teachers, and enhanced mutual recognition of qualifications. Article 127 EC provides that the EU institutions may enact 'measures', in accordance with the 'cooperation' procedure[19] in order to implement a vocational training policy, with a number of aims such as facilitating adaptation to technological change, and promoting cooperation between training establishments and business. Article 127 EC imposes an obligation on Member States to cooperate in 'exchanges of information and experience', for instance by carrying out

---

16. Article 128 EEC.
17. Craig and de Búrca, *EC Law: Text, Cases and Materials* (Clarendon Press, 1995) p 706; Lenaerts, *supra* n 6, pp 25–6.
18. Article 189b EC.   19. Article 189c EC.

consultations or ensuring that national training establishments are able to participate in exchange programmes.[20] Thus, both provisions give quite specific guidelines on policy content.[21]

Article 126 EC covers forms of education (such as pre-school, primary, general secondary education, and general knowledge university courses which do not equip students for a particular occupation) which were not regarded as vocational training within Article 128 EEC, thus extending the EC's competence into these areas.[22] However, Lenaerts posits that, since Article 126 EC concerning education is the *lex generalis*, the EC's competence in educational matters which were previously defined as 'vocational training' but are more properly to be considered as 'education', such as university studies in general, technical secondary and higher education, should also emanate from Article 126 EC. Article 127 EC (the *lex specialis*) is limited to a supplementary role, and to 'vocational training' proper.[23]

However, it might be considered that since the Treaty on European Union expressly preserves the existing *acquis communautaire*, the definitions of vocational training, and rulings of the European Court of Justice concerning educational matters which constitute 'vocational training' in a European Community sense continue to apply. This would limit Article 126 EC to a basis for educational policies in a narrower sense, and give a greater role to Article 127 EC. The 'Leonardo' action programme on vocational training (1995–99) is based on Article 127 EC.[24] However, for the main action programme on educational matters ('Socrates'[25]) the EU institutions have proceeded on the basis of both Article 126 and 127 jointly. The preamble of the decision establishing Socrates explains that part of the measures covered concern vocational training, although the main thrust of the programme concerns education, and explicitly states that Socrates cannot be considered to be part of the EC's vocational training policy. The language here seems to undermine the apparently clear demarcation between Articles 126 and 127 EC, with its legal consequences. However, when (or if) the Treaty of Amsterdam is ratified, the distinction will no longer entail such consequences, as both new Article 126 and new Article 127 will empower the EU institutions to act in accordance with the 'co-decision' procedure.

[20.] Lenaerts, *supra* n 6, pp 37–8. [21.] Shaw, *supra* n 8, pp 307–8.
[22.] Lenaerts, *supra* n 6, pp 25–6. [23.] Lenaerts, *supra* n 6, p 26.
[24.] OJ 1994 L 340/8 [25.] Decision 819/95/EC OJ 1995 L 87/10.

Socrates (1995–99) is the main EC action programme in the area of education. It covers three areas of action: higher education (the previously established Erasmus[26]), school education and 'horizontal activities' (that is, activities at all levels of education) in language skills (Lingua[27]), open and distance learning and information exchange (Eurydice and Arion). Over half of the EC funding available under Socrates is reserved for higher education, to finance cooperation between universities and student mobility. The EC also supports a socio-pedagogical youth exchange programme, known as Youth for Europe,[28] under the aegis of Article 126 EC. These action programmes, and their precursors, along with structural funding for education and training under the European Social Fund, have been instrumental in supporting European-wide networks of educational institutions. These programmes have therefore contributed to the policy-making process by creating and empowering new policy actors, in the form of elite groups, which are likely to feed through to future policy development.[29]

Both Article 126 and 127 EC are subject to the principle of subsidiarity, and expressly exclude power to enact regulatory harmonisation provisions. Both provisions recognise that the primary responsibility for education – 'the content of teaching and the organisation of education systems' – remains with the Member States, whose 'cultural and linguistic diversity' must be respected. The role of the EU institutions is to support and supplement national policies, and to promote cooperation; no more. The diversity of national educational systems is to remain unaffected by European Community law.[30] Thus, the role of the EC is limited to the 'carrot' approach of funding selected projects designed to encourage the development of educational initiatives which promote the spirit and practice of European integration.[31]

Although regulatory harmonisation is excluded by Articles 126

---

26. Decision 87/327/EEC OJ 1987 L 166/20.
27. Decision 89/489/EEC OJ 1989 L 239.
28. The third phase of Youth for Europe (1995–99) was established by Decision 818/95/EC OJ 1995 L 87/1.
29. Milner, *supra* n 1; Beukel, 'Reconstructing Integration Theory: The Case of Educational Policy in the EC' (1994) 29 *Cooperation and Conflict* 33–54.
30. Craig and de Búrca, *supra* n 17, p 706; Lenaerts, *supra* n 6, pp 31–3.
31. Shaw, *supra* n 8, p 309. The 'stick' is the deregulatory aspect of the free movement of persons, which may render unlawful those aspects of national education and training policies that infringe the principle of non-discrimination on grounds of nationality.

and 127 EC, they may provide a legal basis for 'voluntary harmonisation' or convergence, prompted by financial support from the EU institutions, whereby Member States are encouraged (by incentive measures) to attune their educational policy to that of other Member States by means of informal agreements.[32] Shaw considers that it may well be 'acceptable' that EC action in the field of education policy should exclude harmonisation measures, as this is a policy area which is 'more tangential to the specifically economic objectives of the Community per se and more directly related to the wider political objectives of the EU'.[33] However, the limitation imposed on measures in the field of vocational training cannot be so readily justified, especially given that this is a long-established area of EC competence.[34]

The legislative components of the European Community's vocational training policy were established gradually. This is unsurprising, given the 'dead letter' nature of the original Article 128 EEC[35] and the diversity of training systems of the Member States, embedded as they are in state-specific systems of social relations, including industrial organisation and patterns of labour market participation.[36] The general principles of a common European vocational training policy were laid down in Council Decision 63/266/EEC.[37] The Decision does not attempt to set up a common policy in the ordinary sense, and was followed by various provisions of soft law, but no regulatory measures.[38] 'The task of implementing the principles of the common vocational training policy was for the Member States and the Community working in cooperation', as confirmed by the European Court of Justice in Case 242/87 *Commission v Council (Erasmus)*.[39] So, for example, the programme for vocational training for young people,[40] based on Article 128 EEC, which sup-

---

32. Lenaerts, *supra* n 6, p 35.   33. Shaw, *supra* n 8, p 309.
34. Shaw points to the 'strong roots' of vocational training policy in the Treaty, in secondary implementing measures, in institutional structures such as CEDEFOP, and in the case law of the European Court of Justice. Shaw, *supra* n 8, p 309.
35. Flynn contrasts other common policy provisions eg Articles 38-47 EEC agriculture, Articles 110–113 EEC commercial; 'which positively require the creation of an actual policy and themselves set out the general principles on which it is to be based'. Flynn, 'Vocational Training in Community Law and Practice' (1988) 8 YEL 59–85, pp 59–60.
36. Rainbird, *supra* n 5, p 185; Flynn, *supra* n 35, p 60.
37. OJ 1963 L 1338/63; OJ Sp Ed 1963/64, 25. This is an act *sui generis*, not a 'decision' in the sense of Article 189 EC.
38. Flynn, *supra* n 35, p 61.   39. [1989] ECR 1425, para 10.
40. Decision 87/569/EEC OJ 1987 L 346/31.

ported and supplemented national policies and activities in the area in question, was within the competence of the EC institutions.[41]

However, throughout the 1980s, these supporting and cooperative policies proliferated, especially through blurring the distinction between 'vocational training' and 'education' more generally, to the stage that a platform was created for the intervention of the EU institutions in education policy, especially in higher education. This state of affairs was confirmed by the Treaty on European Union amendment to include education within EC competence.[42] During this time, by far the most active institution in establishing the EC's educational policy, especially through this obfuscation of 'vocational training' and 'education', was the European Court of Justice. In a series of 'landmark' judgments, the Court of Justice promoted a broad interpretation of 'vocational training', consequently broadening Community competence, then limited in the sphere of education to 'vocational training'.[43] The contribution of the European Court of Justice is discussed below, with the consideration of the substantive (deregulatory, re-regulatory and coordinating) provisions of European Community law relating to education. These substantive provisions affect both recipients of education and providers of education.

Recipients of education

Children of migrant EUC workers

Regulation 1612/68/EEC,[44] Article 12(1) gives children of migrant EUC workers the right to admission to the general educational and vocational training courses of the host Member State under the same conditions as children of nationals of that state. The children must be resident in the host state. Generally speaking, the European Court of Justice has interpreted 'admission' broadly, to encompass all aspects of access to educational courses, including fees and maintenance grants.[45]

41. Case 56/88 *UK v Council* [1989] ECR 1615.
42. Freedland, 'Vocational Training in EC Law and Policy – Education, Employment or Welfare' (1996) 25 ILJ 110–120, p 113.
43. This is an example of the interplay between the activities of the different institutions. See Shaw, *supra* n 6, p 417; see further Chapter 3.
44. OJ Sp Ed 1968 p 475.
45. See eg Case 9/74 *Casagrande* [1974] ECR 773; but see Case 197/86 *Brown* [1988] ECR 3205, discussed below.

Similarly, the Court has adopted an expansive approach to the personal scope of Article 12 of Regulation 1612/68. Article 12 may apply even if the working parent has returned to their Member State of nationality.[46] The definition given in Regulation 1612/68, Article 10 of 'children of the worker', who have the right to install themselves with the worker, encompasses children under the age of 21 or dependent on the worker. The Court has held that the conditions in Article 10 do not apply to Article 12.[47] Hopkins[48] points to the 'social importance' of this ruling. The child of a migrant worker concerned was orphaned, and dependent on the state orphan's allowance. The Court's judgment ensured that the child was not disadvantaged now that he was dependent on the state *in loco parentis*.

The guarantees of Regulation 1612/68 to basic access to primary and secondary education have not tended to be contentious in the Member States. By contrast, Regulation 1612/68 as a source of a right to access to higher (post-compulsory) education has been much more contentious, and it is here that educational entitlements given by Community law have been the basis of litigation to enforce those legal rights.

As Cullen points out, the measures in Regulation 1612/68 are 'equal access' measures aiming to integrate the migrant child in the host state through assimilation.[49] The assumption is that the needs of the migrant child can be met by simple equal access to the education system of the host state, in the sense of the same provision for migrant children as for nationals; a formal equality approach. A rather more positive assimilation policy, which at least appears to value cultural and linguistic diversity, and seeks to apply the principle of material as opposed to formal equality, may be found in Directive 77/486/EEC.[50] The directive applies to migrant children in the schools of the host Member State. It obliges the Member States to provide free tuition to children of migrant workers 'to facilitate their initial reception' and to ensure the 'teaching of the

---

46. Cases 389-90/87 *Echternach and Moritz* [1989] ECR 723; here the child would otherwise have been unable to continue the course of study.
47. Case C-7/94 *Lubor Gaal* [1995] ECR I-1031.
48. Hopkins, *supra* n 8.
49. Cullen, 'From Migrants to Citizens? European Community Policy on Intercultural Education' (1996) 45 ICLQ 109–129, p 110.
50. OJ 1977 L 199/32. See Cullen, *supra* n 49, p 111; de Witte, *European Community Law of Education* (Nomos, 1989) p 75.

official language of the host state'.[51] In addition, Member States are to promote the 'teaching of a mother tongue and culture of the country of origin'.[52] Although as a matter of Community law the directive applies only to EUC migrants, a Council declaration annexed to the directive pledges the Member States to apply the same principles to migrant TCNs (third country nationals).[53]

The provisions in Directive 77/486 are the only example in the sphere of education rights of an attempt by the EC to establish its own substantive measures of education policy, as opposed to extending the provisions of national policies, on the basis of the non-discrimination principle, to migrants.[54] Perhaps because of this, and also because of the cost factor, Directive 77/486 has never been adequately implemented in the Member States.[55] The European Court of Justice has never ruled on the extent of the rights contained in it, or whether they are directly effective.[56] De Witte comments that the terms of the directive are probably formulated too vaguely to be directly effective in themselves. However, he suggests that even if there is no directly effective claim to a given regime of education, it can be argued that the directive contains a directly effective standstill provision: the Directive could form the basis for a successful action against a Member State that *removes existing facilities* for special language education for migrant children.[57]

Migrant EUC workers themselves

Regulation 1612/68, Article 7(3) provides that migrant EUC workers 'by virtue of the same right and under the same conditions as national workers [shall] have access to training in vocational schools and retraining centres'. A 'vocational school' in this context is narrowly defined as an institution which provides 'only instruction either alternating with or closely linked to an occupational activity, particularly during apprenticeships'.[58] This definition would certainly not cover universities.

---

51. Article 2. 52. Article 3.
53. See COM(88) 787 final p 4; Cullen, *supra* n 49, p 120.
54. Lonbay, *supra* n 7, p 371; De Witte, *supra* n 50, p 75.
55. De Witte, *supra* n 50, p 75; Cullen, *supra* n 49, p 114.
56. Cullen, *supra* n 49, p 111, p 122, p 124.
57. De Witte, *supra* n 50, p 76. 58. Case 39/86 *Lair* [1988] ECR 3161.

However, the entitlement of EUC migrant workers in Regulation 1612/68, Article 7(2) to 'social advantages' on an equal basis with nationals has been used by the Court to develop educational entitlements of EUC migrant workers. The Court has held that Article 7(2) covers 'any advantage available to improve [workers'] professional qualifications or social advancement, such as a maintenance grant in an educational institution not covered by Article 7(3)'.[59] 'Social advantage' is presumably a concept broad enough to include 'education' as well as 'vocational training'.[60] EUC migrant workers are thus entitled, on the same basis as nationals, to a right of access to educational establishments, fees, maintenance grants, and scholarships.[61]

Article 7(2) can only be invoked this way where there is a link between previous employment and the course of education or training; except where the worker became unemployed *involuntarily* and is 'obliged by the conditions on the job market to undertake occupational training in another field of activity'.[62] So, for workers who voluntarily become unemployed in order to take up a full time training or educational course, Article 7(2) applies where there is a link between the previous employment and the course of study undertaken.[63] Otherwise, the individual concerned will have to fall back on the provisions covering migrant students, discussed below.

In order to claim entitlements under Article 7(2), an individual must be a genuine worker. The social benefits available under Article 7(2) are potentially substantial, and those who give up work to pursue education will no longer be economically active, nor contributing to the public finances of the host Member State. The Member States (particularly those with generous provision of public finances for educational access) feared that Article 7(2) could be relied upon by individuals after a short period of employment (say, a summer job) to gain educational benefits.[64] Implicit in these reservations is the idea that Member States, faced with large influxes of such 'worker-students', would be forced to lower their generous provisions for educational access, thus prompting an

---

[59]. Case 235/87 *Matteuchi* [1988] ECR 5589.

[60]. Especially post-TEU, now that the EU enjoys a limited competence in the education field.

[61]. Shaw, *supra* n 6, p 424.   [62]. Case 39/86 *Lair* [1988] ECR 3161, para 37.

[63]. Case C-3/90 *Bernini* [1992] ECR I-1071; see Craig and de Búrca, *supra* n 17, pp 669–70, p 701.

[64]. Craig and de Búrca, *supra* n 17, p 702; Flynn, *supra* n 35, p 73.

undesirable 'race to the bottom' in educational provision in the EU. The Court responded to these fears in Case 197/86 *Brown*.[65] An individual who carries out work prior to a course of study purely in order to prepare for the course of study, may not rely on Article 7(2). Such an individual is still considered a migrant worker in the sense of Article 48 EC, but cannot claim all the advantages – in this case, educational maintenance fees – provided for workers in EC legislation. The ruling appears to introduce a notion of a 'second class EUC migrant worker': someone engaged in genuine and effective work, but purely as a means to becoming a student.[66] Shaw points out that Case 197/86 *Brown* should be seen in the context of the developing student mobility programmes, especially Erasmus, which encouraged mobility, rather than individual free movement, of students. The Court has essentially cooperated with the Council of Ministers in lending its support to regulated mobility of students, rather than by encouraging individual free movement.[67] A different decision in *Brown* would have increased pressure on the UK's system of funding university students (at that time through relatively generous maintenance grants funded from public finances), and might have precipitated removal of their more generous social aspects, on the grounds that the UK 'could not afford' to educate 'for free' EUCs from other Member States – who would presumably return to their home state after graduation to work and pay taxes.

Migrant students

The rights of migrant students in EC law were developed almost exclusively by the European Court of Justice, using an innovative[68] combination of Article 7 EEC (now Article 6 EC), which contains a general prohibition on discrimination on grounds of nationality, and Article 128 EEC, which provided that Council is to lay down the general principles for implementing a common vocational policy.

The landmark ruling of the Court was Case 293/83 *Gravier v City of Liège*.[69] In this ruling the Court developed the principles

---

65. [1988] ECR 3205. 66. Craig and de Búrca, *supra* n 17, p 670.
67. Shaw, *supra* n 6, p 429.
68. Houghton-James, 'The Implication for Member States of the development of an education policy by the Court of Justice' (1993) 5 Education and the Law 15–93, p 91.
69. [1985] ECR 593.

established in the earlier Case 152/82 *Forcheri*,[70] which concerned the Italian spouse of an Italian worker employed in Belgium, who was held to be entitled to admission to Belgian education courses related to vocational training, on the same basis as nationals, that is, without having to pay an enrolment fee. As Gravier had no family member in the host state, and was only a student, he had no residence entitlement independently constituted in EC law. Nevertheless, the Court held that a right of access to education was *not* dependent upon the individual first demonstrating that he or she had derived other rights from the Treaty, for instance by virtue of worker status, or status as a member of the family of a migrant worker.[71] The Court reasserted that 'educational organisation and policy are not as such included in the spheres which the Treaty has entrusted to the Community institutions' but crucially stated that 'access to and participation in courses of instruction and apprenticeship, in particular vocational training, are not unconnected with Community law.'[72] Therefore, since 'the conditions of access to vocational training fall within the scope of the Treaty ... the imposition on students who are nationals of other Member States, of a charge ... as a condition of access to vocational training where the same fee is not imposed on students who are nationals of the host Member State, constitutes discrimination on grounds of nationality contrary to Article 7 of the Treaty'.[73]

The ruling in Case 293/83 *Gravier* had far-reaching potential; if Member States were obliged to treat all EUC students on the same basis as nationals with respect to financial conditions of access to vocational training, a very heavy burden might fall on those Member States which were net importers of such students.[74] The Court's jurisprudence places two limits upon the ruling, with its subsequent jurisprudence on what, in this context, constitutes 'vocational training' and 'conditions of access'.[75]

The definition of 'vocational training' was considered in Case 293/83 *Gravier* itself, and defined as 'any form of education which prepares for a qualification for a particular profession, trade or employment or which provides the necessary skills or training for such a profession, skill or employment ... whatever the age or level

---

70. [1983] ECR 2323.   71. Flynn, *supra* n 35, p 62.   72. Para 19.
73. Paras 25 and 26. See Craig and de Búrca, *supra* n 17, pp 702–3.
74. Green, Hartley and Usher, *The Legal Foundations of the Single Market* (OUP, 1991) p 191; Houghton-James, *supra* n 68, p 91.
75. Craig and de Búrca, *supra* n 17, p 704.

of the training of the pupils or students, and even if the training programme includes an element of general education'.[76] Subsequent jurisprudence[77] narrowed this definition,[78] and also ensured that its application in specific cases is a matter for national courts.[79] Each course is to be considered on its merits, and neither the nature of the institution nor the intention of the relevant student is determinative. In effect, this gives some leeway to national courts to adopt different interpretations, appropriate to their national education and training systems.

The definition of 'conditions of access' was considered by the Court in Case 39/86 *Lair*. The Court held that a maintenance grant for university students was not covered, although registration and tuition fees were.[80] Maintenance grants are a matter of national educational and social policy which falls within the competence of Member States. Moreover, the Court held in Case C-357/89 *Raulin*[81] that although a migrant EUC student admitted to a vocational training course had a right of residence in the host Member State for the duration of the course, conditions of residence 'such as the covering of maintenance costs and health insurance'[82] imposed by that Member State were not contrary to EC law.[83] This ruling may be viewed as a form of 'cooperative dialogue' between the European Court and legislature.[84] The approach adopted in Case C-357/89 *Raulin* is consonant with that in Directive 90/366/EEC, since replaced by the virtually identical Directive 93/96/EEC,[85] which grants residence rights to financially independent EUC migrant students. These students are a sort of 'third class' of EUC migrants, who do not fall into any pre-established category in EC law.[86]

The Court's ruling in Case 293/83 *Gravier* is generally credited with providing the trigger for the European Union's cooperative

76. Para 30.
77. See Case 24/86 *Blaizot v University of Liège* [1988] ECR 379, in which the Court held that although university studies generally fulfil the *Gravier* definition, there are exceptions for 'certain courses of study which, because of their particular nature, are intended for persons wishing to improve their general knowledge rather than prepare themselves for occupations'; para 20.
78. Flynn, *supra* n 35, p 63. 79. Flynn, *supra* n 35, p 71. 80. Para 15.
81. [1992] ECR I-1027. 82. Para 39. 83. Craig and de Búrca, *supra* n 17, p 705.
84. Craig and de Búrca, *supra* n 17, pp 705–6.
85. OJ 1993 L 317/59; following Case C-295/90 *European Parliament v Council* [1992] ECR I-4193, in which the Court held the original directive was invalid on procedural grounds.
86. They are not workers, self-employed persons, providers of services or dependants of any of the above; see Shaw, *supra* n 6, p 427.

incentive policies in the education sphere, especially the Erasmus programme on mobility of university students.[87] Erasmus has now been subsumed in the Socrates programme.[88] Participation in these exchange programmes is voluntary, but has attracted quite large numbers of students. The medium-term objective of the programme is that one in ten university students will spend some time abroad and all will be aware of the European dimension of the subject they are studying. It was argued in Case 242/87 *Commission v Council (Erasmus)* that the Erasmus programme unlawfully affected national education policy (a matter within the competence of the Member States) by financing the establishment of University networks. The Court emphasised that the universities' participation in Erasmus would be on a voluntary basis, and their authority to decide whether to enter into University networks would not be affected. Although these programmes are not regulatory, they do have an integrative function in the sense of shaping (and financing) 'best practice' in higher education,[89] especially in the context of those Member States experiencing decreasing national financing of higher education.

It will be interesting to see the impact of EC law in the UK once the Dearing reforms requiring British students to pay £1,000 per annum towards tuition fees take effect. EUC migrant students who come to the UK to follow a degree programme will presumably be required to pay the fees on a non-discriminatory basis with British students. However, EUC students will also be entitled, in accordance with EC law, to a student loan in order to meet those fees, on the same basis as British students. The student loan for registration and tuition fees will be a 'condition of access' to education, in terms of EC law.[90] The practical difficulty for the UK government will be the recovery of student loans from EUC migrant students who are no longer in the UK.[91] The position of students who come under Socrates to study in the UK for a year, as part of their own degree programmes, is less straightforward. Are these students to be required to pay the annual fee, or is the basis of Socrates – that of exchange of students – such that it is not the 'incoming' Socrates student who meets the cost of their tuition, but an 'outgoing'

87. Shaw, *supra* n 6, p 431.   88. See above.
89. Spokkereef, *supra* n 6, p 343; Lonbay, *supra* n 7, pp 368–9.
90. Case 39/86 *Lair*.
91. The Brussels Convention on Jurisdiction and the Enforcement of Judgments in Civil and Commercial Matters 1968 Articles 26, 28(3) and 31 would enable judgments against the defaulting former students to be enforced across the EU.

British Socrates student? Might not that 'outgoing' student claim that, as they are not receiving tuition in a British university for that year, they need not pay the £1,000? This is an example of the way in which membership of the EU, with its multi-level system of governance, may in practice constrain formally internal matters, in this case, provision of funding for tertiary education.

Freedom to receive services

The possibility that the provisions of the Treaty on the freedom to provide and receive services[92] might form the basis for public educational entitlements of individuals in EC law has been rejected by the Court. Freedom to provide services does not include freedom to go to another Member State and receive services there without restriction.[93] Furthermore, although private education would be a 'service' in EC law,[94] state education is not a service in this sense.[95]

Third country nationals

None of the above provisions of EC law applies to third country nationals (TCNs). However, EC law has had a marginal impact on the provision of education in the Member States for children of migrant TCN workers. In practice it is difficult to separate EUC migrant children from other migrant children. In several Member States, multicultural educational programmes are extended to all migrant children. Even some of the pilot projects sponsored by the Commission have included migrant TCN children.[96] However, the EC has no specific legal basis[97] upon which to build significant provision for migrant TCNs.[98]

92. Article 59 EC.
93. Freedom to provide services is discussed further in Chapter 7 in the context of health services.
94. Case C-109/92 *Wirth* [1993] ECR I-6447.
95. Case 263/86 *Belgian State v Humbel* [1988] ECR 5365. Although, as Nielsen and Szyszczak point out, it is not always easy to distinguish between the 'public/social' and 'private/economic' nature of activities of educational institutions. (Nielsen and Szyszczak, *The Social Dimension of the European Union* (Handelshojskolens Forlag, 1997) pp 147–8). See also Houghton-James, *supra* n 68, p 87.
96. De Witte, *supra* n 50, p 78.
97. Although the general legal basis of Article 235 EC might serve. See De Witte, *supra* n 50, p 79.
98. Cases 281/85, 283/85, 285/85 and 287/85 *Germany and others v Commission* [1988] ECR 3203.

The Tempus programme established in Decision 90/232/EEC[99] operates on the same basis as Erasmus for students from Central and Eastern European countries. The European Training Foundation[100] provides an institutional vehicle for delivering aid in the form of vocational training to the new democracies of Central and Eastern Europe. The aid is provided by the Member States of the EU, and certain other third countries, acting jointly, so as to enhance the effectiveness of the aid provided.[101]

Providers of education

Individual providers (teachers)

The general principle of non-discrimination on grounds of nationality (Article 6 EC), combined with the provisions in Article 48 EC and Article 57 EC on the freedom of movement of workers and the right of establishment, give a general entitlement to equal access to employment or establishment as a teacher in a host Member State for migrant EUC teachers. As teachers in most Member States have civil servant status, teachers were originally viewed as excluded from the Treaty provisions on free movement by the public service exemption in Article 48(4) EEC. At this stage, therefore, cooperative measures were used to promote free movement of teachers.[102] However, the argument from Article 48(4) EC has gradually been eroded by the European Court of Justice. Basically, the Court does not accept that, in general, teachers in the public education sector perform a state function from which non-nationals by definition must be excluded.[103] The Court has

---

[99] OJ 1990 L 131/21.

[100] Regulation 1360/90 OJ 1990 L 131/1 (legal basis Article 235 EEC).

[101] Shaw, *supra* n 8, pp 309–10.

[102] For instance, the resolution of ministers of education meeting within Council 1974 OJ C 98 – para II(vi), which encouraged the freedom of movement of teachers, students and research workers; and the action programme which followed OJ 1976 C 38/1. See Hopkins, 'Recognition of Teaching Qualifications: Community law in the English Context' (1996) 21 ELRev 435–48, p 436.

[103] Case 66/85 *Lawrie Blum* [1986] ECR 2121. See Handoll, 'Foreign Teachers and Public Education', in de Witte (ed), *European Community Law of Education* (Nomos, 1989) p 33. The Commission subsequently issued a notice on Article 48(4) EC, in which teachers were listed in the category excluded from its ambit OJ 1988 C 72/2.

recently confirmed this position in two decisions brought by the Commission under the Article 169 EC procedure, concerning exclusion of non-nationals from teaching posts in nursery, primary and secondary schools, and higher education establishments and universities.[104] The Court's approach here links to the 'state building' functions of education provision as part of social policy generally, and may suggest that the Court's agenda is perhaps one of 'state building' at the European level.

The Court's jurisprudence applies equally to indirect discrimination on grounds of nationality. Detrimental employment conditions of foreign language lecturers, teachers and assistants have been successfully challenged before the Court, on the grounds that these teachers are in practice more likely to be non-nationals.[105] One of the most likely forms of indirect discrimination is the imposition of a language requirement on access to certain teaching posts. A far higher proportion of non-nationals than nationals would be affected by such a requirement. Where a language requirement is a legitimate condition of access to a job, in the sense that, 'by reason of the nature of the post to be filled', the effective execution of the job requires abilities in a particular language, an exemption is provided by Article 3(1) of Regulation 1612/68.

The Court gave a generous interpretation to that provision in Case 379/87 *Groener v Minister for Education*,[106] in which the performance of the duties of the teaching post in question would never actually require the use of the Irish language. Nevertheless, the Court held that this finding 'is not in itself sufficient to enable the national court to decide whether the linguistic requirement is justified by reason of the nature of the post to be filled' within the meaning of the last paragraph of Article 3(1).[107] Subject to the requirement of proportionality, a (long-standing) policy based on the promotion of national identity and culture could justify the imposition of an indirectly discriminatory language requirement for teaching posts.[108] The final decision was left to the national court. Most commentators consider that the *Groener* decision was influenced by the powerful arguments for the preservation of

104. Case C-473/93 *Commission v Luxembourg* [1996] ECR I-3207; Case C-290/94 *Commission v Greece* [1996] ECR I-3285.
105. Case 33/88 *Allué I* [1989] ECR 1591; Case C-259, 331- 2/91 *Allué II* [1993] ECR 4309; Case C-272/92 *Spotti* [1993] ECR 5185; see Shaw, *supra* n 6, p 423.
106. [1989] ECR 3967.   107. Para 16.
108. See Craig and de Búrca, *supra* n 17, p 657.

national cultural heritage, not least those put forward by intervening Member States, and the Advocate General.[109]

Another form of indirect discrimination may arise from a host Member State's failure to recognise teaching qualifications acquired in another Member State. The provisions on mutual recognition of teaching qualifications are discussed below. Teaching may be a 'regulated professional activity' in the sense of these provisions.[110] Hopkins has shown how the Court applies a 'rule of reason' approach to the application of qualifications requirements to teachers and other providers of education. A distinction must be drawn between qualifications requirements resulting in 'duality' (that is, where the individual must comply with the same condition twice, once at home and once in the host state) and those where there is no duality. In the former situation, the host state's requirements may not be applied. In the latter, they may be applied if justified under the rule of reason.[111]

Institutional providers

Institutional providers of education have been affected by the coordination action of the European Union institutions. In the sphere of vocational training, the European Centre for the Development of Vocational Training (CEDEFOP) was set up in 1975[112] with the aims of coordinating and supporting the national vocational training policies of the Member States. Originally, European financial support for educational projects was channelled solely through the structural funds. However, the development in the 1980s of separate programmes such as Erasmus and Commett set up an institutional framework for the Community's intervention in educational policies (still in a supporting and coordinating role) based on Article 128 EEC. The structural funds, especially the ESF, play a role in promoting training and education, especially for young people and other 'excluded' persons.[113] These aspects of EU education and training policy, which are not directly related to

---

109. Craig and de Búrca, *supra* n 17, p 658; Lonbay, *supra* n 7, p 371; Shaw, *supra* n 6, p 423.
110. See Case C-164/94 *Aranitis v Land Berlin* [1996] ECR I-135, paras 16–29; Hopkins, *supra* n 102, pp 439–40.
111. Hopkins, *supra* n 102, pp 442–5.
112. Regulation 1365/75 OJ 1975 L 139/1.
113. Regulation 2052/88/EEC, OJ 1988 L 185/9, Article 1 and Article 3(2), as amended by Regulation 2081/93/EC OJ 1993 L 193/5. See Chapter 9.

mobility or free movement of education providers or recipients within the internal market, are discussed further in Chapter 9, concerned with the EU's structural funds.

In the post-Maastricht era, the European Union institutions are empowered by Articles 126 and 127 EC to encourage cooperation between institutional providers of education. The participation of national educational institutions in the European Union's programmes is strictly on a 'soft' or persuasive (non-regulatory) basis. However, a significant carrot of financial subsidy is offered to national institutions which do participate. Since participation may involve adjustments to national law, policy and practice in the educational field, in the EU's multi-level social policy system, this may be seen as a version of 'cooperative federalism', according to which the central authority uses the power of the purse to steer the course of 'autonomous' cooperating sub-entities. Such mechanisms are familiar in the national spheres of the Member States, especially those in which education is devolved to local or regional governments. As Lenaerts points out, this method of cooperative harmonisation is dependent upon the perception of national governments, or other actors at national or regional level, that it is in their interests to cooperate. These actors are likely to support *supplementary* dimensions[114] to their education policies, where they retain the control of the core of national (or regional) policy in the educational sphere.[115]

Mutual recognition of educational qualifications

In many fields of employment in the Member States, particularly in the professions, entry into certain occupations is limited by national laws to those who hold certain educational qualifications. These national rules on educational and vocational qualifications requirements pose a threat to the free movement of workers, freedom to provide services and the freedom of establishment established by the Treaty of Rome. Accordingly, the European Community regulates the recognition of educational and vocational training qualifications between Member States by means of

---

114. Such as language teaching, mobility of pupils and teachers, distance learning or programmes to improve the transition from education or vocational training to the labour market.
115. Lenaerts, *supra* n 6, p 38.

two general provisions:[116] the 'new approach' Directive 89/48/EEC on the recognition of higher education diplomas,[117] and Decision 92/51/EEC on the recognition of professional education and training qualifications.[118]

Both provisions apply where the host state requires an individual who wishes to take up a professional activity to possess a diploma. Directive 89/48 applies where the diploma requires at least equivalent of three years' full-time study at a university or similar institution. Directive 92/51 applies where the profession requires a post-secondary course at least equivalent to one year's full-time study.[119] The provisions operate on the same basis, by prohibiting the host state from denying the individual who either has the requisite qualifications to practise the profession in the host state, or has pursued the profession in a host state in which it is unregulated, and incidentally holds some qualifications, the entitlement to practise the profession in the host state. Although the directives have passed their date for implementation, there are still problems in practice in some Member States.

These provisions are based on the mutual recognition, between Member States, of educational qualifications. They operate on the basis of the fulfilment of minimum conditions by the individual, and on mutual cooperation and trust between Member States. Zilioli points to the Member States' common educational and cultural heritage, in particular the institution of the university, as the structural underpinning for this mutual trust.[120] The benefit of the mutual recognition approach is that it allows for free movement, without necessitating regulatory harmonisation, which would almost certainly have to be on the basis of the lowest level of qualification permitted in any Member State. The spectre of the lowering of educational standards in those Member States with higher standards is thereby avoided.[121]

---

116. In addition there are various 'old approach' directives in specific professional fields, eg Directive 80/154/EEC and 80/155/EEC OJ 1980 L 33/1 and 8 (midwives); Directive 85/384/EEC OJ 1985 L 223/15 (architects); Directive 77/249/EEC OJ 1977 L 78/16 (lawyers).
117. OJ L 1989 19/16 (legal basis Articles 49, 57(1) 66 EEC).
118. OJ L 1992 209/25 (legal basis Articles 49, 57(1) 66 EEC).
119. Hopkins, *supra* n 102, p 439.
120. Zilioli, 'The Recognition of Diplomas and its Impact on Educational Policies', in de Witte (ed), *European Community Law of Education* (Nomos, 1989) p 59.
121. Zilioli, *supra* n 120, p 60.

Conclusions

Education and training in the EU is a policy field which is influenced by actors at European, national and subnational levels: another example of the multi-level nature of European social policy.[122] From the point of view of individuals, the most significant legal influences on national education systems emanating from the EU institutions are probably the deregulatory internal market measures on the free movement of persons, and the coordination measures (based on mutual recognition of qualifications) enacted by the EU institutions to make that free movement a practical reality. However, it will be remembered that the free movement provisions apply only to workers (and their families), and only a very small proportion of EUCs are migrant workers. Migrant students have only the 'third class' status granted by EC law, and in particular are not entitled to social advantages of maintenance grants while they complete their studies.

Moreover, the provisions of EC law on education for migrants may be said to be focused on educational 'achievers', rather than those who are disadvantaged and may benefit from social assistance by means of the education system. For instance, the entitlements given by Regulation 1612/68 tend to give most financial help to EUC migrant children who are sufficiently integrated in the host Member State to proceed to tertiary education there. No provision is made at the EU level for less advantaged children, for instance, those with special linguistic needs or TCNs.[123] Free movement of persons within the European Union, although in principle open to all, in practice consists mainly of the movement of skilled workers.[124] Hence, European action focuses upon, for instance, opportunities to study abroad, improving university education, and language learning. Support for the movement of students may promote 'a Community labour market in professionals and a cross-frontier provision of [professional] services'.[125] Only a very small proportion of EC action fosters the 'social' dimension

---

122. Pierson and Leibfried 'Multitiered Institutions and the Making of Social Policy', in Leibfried and Pierson (eds), *European Social Policy: Between Fragmentation and Integration* (Brookings, 1995); Milner, *supra* n 1.
123. See Cullen, *supra* n 49, p 119.
124. The demand for semi-skilled or unskilled workers is largely met by TCN migrants.
125. Shaw, *supra* n 6, pp 431–3.

of education and training, aimed at alleviating disadvantage, mainly the ESF measures on retraining of the unemployed.[126]

Generally, responsibility for education and training policies remains firmly with the Member States. The costs of public education and training programmes fall at the national level, and, save the small amounts administered through the structural funds and other EC education policies, are not redistributed at EU level. The principle of subsidiarity, and the specific provisions in Articles 126 and 127 EC[127] ensure that national (or regional) governments retain their control. National education policies remain closely tied to national cultural traditions. Any convergence of policies is more likely to come about in response to economic and social trends which apply within and beyond the EU, such as rising youth unemployment,[128] not as a direct response to EU action.

However, the EU institutions are likely to continue to influence development of education and training policies within the EU. The Commission (and especially DG XXII) may help to prompt convergence by its role as gatherer and disseminator of information and expertise in education and training policy, to provide national policy actors with a number of choices informed by practice in other Member States. Education policy networks, supported by the Commission, also provide a means of such information exchange. Freedland has sought to argue that the EU institutions have attempted to 'relocate' vocational training issues in the sphere of education, on the grounds that they meet less ideological resistance from Member States on that basis. The Commission has sought to reconceptualise matters relating to vocational training, traditionally viewed as an aspect of national employment policies, as part of education policy. Education is seen as less politically charged than employment, and therefore an area where the Commission may be more likely to exert its influence as against Council.[129] However, if this is so, the attempt has been undermined by recent developments. A new emphasis in Commission documents on 'lifelong learning'[130] and 'the learning society' may well signal an attempt (at least on the part of DG XXII) to situate both training *and*

---

126. See Chapter 9.
127. Excluding harmonisation, even though they permit action by qualified majority.
128. Milner, *supra* n 1.   129. Freedland, *supra* n 42, pp 111–14.
130. 'The on-going access to the renewing of skills and the acquisition of knowledge' COM (95) 590 final.

education issues firmly in the employment and competitiveness sphere.[131] This new approach of the Commission reflects changing employment patterns and the social reality of unemployment, short-term jobs, and frequent career changes. It attempts to underpin the resultant social insecurity with education and training, focused upon a broad knowledge base and transferable employment skills. The Commission's White Paper on Education and Training[132] specifically aims to encourage the acquisition of new knowledge; bring school and business sector closer together; combat exclusion; develop proficiency in three European languages; and treat capital investment and investment in training on an equal basis. The implication is that in the future a much greater 'flexibility' in education and training systems will be required. If the EU institutions underpin these aspirations with funding subsidies, this could promote quite fundamental changes in European education and training systems. However, no such dramatic change is likely to take place in the short term. The Council Conclusions on the White Paper[133] are lukewarm, calling for further discussion. The cultural aspects of education and training are explicitly placed firmly back into the frame, and the 'risk' of an over-simplistic interpretation of the relationship between learning, economic development and employment growth is stressed.

The main influence of EU action on national education and vocational training policies may simply turn out to be the introduction, within the internal market, of some measure of competition between different national educational regimes, as individual 'consumers' and providers of educational services are enabled to seek or provide those services without hindrance on grounds of their nationality. However, EU action in the education and vocational training sphere does extend further. The 'market building' aspects of EU education, and especially vocational training policy, are evident in the ESF provisions, and are indicated more strongly in recent initiatives. According to this view, education and vocational

131. COM(95) 590 final; COM(96) 471 final; *Learning in the Information Society action plan for a European Education Initiative (1996–98)*.
132. *Teaching and Learning: Towards the Learning Society* COM(95) 590 final. Based on *White Paper on Growth, Competitiveness and Employment* COM(93) 700 final and statement of Cannes European Council that 'training ... policies, which are fundamental for improving employment and competitiveness, must be strengthened, especially continuing training'.
133. OJ 1996 C 195/1. See also Council Conclusion on Lifelong Learning OJ 1997 C 7/6.

training policy is a tool in the creation of a more competitive EU.

Moreover, in the long term, perhaps the most significant aspect of European educational policy may yet turn out to be its role in raising European and 'cross-cultural' consciousness.[134] If education policy were reconceptualised as part of an emergent notion of 'European social citizenship', either in addition to, or even in conflict with, the rather commodifying market-building aspects which have hitherto received much support, this could pave the way to wider EU-level intervention in education, perhaps contributing, in time, to a process of creating a 'Europeanisation' of the 'hearts and minds' of the people of Europe.

[134.] Shaw, *supra* n 6, p 419; Spokkereef, *supra* n 6, p 340; Ryba, *supra* n 14, p 24.

CHAPTER SEVEN

Health

Introduction

Health policy and national health care systems are traditionally viewed as a central plank of national social policies. Health policy may be broadly defined as concerned with all aspects of provision of health care – both publicly and privately financed – ranging from regulation of health professionals and producers of medical products such as pharmaceuticals, individual entitlements to provision of medical treatment, and health promotion generally. Health policy is closely related to welfare and social security policies, as those who are most in need of medical treatment are often those who are 'excluded' from society – *inter alia* through their inability to work – and who therefore require social security or welfare provision. Health, along with social security, housing, social work and education, is one of the 'big five' social services.[1]

The EU has no general competence to regulate in the field of health policy. Although Article 30 EC provides that the activities of the Community include 'a contribution to the attainment of a high level of health protection', that 'contribution' is explicitly limited[2] to support for cooperation between Member States and coordination of national policies. There is no such thing as the 'European Union health system'. Wide disparities exist between health care systems within the European Union; both in terms of level of provision, and in terms of organisation and financing. These differences are attributable to different policy choices in the trade-off between the goals of solidarity, efficiency and individual

1. Spicker, *Social Policy: Themes and Approaches* (Prentice Hall/Harvester Wheatsheaf, 1995) p 3.
2. Article 129 EC.

freedom of choice, each of which to a greater or lesser extent informs national health care systems.[3] Levels of health expenditure reflect the relative value attributed to health care as opposed to other sectors competing for public finance.[4] These policy choices are made in the context of political, historical, cultural and socio-economic factors which are (at least to some extent) unique to each Member State.

However, as with the other areas of social policy discussed in this book, health policy within the Member States of the EU is affected by policy decisions and legal acts taken at European level. The coordination of national health policies at European level may lead to voluntary convergence of national policies. In particular, the phenomenon of common problems in health provision may lead to the adoption by national health executives of policy measures that are seen as having been successful in other Member States. Health issues which preoccupy Europe as a whole pose common problems to all Member States.[5] A report prepared recently for the European Commission identifies 'ageing, population mobility, disease from environmental change and hazardous workplaces and socio-economic problems, especially social exclusion' as areas where cooperation and collaboration between Member States in health care and health policy could give 'added value' to national efforts.[6] Effective health education is a central part of all national health promotion and preventative policies of the Member States. So far as organisation of health systems is concerned, all Member States[7] have cost containment of health care as a central aim of their social policies. A certain convergence of methods to meet this aim is to be expected.[8] These issues are reflected in the agendas of the meetings of the ministers for public health and the Commission,

---

3. Admiraal, 'Introduction to in Health Care' in Hermans, Casparie and Paelinck (eds), *Health Care in Europe After 1992* (Dartmouth, 1992) p 51.

4. Abel-Smith, Figueras, Holland, McKee and Mossialos (eds), *Choices in Health Policy: An Agenda for the European Union* (Dartmouth, 1995) p 23.

5. Eg, the ageing of the population, AIDS, cancer, alcohol and drug abuse; Berlin, 'Current Trends likely to Affect Health Care in Europe After 1992', in Hermans, Casparie and Paelinck (eds), *Health Care in Europe After 1992* (Dartmouth, 1992) p 3.

6. Abel-Smith et al, *supra* n 4, p xix, pp 1, 21–2.

7. With the possible exception of Greece, where cost containment policies have had a more limited impact.

8. Abel-Smith, *Cost Containment and New Priorities in Health Care: A study of the European Community* (Avebury, 1991) pp vii, 129; Berlin, *supra* n 5, p 5; Abel-Smith et al, *supra* n 4, p 39.

held since the late 1970s.[9] Moreover, and perhaps more significantly, the deregulatory[10] provisions of EC law relating to the establishment of the internal market, and the 'four freedoms', in particular the freedom of movement of goods, persons and services,[11] have an impact on some aspects of national health policies. These provisions are discussed in more detail below.

The relevant Treaty provisions and legislation: context

The Treaty on European Union introduced the new provision of Article 129 EC on 'Public Health' into the Treaty of Rome. Article 129 EC provides that 'the Community shall contribute towards a high level of human health protection by encouraging cooperation between Member States and, if necessary, lending support to their action'. Action of the EU institutions is to be directed towards a number of particular areas, listed in Article 129 EC. These are the prevention of diseases, in particular major health scourges (including drug dependence); research into causes and transmission of these diseases; and provision of information and education on health. Article 129 EC also provides that health protection requirements are to form a constituent part of the EC's other policies.

Article 129 EC establishes a 'flanking policy': an area in which activities of the EU institutions are limited to coordination, and harmonisation of national laws is explicitly excluded from Community competence. Member States are placed under an obligation to liaise with the Commission and to coordinate policies and programmes in the areas referred to above. The Commission is granted a general power of initiative to propose measures which will promote cooperation between the Member States in those areas. Article 129 EC forms a legal basis upon which Council and Parliament may adopt 'incentive measures' according to the co-decision procedure,[12] or recommendations, by qualified majority

9. Roscam Abbing, 'European Community and the Right to Health Care', in Hermans, Casparie and Paelinck (eds), *Health Care in Europe After 1992* (Dartmouth, 1992) p 24.
10. And consequent pressure to re-regulate.
11. Leibfried and Pierson, 'Social Policy', in Wallace and Wallace (eds), *Policy-Making in the European Union* (OUP, 1996) p 198.
12. Article 189b procedure.

on a proposal from the Commission, in order to contribute to the achievement of the objectives set out in the provision.

Coordination activity in the health field between the Member States, supported by the European Commission, actually predates the amendment introduced by the Treaty on European Union. For instance, the 'Europe against Cancer' programme[13] commenced in 1989 and the similar 'Europe against AIDS' programme[14] in 1991. Article 129 EC represents a compromise between those Member States who did not want any European Community mandate in health, and those who wanted to go further. Article 129 EC was seen by some as setting limits to the expansion of EU-level activities in the public health field, which had occurred in the past without any specific legal basis. For others, it was a mere formalisation of what was already taking place.[15]

Although legislative regulatory harmonisation at EU level is explicitly excluded by Article 129 EC, coordination of national health policies is likely to produce a certain degree of convergence. Convergence will be promoted not least by the financial inducements attached to participation in European health programmes. 'Incentive measures' in the health field supported by the European Community will promote common objectives and practices, by encouraging 'voluntary' conformity of national policies, or at least new developments within those policies, by means of the financial benefits available to those national bodies which choose to participate.[16]

The competence of the European Community in the field of public health was expressed at greater length in the Council Resolution on future action in the field of public health.[17] This resolution reiterates that 'public health policy as such, except where the

---

13. Decision 88/351/EEC of the Council and Representatives of the Governments of the Member States meeting within the Council OJ 1988 L 160/52. The programme encompassed anti- tobacco campaigns, improvements in nutrition, protection against carcinogenic agents, promotion of screening policies, provision of information to public and professionals, and research. The decision presents as its basis simply 'the Treaty establishing the EC'.

14. Decision 91/317/EEC of Council and Minsters of Health of the Member States adopting a plan of action in the framework of the 'Europe against AIDS' programme OJ 1991 L 175/26, encompassing training provision, information exchange on services, research and measures to promote the safety of blood. McKee, Mossialos and Belcher, 'The Influence of European Law on National Health Policy' (1996) 6 JESP 263–86, p 265.

15. McKee, Mossialos and Belcher, *supra* n 14, p 267.

16. McKee, Mossialos and Belcher, *supra* n 14, p 266.

17. OJ 1993 C 174/1.

Treaties provide otherwise, is the responsibility of the Member States'. Four basic criteria for Community action in the field are set out. First, there must be a significant health problem, for which appropriate preventative actions are possible. Second, the proposed activity must supplement or promote other EC policies such as the operation of the internal market. Third, EC activities are to be consistent with those of other international organisations, for instance the World Health Organisation. To this effect, the desirability of European Community cooperation with other international organisations concerned with health is expressly noted.[18] It is important to view the formation of European Community health policies in this international context. Many EC action programmes in the health field, for instance the Cancer and AIDS programmes, are the fruits of long-standing collaboration between the World Health Organisation's regional office for Europe, and the institutions of the EU.[19]

Fourth, the Resolution provides that the aim of the Community action must be such that it cannot be sufficiently achieved by Member States acting alone; a specific application of the principle of subsidiarity.[20] Subsidiarity requires that proposed activities and functions are demonstrably better performed at European, rather than national, level. In the health field, criteria to test proposed activities for compliance with subsidiary might include a clear need for coordination of activity or for enabling Member States to learn from each other's experience in health care reform or innovation; functions which might be performed more cheaply for the EU as a whole;[21] issues which cross country boundaries;[22] and actions to make information exchange beneficial.[23]

The Council Resolution is fleshed out by the Commission action programme for health promotion, information, education and training in the field of public health.[24] This was agreed in 1995 after lengthy negotiations over budget size. As the budget is rela-

---

18. McKee, Mossialos and Belcher, *supra* n 14, p 267.
19. Altenstetter, 'The Effects of European Policies on Health and Health Care' in Hermans, Casparie and Paelinck (eds), *Health Care in Europe After 1992* (Dartmouth, 1992) p 34.
20. Article 3b EC.
21. Eg, research into rare diseases which would be too expensive for one Member State acting alone.
22. For example, epidemics, the environment or consequences of free movement of personnel.
23. For example, to standardise definitions. Abel-Smith et al, *supra* n 4, p 126.
24. COM(94) 202 final.

tively modest, the setting of priorities for Community action is crucial. It was agreed that action should not be spread superficially over a large area, rather that limited resources be directed at a few carefully chosen areas.[25] The priority areas are drug dependence, cancer, AIDS and other communicable diseases, health data, information, accidents and injuries, pollution-related diseases, and rare diseases. The Commission's action programme suggests a slight refocussing of policy, towards health promotion and the broader determinants of good health, from the direction suggested by the wording of Article 129 EC, which appears to be more focused on the prevention of major diseases. This refocus appears to emanate from the Commission itself, and the agenda of those responsible in DG V.[26]

In addition to the coordination action under Article 129 EC, various other provisions of EC law have an impact on health policy. Measures aimed at completion of the internal market[27] may have some effect on health systems. For instance, the provisions on the free movement of persons have an impact on health professionals and patients; those on freedom to provide services may affect health care services, and also health insurance; and those on the free movement of goods include the free movement of pharmaceuticals and other medical products. Moreover, in some circumstances, Member States may restrict free movement of persons and goods on the ground of health protection. Where the provisions on the completion of the internal market interface with health policy or national health systems, the context for their construction and effect in the national legal orders is the centrality of the 'four freedoms' to EC law. This centrality is reflected, for instance, in the extremely restrictive jurisprudence of the European Court of Justice on exclusions to the provisions establishing the internal market.[28]

The impact of the internal market provisions of EC law on national health systems may prove to be a significant force for their future convergence. If pressures arise from increasing patient mobility, deregulation of private health insurance, increased border crossing of health professionals, a growing number of internationally

---

[25.] McKee, Mossialos and Belcher, *supra* n 14, p 269.
[26.] McKee, Mossialos and Belcher, *supra* n 14, p 266.
[27.] Based on Articles 49, 57(3), 66, 100a EC.
[28.] For example, in Case 30/77 *R v Bouchereau* [1977] ECR 1999 the Court held that the policy justifying the exclusion must be a threat to 'one of the fundamental interests of society'.

operated hospital chains, and free trade in pharmaceutical products, these are likely to have more of an effect on national health systems than coordinating measures emanating from the European Commission.[29] Such pressures may contribute to a 'regulatory gap' in health care, which some may regard as undesirable. If public provision of health care decreases, and 'privatised' market models and competition in health care increase, coupled with the measures on the internal market, price competition and decentralisation of decision making may have a destabilising effect on national health systems.[30] So far, the practical impact of the internal market on national health care systems has been rather limited. If, however, in the future, pressures imposed, *inter alia*, by the internal market lead to a 'privatisation' of health care provision in the Member States, this may in turn increase support for a European health care system more firmly based on the social justice model. Such a scenario must at present remain purely at the level of speculation.

Recipients of health care and health protection

Although health care and health protection in the Member States is at present almost exclusively within the remit of national legal systems, some measures of European regulation may affect health-related rights of all individuals in the Member States. In addition, free movers may derive specific rights relating to health care from provisions of EC law. Potential free movers may also have their freedom of movement restricted on health grounds, under certain circumstances provided for in EC measures.

Rights of all European citizens/residents

Generally speaking, rights and entitlements to health care and health protection of EUCs and those resident within the territory of the European Union are determined by national law. However,

29. Leibfried and Pierson, 'Semisovereign Welfare States: Social Policy in a Multitiered Europe', in Leibfried and Pierson (eds), *European Social Policy* (Brookings, 1995) p 66; Leibfried and Pierson, *supra* n 11, p 198; Graf von der Schulenburg, 'Competition, Solidarity and Cost Containment in Medical Care' in Hermans, Casparie and Paelinck (eds), *Health Care in Europe After 1992* (Dartmouth, 1992) p 71.
30. Admiraal, *supra* n 3, p 51.

some aspects of this field are subject to European-level regulation. This regulation may be divided into three broad areas. The first may be characterised as European-level regulation to ensure the protection of consumers from harmful medical products. The second related area concerns the application of the deregulatory free movement of goods provisions to medical products and in particular from their application on health grounds; again, this is concerned with consumer protection from harmful or potentially harmful medical goods, although here protection is imposed at national level. The third concerns protection of consumers from goods in general which may be harmful to health, in the context of the internal market in goods.[31]

Directive 65/65/EEC[32] is the earliest European-level measure with the aim of harmonising safety and efficacy standards for medical products. Enacted in response to the thalidomide tragedies of the early 1960s,[33] the directive required Member States to enact laws to ensure that new medical products may not be marketed on their territories without the approval of a competent regulatory body.

More detailed harmonisation provisions for the criteria and procedures according to which approval may be given by national regulatory bodies for new medical products followed. A large number of detailed provisions of secondary legislation now cover all industrially produced medicines, including vaccines, blood products and radio pharmaceuticals. Technical requirements governing testing of new medical products are regularly updated by the Commission, in accordance with power delegated for this purpose by the Council.[34] In addition to criteria relating to quality, safety

---

31. This is not discussed in detail in this book; see Weatherill *EC Consumer Law and Policy* (Longman: 1996).

32. OJ 1965 L 369/65; OJ Sp Ed p 20. Now amended and consolidated by Directive 93/39/EEC OJ 1993 L 214/22.

33. White, 'Whither the Pharmaceutical Trade Mark?' (1996) 8 European Intellectual Property Rev 441–5, p 441; Gardner, 'The European Agency for the Evaluation of Medicines and European Regulation of Pharmaceuticals' (1996) 2 ELJ 48–82, p 52; Kaufer, 'The Regulation of New Product Development in the Drug Industry', in Majone (ed), *Deregulation or Re-regulation? Regulatory Reform in Europe and the United States* (Pinter, 1990) p 157.

34. Sauer, 'The European Community's Pharmaceutical Policy' in Hermans, Casparie and Paelinck (eds), *Health Care in Europe After 1992* (Dartmouth, 1992) p 133. Amendments are made according to the 'regulatory committee procedure', under which the Committee must support the Commission proposal by a qualified majority in order for the amendment to be adopted. Shaw, *Law of the European Union* (Macmillan, 1996) p 161.

and efficacy, rules relating to procedures for marketing authorisation (time limits, giving of reasons, publication),[35] to manufacture (quality control, inspections),[36] to labelling (packaging to include information relating to dose, ingredients, side effects)[37] and to advertising of medical products (advertisement to the general public of prescription drugs is prohibited)[38] have been harmonised. These provisions are consolidated in the Commission's six volume publication 'The Rules governing Medicinal Products in the European Community'.

Approval of most new medical products[39] is still basically a matter for national authorities. However, exercise of this national competence is curtailed to a certain extent by European-level provisions which set out a 'decentralised procedure' for approval of a new medical product in other Member States, once it has been approved in one Member State. This procedure is essentially an application of the principle of mutual recognition, according to which Member States must provide a good reason for non-recognition of an approval of a new medical product granted by another Member State and therefore is an example of regulatory coordination of national laws.

The decentralised procedure, provided for in Regulation 2309/93/EC[40] and Directive 93/39/EEC, is the successor to the 'multi-state procedure',[41] according to which a producer of a medical product authorised in one Member State could request extension of this authorisation to two or more (originally five or more[42]) other Member States. A formal opinion on authorisation was to be provided by the Committee for Proprietary Medical Products (CPMP), comprised of national experts and members of the Commission, established by Directive 75/319/EEC.[43]

Under the decentralised procedure, a producer who has obtained approval in one Member State may seek approval in another Member State, simultaneously submitting their application to the CPMP and the first Member State. The first Member State is

35. Directive 93/39/EEC amending Directive 65/65/EEC and Directives 75/318/EEC, 75/319/EEC OJ 1975 L 147/1.
36. Directives 75/318 and 75/319/EEC. 37. Directive 92/27 OJ 1992 L 113.
38. Directive 92/28 OJ 1992 L 113. Officially supported vaccination campaigns are exempted (Article 3(5)). See also Directives 92/25 and 92/26 OJ 1992 L 113.
39. With the exception of products resulting from biotechnology and 'high technology'; see below.
40. OJ 1993 L 214/1. 41. Sauer, *supra* n 34, p 135; Gardner, *supra* n 33, pp 53–4.
42. According to Directive 75/319. 43. OJ 1975 L 147/1.

required to provide an assessment report for the relevant product. The second Member State must make a decision on approval within 90 days. Approval may be refused only on grounds of risk to public health, that is to say on quality, safety or efficacy grounds.[44] If the Member State is minded to reject, the parties may request arbitration in the CPMP, and from 1 January 1998 arbitration will be obligatory if approval is not given.

The CPMP provides an institutional forum for coordination of national approval systems within which the gradual convergence of national approval systems is likely to be fostered. Differences in approaches of national authorities granting marketing permission for new medical products, and consequently in their decisions, are reduced by cooperation of national experts within the CPMP.[45]

In addition to the decentralised procedure, a new 'centralised procedure', according to which European-level approval may be given to certain medical products, was set up by Regulation 2309/93/EC.[46] The centralised procedure applies to new biotechnological products and high-technology products.[47] Regulation 2309/93 establishes the new European Medicines Evaluation Agency (EMEA), which began operation in February 1995. The Agency is responsible for the centralised procedure for authorisation, according to which the CPMP is required to give an opinion within 210 days of receipt of the application[48] and the Commission gives the final decision.[49] An EMEA authorisation is compulsory for products derived from biotechnology, and is optional for other high-technology products.[50] These provisions supersede the earlier Directive 87/22/EEC, under which producers of certain products derived from biotechnology and high-technology were granted a ten-year exclusive entitlement to market the product in the EU, in accordance with a procedure imposing obligations of consultation on national authorities.[51]

A product licence granted under the centralised procedure is valid in all fifteen Member States, and the product is entered on

44. Gardner, *supra* n 33, p 60.   45. Gardner, *supra* n 33, pp 59–60.
46. OJ 1993 L 214. See Gardner, *supra* n 33, pp 56–7.
47. As defined in the Annex (parts A and B) to Regulation 2309/93/EC.
48. Regulation 2309/93, Article 6(4).   49. Regulation 2309/93, Article 10.
50. Regulation 2309/93, Article 3(1) and (2).
51. Sauer, *supra* n 34, p 135; Taylor, 'Europe Without Frontiers? Balancing Pharmaceutical Interests' in Normand and Vaughan (eds), *Europe Without Frontiers: The Implications for Health* (Wiley, 1993) p 285; Gardner, *supra* n 33, p 54.

the Community Register of Medicinal Products.[52] Authorisations are valid for five years, and are renewable on application and presentation to the EMEA of an up-to-date dossier containing 'pharmacovigilance' information.[53] The EMEA, in cooperation with competent national authorities, is given a significant role in the process of pharmacovigilance.[54] This is a process which, in accordance with the principle of subsidiarity, is better done at EU, rather than national level.[55] It is expected that EMEA will give only a small number of authorisations per annum; for most new medical products, approval will continue to be given by national authorities, within the framework of consultation in the CPMP.

In terms of protection of consumers from potentially harmful medical products, the Product Liability Directive 85/374/EEC[56] gives consumers the right to compensation for defective products,[57] including medical products.[58] However, if, at the time of manufacture of the product, the state of scientific and technical knowledge was such that the risk of harm was not foreseeable, the producer will not be liable under the directive.[59]

The internal market in goods was established by the Treaty of Rome, Articles 9–16 and 30–36 EC. The '1992 programme' – a major legislative drive to complete the internal market – aimed to remove all technical barriers to free movement of goods by 1 January 1993. The Treaty requires that all customs duties, quantitative restrictions on imports, and measures having equivalent effect be abolished between Member States. Such measures may be applicable only to imported goods, or may be equally applicable to domestically produced and imported goods, but have a disproportionate impact on imported goods.[60] The Treaty provisions concerning free movement of goods are directly effective, and form the source of rights for individual importers and exporters of goods.

---

52. Regulation 2309/93, Article 12.
53. Regulation 2309/93, Article 13.
54. See Regulation 2309/93, Articles 19–26, which impose obligations on the person responsible for placing authorised medical products on the market to notify the EMEA of any serious adverse reactions to the product. Regulation 540/95 OJ 1995 L 55/5 imposes similar obligations in respect of non-serious adverse reactions.
55. Gardner, *supra* n 33, p 58.
56. OJ 1985 L 210/29, legal basis, Article 100 EEC.   57. Article 1.
58. Article 2: '"Product" means all movables, with the exception of primary agricultural products and game.'
59. The so-called 'development risks defence'; Article 7(e).
60. Sometimes called 'distinctly' and 'indistinctly applicable' measures.

The Treaty grants a limited exclusion to the general principle that goods be allowed to move freely within the territory of the European Union in Article 36 EC. Article 36 EC provides, *inter alia*, that the Treaty 'shall not preclude prohibitions or restrictions on imports ... justified on grounds of ... the protection of health and life of humans ...'. However, such prohibitions must be justified in accordance with the principle of proportionality, and may not 'constitute a means of arbitrary discrimination or a disguised restriction on trade between Member States'.

Provided these latter requirements of non-discrimination and proportionality are met, the European Court of Justice has granted a reasonable margin of discretion to Member States in terms of national rules which restrict free movement of goods, but are justified on grounds of protection of human health. In Case 104/75 *De Peijper*[61] the Court held that 'the health and life of humans rank first among the property or interests protected by Article 36 and it is for the Member States, within the limits imposed by the Treaty, to decide what degree of protection they intend to assure, and in particular how strict the checks to be carried out are to be'. So long as the risk to human health is genuine, Member States may choose the steps they impose to prevent it.[62]

So, for instance, national rules according to which only authorised dispensing pharmacies are permitted to sell proprietary medical products (as defined in Directive 65/65/EEC) are justified on public health grounds.[63] A ban on pharmacists substituting (save in emergencies) one medical product for another prescribed by name was also upheld by the Court, in spite of its 'devastating effect' on imports of medical products from other Member States, on the grounds that the aim of the ban was 'to leave the entire responsibility for the treatment of the patient in the hands of the doctor treating him' and that the ban was not disproportionate to this aim.[64] However, a prohibition on the private importation of pharmaceuticals, either non-prescription,[65] or prescription-only,[66]

---

61. [1976] ECR 613.
62. Oliver, *Free Movement of Goods in the European Community* (Sweet and Maxwell, 1996) p 204.
63. Case C-369/88 *Delattre* [1991] ECR I-1487; Oliver, *supra* n 62, pp 213–14.
64. Case C-266–7/87 *R v Royal Pharmaceutical Society of Great Britain* [1989] ECR 1295. See Oliver, *supra* n 62, p 215, who is mildly sceptical about the objectivity of this decision.
65. Case 215/87 *Schumacher v HZA Frankfurt* [1989] ECR 617.
66. Case C-62/90 *Commission v Germany* [1992] ECR I-2575.

lawfully purchased in another Member State, is not justified. The consumer is entitled to equivalent guarantees of information concerning the product, and the qualifications of pharmacists have been harmonised by EC law.[67] Such a rule is therefore a disproportionate restriction on the free movement of goods.[68]

The exemptions granted in Article 36 EC to the free movement of goods may also apply in the case of non-medical goods which may be harmful to human health. The requirements of non-discrimination and proportionality have been interpreted by the European Court of Justice in this context to require that national rules purportedly justifying restrictions on health grounds must constitute a 'seriously considered health policy'.[69] Evidence that the restriction has been applied for an external reason – for instance, to protect the domestic market in the allegedly harmful good – will tend to suggest discrimination, or disproportionality.[70] However, if there is genuine doubt about the safety of a good, the Court will normally accept a public health exemption, leaving a margin of discretion to the Member States in this respect.[71] Where re-regulation at European level has established harmonised minimum levels of health protection, Member States may retain higher standards.[72]

Rights of free movers only

Generally speaking, all EUCs have the right, in accordance with EC law, to move to another Member State to work,[73] to establish

67. Directives 85/432/EEC and 85/433/EEC OJ 1985 L 253; see below.
68. Oliver, *supra* n 62, p 214.
69. Case 40/82 *Commission v UK* [1982] ECR 2793.
70. Eg, in Case 40/82 *Commission v UK*, *supra* n 69, the ban on poultry imports imposed by the UK before Christmas, purportedly to protect against Newcastle disease, was actually to block imports of French turkeys.
71. See Case 53/80 *Eyssen* [1981] ECR 409, in which a ban on nisin in cheese was accepted by the ECJ, even though the scientific evidence concerning its harmful nature was equivocal. Oliver, *supra* n 62, p 207.
72. Eg Case C-11/92 *Gallaher* [1993] ECR I-3345, in which the UK's labelling requirements for *nationally produced* tobacco products were challenged as being inconsistent with EC law. Directive 89/662/EEC OJ 1989 L 359/1, Article 8(1), provided that Member States were not permitted to restrict sales of products complying with the Directive. The UK's requirements were that 6% of the packaging include a health warning about tar and nicotine yields; the Directive provided for 4%. The Court found for the UK. See Slot, 'Harmonisation' (1996) 21 ELRev 378–97, p 385.
73. Article 48 EC; Regulation 1612/68/EEC OJ Sp Ed 1968 II p. 475; Directive 68/360/EEC OJ Sp Ed 1968 II p 485.

themselves[74] or to provide services.[75] EC law prohibits a Member State from excluding an EUC free mover worker, self-employed person or provider of services on the grounds of their ill-health, or because the free mover will be an extra burden on the public health system of the host state. Workers and self-employed persons may not be refused a residence permit on these grounds. Those exercising the 'residual' free movement rights, to study[76] or simply to reside[77] in another Member State could not be refused entry simply on grounds of ill-health, but they must show that they will they impose no burden on the public finances of the host state, so would not be entitled to public health care in the host state.[78]

An exception to the rights of free movement of persons is granted in Article 48(4) EC, which permits Member States to limit the free movement of persons 'on grounds of public policy, public security or public health'. The application of the derogation in Article 48(4) EC is governed by Directive 64/221/EEC,[79] which applies to workers, the self-employed and recipients of services.[80] Article 4 provides that the only diseases or disabilities justifying exclusion of an individual are those listed in the Annex to the directive. The Annex defines 'diseases which might endanger public health' as WHO-designated contagious diseases, tuberculosis, syphilis and 'other infectious diseases or contagious parasitic diseases if they are the subject of provisions for the protection of nationals of the host country'. Furthermore, a Member State may not exclude from their territory an EUC whose disease occurs after a residence permit has been granted.

The provision in Article 3 of Directive 64/221, that EUCs may be excluded where there is a threat to public policy or public security, may also have some relevance in the health field. Annex B defines 'diseases and disabilities which might threaten public policy or public security' as drug addiction, profound mental disturbance, and manifest psychotic disturbance. However, measures taken on the grounds of public policy or public security must be based solely on the 'personal conduct of the individual con-

---

[74]. Article 52 EEC; Directive 73/148/EEC OJ 1973 L 172/14.
[75]. Article 59 EC; Directive 73/148/EEC OJ 1973 L 172/14. In some circumstances EC law also provides a right to travel to *receive* services.
[76]. Directive 93/96/EEC OJ 1993 L 317/59.
[77]. Directive 90/364/EEC OJ 1990 L 180/26.
[78]. See Chapter 5.   [79]. OJ Sp Ed 1963–4 p 117.   [80]. Article 1.

cerned'.[81] The public policy and public security exemption is particularly significant in terms of restrictions on the movement of users of illicit drugs. The exemption is construed restrictively; therefore it would not constitute a grounds for refusal of entry or residence to someone convicted for drug possession or consumption, as opposed to a drug addict.[82] However, it is important to remember that this entitlement only extends protection to those EUCs who enjoy a right to move in EC law by virtue of their worker or self-employed status.[83]

Regulations 1408/71/EEC and 574/74/EEC cover entitlement of migrant EUCs to medical treatment from the public health service of the host Member State. These provisions were considered in Chapter 5. Entitlement is to the level of health care (for instance, coverage of services by the national health system, level of co-payment) provided for in the competent Member State.

Private health care is a separate issue. Any individual EUC may travel to another Member State to receive health care on a privately financed basis, or with private health insurance. Privately provided health services are services in the sense of Article 59 EC, which abolishes restrictions on the freedom to provide services within the EC.[84] The right to move to another Member State to receive medical services has particular significance where the particular health service sought is not available – or is unlawful – in the individual's country of nationality or residence. Activities which are unlawful in one Member State, but not in others, may constitute 'services' in the sense of Article 59 EC.[85] So, for instance, the implication of the Court's ruling in Case 159/90 *Grogan*[86] is that abortion may be a service in EC law, and Member States may not prevent their nationals from travelling to another Member State for an abor-

---

81. See Case 67/74 *Bonsignore* [1975] ECR 297; Case 30/77 *Bouchereau* [1977] ECR 1999.
82. Case 30/77 *R v Bouchereau, supra* n 81. Dorn, 'Health policies, drug control and the European Community' in Normand and Vaughan, *Europe Without Frontiers: The implications for health* (Wiley, 1993) p 318.
83. See Case 344/87 *Bettray* [1989] ECR 1621, in which former drug users in Dutch sheltered work premises were held not to be 'workers', therefore Article 48 EEC did not apply. Dorn, *supra* n 82, p 319.
84. Cases 286/82 and 26/84 *Luisi and Carbone* [1984] ECR 377.
85. Case C-275/92 *Schindler* [1994] ECR I-1039; Craig and de Búrca, *EC Law: Text, Cases and Materials* (Clarendon Press, 1995) pp 761–2.
86. [1991] ECR 4685.

tion.[87] This rule may have significance for individuals such as Diane Blood, who wished to travel to Belgium for artificial insemination with the sperm of her deceased husband – a procedure which is unlawful in the United Kingdom without the husband's written consent.[88]

Article 59 EC does not apply to public health services because, in order to fall within Article 59 EC, the service must be provided for remuneration.[89] Public health services are received either free of charge, or paid for with a grant given by the state, or reimbursed by the state; at present, generally speaking, they are not provided for remuneration.[90] However, those parts of national public health service systems which are organised on a 'privatised' basis – for instance, the social insurance systems in France and Germany which are based on free access and open competition between public and private suppliers – are open to competition from other Member States in accordance with the provisions on freedom to provide services.[91]

Providers of health care

As with recipients of health care, generally speaking, the legal regime governing providers of health care emanates from national law. However, some provisions of EC law on the 'four freedoms', and the internal market in goods, persons and services, also affect providers of health care.

Health professionals

Approximately 4% of the total EU labour force is made up of health professionals.[92] These professionals enjoy freedom of movement to work and the right of establishment in a Member State

---

87. The application in Ireland of the prohibition on abortion, enshrined in the Irish Constitution Article 40.3.3, remains unaffected by EC law; see Protocol 17 annexed to the Treaty of Rome by the Treaty of Maastricht, and the Declaration of the Member States on Protocol 17 of 1 May 1992.
88. See Hervey, 'Buy Baby: The European Union and regulation of human reproduction' (forthcoming (1998) OJLS).
89. There is no direct authority on this in the public health field, but see cases in other sectors, for instance Case 263/86 *Humbel* [1988] ECR 5365, Case C-109/92 *Wirth* [1993] ECR 6447 in the field of education.
90. McKee, Mossialos and Belcher, *supra* n 14, p 277.
91. Leibfried and Pierson, *supra* n 29, p 66; Leibfried and Pierson, *supra* n 11, p 198.
92. Berlin, *supra* n 5, p 3.

other than that of their nationality in accordance with EC law. The basic Treaty provisions of Articles 48–66 EC apply. The exemption provided in Article 48(4) allowing restrictions on the grounds of public policy, security, and health only applies to individuals and cannot be used by Member States to restrict access to the medical profession, or branches of the medical profession, as a whole.[93]

To facilitate the movement of health professionals, a number of directives on the mutual recognition of qualifications in the health field have been enacted by the EU institutions. These apply to doctors,[94] dentists,[95] pharmacists,[96] nurses[97] and midwives.[98] Basically, these directives set out an agreed core of requirements for professional training in each profession, and abolish restrictions on freedom of establishment based on the fact that a professional qualification was obtained in a Member State other than that in which the professional wishes to practise. National authorities giving authorisation to health professionals practising within their territory are obliged to recognise qualifications obtained in another Member State.

Other health professionals, for instance those whose work is not regulated in all Member States,[99] may rely on the general 'new approach' Directive 89/48/EEC on the recognition of higher education diplomas.[100] This directive prohibits Member States from excluding from practice, on the grounds of inadequate qualifications, a medical professional who has either been awarded a diploma for that profession in another Member State, or, if the Member State does not regulate the profession concerned, has pursued the activity for a certain amount of time, and holds some formal qualifications.[101] However, the directive does not provide for an

---

93. Case 131/85 *Gül* [1986] ECR 1573; Case 307/84 *Commission v France* [1986] ECR 1725; see ter Kuile, du Pré and Sevinga, 'Health Care in Europe after 1992: the European dimension', in Hermans, Casparie and Paelinck (eds), *Health Care in Europe After 1992* (Dartmouth, 1992) p 12.

94. Directives 75/362/EEC and 75/363/EEC OJ 1975 L 167.

95. Directives 78/686/EEC and 78/687/EEC OJ 1978 L 233.

96. Directives 85/432/EEC and 85/433/EEC OJ 1985 L 253; pharmacists do not, however, have an automatic right to establish a pharmacy in another Member State, as some Member States control the geographical distribution of pharmacies.

97. Directives 77/452/EEC and 77/453/EEC OJ 1977 L 176.

98. Directives 80/154/EEC and 80/155/EEC OJ 1980 L 33.

99. For instance, physiotherapists; see McKee, Mossialos and Belcher, *supra* n 14, p 270.

100. OJ L 1989 19/16. See Chapter 6.

101. Article 3.

automatic right to practise, as the host Member State may, in certain circumstances, require evidence of professional experience, or a period of adaptation, or an aptitude test.[102] In practice, the level of migration of health professionals is fairly low, with the exception of movement between Member States with a shared language,[103] and movement at the borders of Member States.[104] There remains (at least circumstantial) evidence of administrative or bureaucratic factors limiting migration.[105] Here the role of EC law, and especially the European Court of Justice, in removing these barriers to movement may prove to be increasingly significant.[106]

Institutions

National health institutions, purchasers of health care and medicinal products are (at least in theory) affected by provisions of EC law designed to make the internal market a reality. However, as provision of public health care is part of the social policy of each Member State and is, generally speaking, not organised on principles of free competition between providers of goods and services, the penetration of the internal market rules into national health service provision is incomplete.

From the point of view of the (private) medical industry, and in particular the pharmaceutical industry, the creation of the internal market should in theory bring significant opportunities to trade into other Member States. Pharmaceuticals and medical equipment are obviously 'goods' in the sense of EC law.[107] However, at present there is no single internal market in pharmaceuticals and medical products in the EU. Huge differences remain between Member States in matters such as which pharmaceuticals are available,

---

102. Article 4.
103. For example, the UK and Ireland; Belgium and France.
104. For example, Dutch dentists providing services on German territory because the Netherlands restricts numbers of dentists to one for every 3,250 inhabitants, whereas German law has no such restriction; see Pierson and Leibfried *supra* n 29, p 24.
105. See McKee, Mossialos and Belcher, *supra* n 14, p 273.
106. See Case 307/84 *Commission v France*, *supra* n 93, in which the French nursing profession was opened up to nurses from other Member States by a ruling of the ECJ that the public health exemption in Article 48(4) EEC did not apply to the nursing profession as a whole. Compare the role of the Court in the field of education; see Chapter 6.
107. ter Kuile, du Pré and Sevinga, *supra* n 93, p 15.

which are available on a prescription-only basis, which will be paid for or reimbursed by the national health system, the market names of particular products, and, most significantly, the prices of particular pharmaceuticals and other medical products.[108] These differences tend to operate to the disadvantage of non-domestically produced medical products.[109] The reason for these differences is that, as the major purchaser of medical products, the national authorities in the Member States control pricing and availability of pharmaceuticals as part of their general social policies, and especially the cost containment aims of those policies. Almost all the Member States control either profits or prices in the pharmaceutical industry, for instance by setting prices for products, or by establishing positive (or negative) lists of pharmaceuticals which may be reimbursed by the national health service or insurance institutions, or by agreement of profit levels by means of bargaining with industry.[110]

Challenges to these types of national measures on the grounds that they are measures having equivalent effect to quantitative restrictions on goods, in terms of Article 30 EC, have failed. In Case 238/82 *Duphar*[111] the Court held that, provided national rules and practices on the purchase of medical products do not discriminate between products on grounds of nationality, Member States are free to establish restrictive national purchasing systems, for instance to protect the financial basis of the health system.[112] These rules will not breach Article 30 EC.[113]

Some very limited intervention by the European Community exists in this area. The *Duphar* case was followed by a Commission Communication[114] on price controls and the reimbursement of medical products. Directive 89/105/EEC[115] concerning

---

108. McKee, Mossialos and Belcher, *supra* n 14, p 278; Hancher, 'Creating the Internal Market for Pharmaceutical Medicines – An Echternach Jumping Process' (1991) 28 CMLRev 821–853.

109. Hancher, *supra* n 108, pp 843, 852; Kaufer, *supra* n 33, p 168.

110. McKee, Mossialos and Belcher, *supra* n 14, p 278; Abel-Smith et al, *supra* n 4, p 47.

111. [1984] ECR 523.

112. See McKee, Mossialos, and Belcher, *supra* n 14, p 279; Weatherill and Beaumont, *EC Law* (Penguin, 1995) p 444; ter Kuile, du Pré and Sevinga, *supra* n 93, p 15; Gardner, *supra* n 33, pp 76–80.

113. See Cases C-267 and 268/91 *Keck and Mithouard* [1993] ECR 6097, in which the Court held that non-discriminatory rules relating to selling arrangements, which might otherwise constitute 'indistinctly applicable' measures having equivalent effect to quantitative restrictions, fall outside the scope of Article 30 EC.

114. OJ 1986 C 310/7, 9–10.

transparency of measures regulating pricing of medicinal products for human use and their inclusion in the scope of national health insurance systems provides that the process of setting pharmaceuticals prices must be transparent, in the sense of being based on objective and determinable criteria. The Directive aims to ensure that any advantage given to domestic products is removed, by setting out various procedural provisions, for instance relating to time limits for decisions, a duty to give reasons, rights of appeal and the publication of decisions.[116] This may be a (very small) first step towards the establishment of a single market in the area, but the discretion which remains with Member States for the organisation and financing of their health systems remains central and (at least apparently) unassailable.[117]

The pharmaceutical industry has argued strongly that a single market in pharmaceuticals should be created for the EU. In particular, the industry relies on the argument that national cost containment policies tend to operate to restrain investment in research and hence impede the global competitiveness of European pharmaceuticals companies. The European Commission, and especially DG IV charged with competition policy, has traditionally supported this view. However, it should be borne in mind that most pharmaceuticals companies operate on an international basis in any case. Moreover, national cost containment policies are in place for good reasons, and national governments are likely to oppose any moves to remove their discretion in this area. It may be that the new requirement in Article 129 EC that health be considered as a part of other policies may prompt a change of direction in the Commission's support for the pharmaceuticals industry, and predominance of its 'competition views', and allow the perspectives of other DGs, for instance DG V, to take a more central role.[118]

In addition to these (limited) rules relating to pricing of pharmaceuticals and other medical products, EC law may also affect the pharmaceutical industry as innovator: as inventor or producer of new medical products or new medical techniques. The ability of an

---

115. OJ 1989 L 40/8. 116. Sauer, *supra* n 34, p 136.
117. Leidl, 'EC Health Care Systems Entering the Single Market', in Normand and Vaughan (eds), *Europe Without Frontiers: The Implications for Health* (Wiley, 1993) p 115.
118. McKee, Mossialos and Belcher, *supra* n 14, pp 279–80.

inventor of a new medical product or process to protect their invention from exploitation by others by means of trade marks and patents is to a certain extent affected by EC law. All of the Member States, along with several non-EU states, are signatories to the European Patent Convention 1973, which empowers the European Patent Office (a non-EU institution) to grant, on a single application, patents for all signatory states. Attempts to establish an EC patent system are proving difficult.[119] For trade marks, Regulation 40/94/EC[120] establishes a system whereby firms may apply for a 'Community trade mark' which will coexist with national trade marks. In the area of medical products, this may prove problematic as it may be difficult to find a single trade mark for a new medical product which will be appropriate, or even available, in all Member States. Regulation 2309/93/EEC,[121] which established the European licensing system for new biotechnological and other 'innovative' products, requires that application for approval be 'accompanied' by 'the name' of the product.[122] The EMEA has indicated that its approval of a new product is to be granted on the basis of a single 'European' trade mark. White is extremely critical of this position, pointing to the burdens this will place on inventors of new products.[123]

As far as patents for medical inventions are concerned, the area of most controversy is inventions in the biotechnology area. The European Patent Convention 1973 implies that micro-organisms are patentable in Europe.[124] An exclusion is given in Article 53(a), which provides that 'European patents shall not be granted in respect of inventions the publication or exploitation of which would be contrary to *ordre public* or morality'. The flexibility of the language in this provision – '*ordre public* or morality' – is such that it is open to various interpretations. To resolve disputes arising from these differences within the European Union, the European Commission proposed a directive on the legal protection of biotechnological inventions. However, this proposal was defeated in the European Parliament,[125] as a result of successful pressure from various lobbying groups concerned with the ethical implications of the directive.

119. See Weatherill and Beaumont, *supra* n 112, p 855.
120. OJ 1994 L 11/1.   121. OJ 1993 L 214.   122. Article 6.
123. White, *supra* n 33, pp 441–4.   124. Article 53(b).
125. On 1 March 1994, using its power of veto in the Article 189b EC procedure.

The Commission has proposed a new draft directive,[126] emanating from its continuing concern that lack of harmonisation will prevent the formation of an internal market in patented biotechnological products in the EU, hinder the free movement of goods, and discourage European research.[127] In an attempt to assuage the ethical concerns, the Commission has set up a Group of Advisers on the ethical implications of biotechnology, comprising various experts in fields such as ethics, science and religion.[128] The Group of Advisers gives opinions at the Commission's request and undertakes own-initiative reports. Given the lack of moral consensus in Europe, and the fact that differences are deeply rooted in cultural traditions, it is likely to prove exceedingly difficult, if not impossible, to establish agreed 'European' values in this, or indeed any other[129] ethically contentious area of health care.[130]

Conclusions

Provisions of EC law relating to health policy suffer from the lack of policy coherence which is typical of many areas of European social policy. European policy provisions in various areas, especially the internal market programme, may have an effect on national health policies, and indirectly on policy provision made to safeguard the health of citizens of the EU and provide care for those in ill-health. But these provisions are not subject to any overall 'European health policy'.

'Consumers' of medical products in the EU are protected from harmful products through a combination of national regulation of the medical industry, which is justified according to EC internal market law, and a limited regulation at EU level through the

---

126. COM(95) 661 final; adopted by the European Parliament on 16 July 1997; *Agence Europe* No 7018 17 July 1997.
127. Commissioner Mario Monti, press release 13 Dec 1995; Jones, 'The New Draft Biotechnology Directive' (1996) 6 European Intellectual Property Review 363–365, p 363.
128. SEC(91) 629 final.
129. For instance, the concept of 'informed consent' to medical treatment – an issue on which there is broad consensus in the EU, but with widely differing interpretations and approaches.
130. Verkerk, 'Introduction to Medical Ethics', in Hermans, Casparie and Paelinck (eds), *Health Care in Europe After 1992* (Dartmouth, 1992) pp 89–90; Buise, 'Harmonization of Medical Ethics; A Civil Servant's View', in Hermans, Casparie and Paelinck, *supra*, p 91.

EMEA's authorisation procedure. The benefits to the medical industry through economies of scale by operating in the internal market are, so far, largely unrealised, although there is potential for future developments, if not through litigation, through EU-level legislation. Many actors in the medical industry are multi-national companies operating on a global basis in any case.

It is possible that the application of EC internal market law may place pressures on financial aspects of national health systems in the Member States, at least those aspects which are funded through private means such as health insurance, rather than through public taxation.

Moreover, there is scope for the EU to lead the way in future developments of health policy. The current focus on provision for medical products, and research into diseases suggests a rather narrow definition of 'health' at the EU level, which is at odds with the more innovative trends in health care, nationally and interna-tionally. For instance, the Dutch Dunning Committee report on Choices in Health Care[131] defines 'health' as 'the ability to partici-pate in society'. According to this view, health policy should not be simply about extending the length of lives, but should be about improving *quality* of life. If the EU channels its financial support in the health field towards quality of life issues, perhaps through link-ing health entitlements – thus broadly defined – to notions of social citizenship, participation in society and social justice, this could help promote a sea change in health policy in the Member States. Focusing health policy on inability to participate in society would link health firmly to central areas of social policy such as social exclusion, disadvantage and poverty.

131. 1993; cited in Abel-Smith et al, *supra* n 4, pp 99–100.

CHAPTER EIGHT

Social assistance and social welfare

Introduction

Measures of social assistance and social welfare form the 'safety net' of national social policies. Social assistance may be defined as providing a minimum level of protection to ensure that the basic human living requirements of individuals who are unable to provide for themselves through employment or earned social security entitlements are met.[1] Social assistance and social welfare are concerned with providing resources for the least privileged (economically and socially) in society. Persons whose material and social resources are so limited as to exclude them from the minimum acceptable way of life in the state in which they live may be defined as living in poverty. Social assistance programmes may therefore be said to be concerned with the alleviation of poverty and 'social exclusion'.

Apart from the provision in Regulation 1612/68, Article 7(2), as interpreted by the European Court of Justice,[2] extending the principle of non-discrimination to access to social assistance for EUC migrant workers, there are no regulatory European-level harmonising measures on social assistance. Lacking legal competence to do so, the EC has not introduced binding measures aimed at harmonising welfare provision in the Member States, and has certainly not attempted to introduce directly effective measures of 'European welfare law' upon which individuals in the Member States might rely. The types, methods and levels of provision of social assistance and welfare remain entirely within the competence

---

[1.] Holloway, *Social Policy Harmonisation in the European Community* (Gower, 1981) p 6; see Chapter 5.

[2.] See Chapter 5.

of the Member States. Moreover, the phenomena of poverty and social exclusion differ in complexion between the Member States: for instance, in the southern Member States poverty in the sense of lack of material income is much higher than in northern Member States, but social links at family and neighbourhood level inhibit social exclusion.[3] The Member States have adopted very different national approaches to the problems of poverty and social exclusion, ranging from the corporatist model, based on income security (typified by Germany); the social democratic welfare regimes (such as Denmark and Sweden); residual state welfare (typified by the UK) and rudimentary or formative systems (such as Greece, Spain, and Portugal).[4] Some Member States have provided minimum subsistence benefits for several decades;[5] others have such measures only on a local, experimental basis.[6]

However, EC legislative action concerned with social assistance and social welfare has had a limited impact, or at least has the potential to affect national social policies. The enactment by the EU institutions of non-binding measures of soft law may encourage the convergence of national practice in welfare provision. Furthermore, the EC's direct expenditure action programmes, in the field of social exclusion, have influenced social assistance welfare provision in the Member States. A further significant aspect of the EC's role is that of information gatherer and disseminator. The EC has set up specialist agencies with the task of gathering and disseminating information on various aspects of exclusion in European society, related to social assistance and social welfare in their broadest sense. These types of activities may be significant in that they allow the Commission to establish a 'Community interest' in the field, in the absence of formal legal competence, and may prove to be the catalyst for future policy proposals, either at European level (contributing either to eventual regulatory harmonisation or to financial support from EC funds) or at national level (contributing to convergence of national welfare policies).

The influence or interest of the EC in this area is limited. Some

---

3. Paugam, 'Poverty and Social Disqualification: A Comparative Analysis of Social Disadvantage in Europe' (1996) 6 JESP 287–303, p 297.
4. See chapter 4; Hantrais, *Social Policy in the European Union* (Macmillan, 1995) pp 134–7; see further George and Taylor-Gooby (eds), *European Welfare Policy: Squaring the Welfare Circle* (Macmillan, 1996).
5. Denmark 1933, UK 1948, Germany 1961, Netherlands 1963, Belgium 1974, Ireland 1977. See Paugam, *supra* n 3, p 297.
6. Spain, Italy, Portugal, Greece. See Paugam, *supra* n 3, p 297.

aspects of national welfare policies, for instance housing policies, have hardly been influenced at all by EC action.[7] Action taken by the EU institutions tends to be related to the internal market endeavour in some way, most commonly by direct or indirect reference to employment, or rather unemployment. The coordinating provisions of EC social security law are firmly based on the creation of an internal market in labour, and the free movement of persons not only as workers, but also, for instance, as recipients of services. By contrast, the EC's action in the social assistance field is not based directly on dealing with the consequences of the free movement of labour. Rather, it is based on the perception that establishing the internal market is likely to bring about restructuring of national industries, in particular centralisation, which may be disruptive to traditional national patterns of work, and may produce, or at least exacerbate, social and economic dislocation or exclusion. These phenomena may be linked to what is termed the 'new poverty'. Before the 1970s, most people in poverty were older people. By the 1990s, all Member States were experiencing the problem of an increasing number of younger people, of working age, falling into poverty as a result of, among other things, long-term unemployment.[8] The EC's action is concerned with what are perceived to be problems common to the Member States.

Relevant legislation: context

There are two types of EC legislation concerned with social assistance and social welfare, or to put it another way, concerned with poverty and social exclusion. These are general provisions, and provisions focused on specific marginalised or excluded groups. The phenomena of poverty and the need for social assistance are complex, arising not simply from a lack of access to material resources, but from social and economic structures which tend to place certain groups of persons at a higher risk of exclusion. Specific provisions to combat the exclusion from society of such social

---

7. Although some Commission sponsored action programmes deal, *inter alia*, with homelessness. Even here, some collaboration and exchange of information takes place at EU level. The housing ministers of the Member States meet once a year, with the Social Affairs Commissioner, for systematic exchange of information; Agence Europe, No 6843 30 Oct 1996.
8. Hantrais, *supra* n 4, pp 146–7.

groups as the elderly, the disabled, the young, members of racial minorities, and women are therefore an appropriate mechanism for tackling poverty. The EC has addressed itself to at least some of these 'excluded groups'.

The Commission defines as living in poverty 'persons, families or groups of persons, whose resources (material, cultural and social) are so limited as to exclude them from the minimum acceptable way of life in the Member State in which they live'.[9] The Commission also refers sometimes to 'people with incomes of less than half the average income per capita in each Member State'.[10] These are relative and national level definitions, based on the acceptable way of life in a particular Member State, rather than a European-level acceptable standard of living.[11] The national aspect of EC definitions of poverty reflects the fact that the internal market, and in particular its social dimension, is not so established as to make meaningful a concept of 'the European standard of living'. The definitions are also relative in the sense of being focused on inequality in living standards. Poverty includes relative shortage of money, but also entails relative deprivation in relation to matters such as education and vocational training, the ability to work, health and incapacity, and housing.[12] The Commission has drawn on the general principle of equality in promoting its specific provisions aimed at combatting exclusion of certain disadvantaged groups.

General provisions

The historical context of the EC's general provisions concerned with poverty and social assistance may be traced to efforts of the European Commission in the 1970s to link debates in the Member States concerning the 'new poverty' with the need to establish poverty as a priority area for action at the European, as well as national, level.[13] The Commission referred to Treaty provisions such as

---

9. Poverty 1, Final Report; Council Decision 85/8/EEC OJ 1985 L 2/24.

10. See European Commission *Proposal for a Medium-Term Action Programme to Combat Exclusion and Promote Solidarity* (1994–1999) COM(93) 435 final p 4 ('Poverty 4').

11. Ramprakash, 'Poverty in the Countries of the European Union: a synthesis of Eurostat's statistical research on poverty' (1994) 4 JESP 117–128, p 118.

12. Schulte, 'Guaranteed minimum resources and the European Community', in Walker and Simpson (eds), *Europe: for richer or poorer?* (CPAG, 1993) p 41.

13. Schulte, *supra* n 12, p 40.

Article 117 EEC, according to which Member States agreed on the need to 'promote ... an improved standard of living' and Article 123 EEC, by which the European Social Fund is established in order to 'contribute ... to raising the standard of living' and to 'facilitate adaptation to industrial changes'. However, these provisions are expressed in terms of the living conditions of workers, not persons in general. This focus on workers underpins many of the EC's provisions on social exclusion, most recently the provisions concerning combatting unemployment in the EC, such as the 'confidence pact' for employment,[14] and the Council Resolution on the role of social protection systems in the fight against unemployment.[15]

Soft law

The Community Charter of 1989, point 10, provides that:

> According to the arrangements applying in each country:

> Persons who have been unable either to enter or re-enter the labour market and have no means of subsistence must be able to receive sufficient resources and social assistance in keeping with their particular situation.

It will be remembered that the Charter is a provision of soft law, and is therefore not enforceable by individuals. This provision did not feature in the Social Policy Agreement, nor is it included in the amendments made at Amsterdam. However, new Article 117 EC – based on the SPA – refers to the 'combating of exclusion' as one of the objectives of the Community and the Member States, and new Article 118 EC will give competence for EC measures, including setting down of minimum requirements by directives, to support and complement those of the Member States in the field of 'integration of persons excluded from the labour market'. Unanimous agreement of Council is required for the areas of 'social security and social protection of workers ... and financial contributions for promotion of employment and job creation'. These new legal basis provisions have (obviously) not so far been used as a sole legal

---

14. Bull. EU Supp 4/96.
15. Resolution of Council and the Representatives of the Governments of the Member States meeting within Council on the role of social protection systems in the fight against unemployment OJ 1996 C 386/3.

basis for 'hard' legislative measures concerned with poverty or social exclusion.[16]

The Council of Ministers enacted two recommendations on social assistance in 1992. Recommendations are non-binding provisions of EC legislation, which may prompt convergence of national laws or practices. Recommendation 92/441/EEC[17] recommends that Member States 'recognise the basic right of a person to sufficient resources and social assistance to live in a manner compatible with human dignity'.[18] The recommendation sets out a number of principles by which this right should be governed, such as the individual basis of the right,[19] and its permanence,[20] and establishes practical guidelines by which the right should be implemented in Member States.[21] These guidelines recommend that Member States should fix 'the amount of resources considered sufficient to cover essential needs ... taking account of living standards and price levels in the Member State'.[22] The relative and national basis of the European definition of poverty is thus reflected in the recommendation. Moreover, Recommendation 92/441/EEC is very limited in scope, with clear respect for the principle of subsidiarity, and the divergence of social assistance and social welfare schemes in the Member States.

Recommendation 92/442/EEC[23] on the convergence of social protection objectives and policies is a little more ambitious. Section IA recommends that Member States should 'allow their general policy in the area of social protection ... to be guided by the following principles'. The principles set out concern the tasks which national social protections should attempt to fulfil[24] and the principles according to which social benefits should be granted.[25] These are the principle of equal treatment on grounds of nationality, race, sex, religion, customs or political opinion;[26] the principle

---

16. Although the SPA has been used as the legal basis for some soft law measures in the field, eg Council Resolution on certain aspects for a European Union social policy: a contribution to economic and social convergence in the Union OJ 1994 C 368/6.

17. OJ 1992 L 245/46.   18. Section IA.   19. Section IB(2).   20. Section IB(4).

21. Section IC.   22. Section IC(1)(a).   23. OJ 1992 L 245/49.

24. Section IA(1). These are: (a) to guarantee a level of resources consistent with human dignity; (b) to guarantee access for lawful residents to national health systems; (c) to further social integration for lawful residents, and integration into the labour market for 'those in a position to exercise a gainful activity'; (d) to ensure replacement income for those who have ceased work; and (e) to develop social protection for the self-employed.

25. Section IA(2).   26. Section IA(2)(a).

of fairness, in the sense that levels of social benefits should be linked to the standard of living in a Member State;[27] the principle of adaptability and responsiveness to changes in the labour market, demographic changes, and changes in family patterns;[28] and the principle of efficiency.[29] The recommendation then sets out, in relation to six specific policy areas (sickness, maternity, unemployment, incapacity for work, the elderly and the family), specific aims towards which Member States are recommended to adapt and develop their social assistance and social welfare systems.

Direct expenditure action programmes

In addition to non-binding measures of soft law, the EC has established a number of direct expenditure action programmes in the field of social exclusion. The European Commission's poverty programmes began in the 1970s, with the general aim of promoting the debate on how to alleviate poverty and social exclusion. This was to be done by providing exchange of information and experience between actors concerned with social exclusion within the Member States, by setting up networks of experts, practitioners and policy makers and by the Commission coordinating national activities concerned with combatting poverty and social exclusion.[30] These programmes are linked with the Commission's activities under the aegis of the structural funds.[31]

The SAP of 1974 included a Commission proposal for a short-term (two-year) anti-poverty programme, on an experimental basis. This was apparently based on the popularity and success of a similar programme in Ireland, at that time one of the new Member States.[32] With a legal basis of Article 235 EEC, unanimous support was required in Council. This was found, in spite of the difficulties of establishing a new programme in the context of the oil crisis, and national tendencies to retrenchment at such a time of economic difficulty.[33] The pilot programme was established by Council Decision 75/458/EEC,[34] subsequently amended by Decision

27. Section IA(2)(b).   28. Section IA(2)(c).   29. Section IA(2)(d).
30. Schulte, *supra* n 12, p 40; Hantrais, *supra* n 4, p 147.
31. See Chapter 9.
32. See Dennett, James, Room and Watson, *Europe Against Poverty: The European Poverty Programme 1975–1980* (Bedford Square Press, 1982) pp 4–5.
33. Germany in particular was reluctant; see Hantrais, *supra* n 4, p 151; Dennett et al, *supra* n 32, pp 7–9. See Chapter 2.
34. OJ 1975 L 199/34.

77/779/EEC,[35] which approved a second phase for three years, until 1980. Under the so-called 'Poverty 1' programme, the Commission launched a modest number of pilot or action projects, each containing a significant component related to research into the dimensions and nature of poverty. Cross-national studies, designed to provide national data on the causes, nature and extent of poverty within the Member States, to compare national systems for tackling poverty, and to establish research methods for comparative assessment of national systems, were also funded.[36]

Poverty 1 was followed by Poverty 2 (1985–88) and Poverty 3 (1989–93), each involving an expansion in the budget. However, the total budget remained limited. Poverty 3[37] – the 'medium term Community action programme concerning the economic and social integration of economically and socially less privileged groups in society' – saw a new approach by the Commission, which sought to relate the need for the programme explicitly to alterations in the structure and nature of poverty in Europe brought about by the 1992 programme on completing the internal market and the concept of 'economic and social cohesion', introduced to the Treaty by the Single European Act.[38] The key concepts underpinning Poverty 3 are 'partnership, active participation and multi-dimensional strategy'. Partnership and active participation are concerned with ensuring that the Commission supports projects constituting collaboration between government bodies, non-governmental organisations, associations, community groups and the individuals concerned, as the experience of Poverty 1 and Poverty 2 suggested that these projects were the most successful. The idea of a 'multi-dimensional strategy' shows the Commission's sensitivity to the very complex structures and processes which contribute to create situations of poverty and social exclusion.[39] These key concepts were carried forward to the proposal for Poverty 4.

Poverty 4 – a 'medium-term action programme to combat exclusion and promote solidarity' – was proposed by the Commission in 1993 to run from 1994–1999.[40] However, despite the Commission's view that the previous programmes had shown that targeted action over several years was producing positive results,[41]

---

35. OJ 1977 L 322/28. 36. Hantrais, *supra* n 4, p 151.
37. Decision 89/457/EEC OJ 1989 L 224/10.
38. Article 130a EC. Hantrais, *supra* n 4, pp 152–3.
39. Hantrais, *supra* n 4, p 153. 40. COM(93) 435 final.
41. Hantrais, *supra* n 4, pp 153–4.

Poverty 4 has not been adopted by Council. This is apparently due to opposition from Germany, and in particular the German Länder, based on the principle of subsidiarity. The Länder and the Federal Government consider that combatting exclusion is a matter of national, not EC, competence.[42] The European Commission, hoping for agreement of Poverty 4 within a few months, continued to fund projects under Budget Line B3–4103 'measures to combat poverty and social exclusion' in 1994. This action has been challenged by the UK under Article 173 EC, on the grounds that the Commission had no legal competence to do so.[43] The European Court of Justice gave an interim ruling on the issue, to the effect that the projects could not continue to be supported while the substantive issue was decided by the Court.[44] The final decision of the Court is expected in early 1998, and is likely to be in favour of the UK.

Commission as information expert

Both the measures of soft law and the EC's direct expenditure action programmes, concerned with poverty and social exclusion, delegate to the Commission responsibility for providing and disseminating various aspects of information related to the combatting of poverty and social exclusion. This information is gathered partly by independent agencies reporting to the Commission, and partly by the bodies involved, at a local level, with EC sponsored projects.

The longest established independent agency of this type is the European Foundation for the Improvement of Living and Working Conditions, set up in Dublin in 1976, which advises the Commission and national policy makers on issues such as social consequences of economic and environmental developments, and regional disparities in living and working conditions.[45] The work of the European Observatory on National Policies to Combat Social Exclusion, established in 1989, is more closely focused upon issues related to poverty and social exclusion. The Observatory provides analysis of national policies, fosters exchanges of information and experience at national and local levels, and monitors developments and trends in the Member States.

[42.] Pochet et al, 'European Briefing' (1996) 6 JESP 241–246, p 245.
[43.] Case C-106/96 *United Kingdom v Commission* OJ 1996 C 145/7.
[44.] Cases C-239 & 240/96 R *United Kingdom v Commission* [1996] ECR I-4475.
[45.] Regulation 1365/75/EEC OJ 1975 L 139/1.

Both Recommendation 92/441/EEC and Recommendation 92/442/EEC charge the Commission with a role in organising systematic exchange of information between the Member States on the provisions and policy developments adopted in pursuit of the recommendations at national level.[46] They also give the Commission power to analyse and assess developments in the Member States, including the power to set criteria for evaluation.[47] This power may be used by the Commission to promote a particular normative view of developments at national level. The Member States are required to supply information on progress to the Commission, to enable the Commission to carry out these tasks.[48]

The poverty programmes have led to the establishment of various European-wide networks of NGOs, for instance the European Anti-Poverty Network of NGOs,[49] which is supported by and has close contact with the Commission (DG V). Networks such as these both promote coordination of best practice and dissemination of innovations across the Member States, and support the 'poverty lobby' both at European and at national level.

Although the Commission's role as an information expert makes a significant contribution to the development of European policy related to poverty and social exclusion, it is important to remember that it is of course the case that simply measuring and observing poverty and social exclusion does not in fact make any direct contribution to the eradication or alleviation of the problem.[50]

Specific 'excluded' categories

In addition to the general provisions of EC soft law, and direct action programmes in the area of poverty and social exclusion, a number of provisions (also taking the form of soft law and direct action programmes) of EC legislation are aimed at promoting convergence of social assistance provisions for particular 'excluded' or 'marginalised' groups. In contrast to the 'universalist'

---

46. Recommendation 92/441/EEC, Section II 1; Recommendation 92/442/EEC, Section II 2.
47. Recommendation 92/441/EEC, Section II 1 and 2; Recommendation 92/442/EEC, Section II 1.
48. Recommendation 92/441/EEC, Section II 2.
49. Hantrais, *supra* n 4, p 153.
50. Walker and Simpson, 'Introduction', in Walker and Simpson (eds), *Europe: for richer or poorer?* (CPAG, 1994); Hantrais, *supra* n 4, p 160.

social democratic (Scandinavian) and corporatist (Bismarckian) systems, this approach to welfare, which treats each category of person differently, has a historical basis in residual state welfare (Anglo-Saxon) systems, and strong resonances with concepts such as 'the deserving poor'.[51] The EC has taken action of this nature to protect women,[52] the elderly,[53] people with disabilities, the young,[54] and the long-term unemployed,[55] as excluded groups. The category of people with disabilities will be discussed here, as exemplifying the general approach.

Hantrais considers that provisions of the original Treaty of Rome, such as Articles 51 EEC, 117-118 EEC and 121 EEC, im-

51. Leibfried, 'Towards a European Welfare State? On integrating poverty regimes in the European Community', in Ferge and Eivind (eds), *Social Policy in a Changing Europe* (Westview, 1992) p 259.

52. Recently, Council Resolution on the Third Medium Term Action Programme on equal opportunities for women and men (1991–1995) OJ 1991 C 142/1; Council Decision 95/593/EC on Fourth Action programme on equal opportunities for men and women (1996–2000) OJ 1995 L 335/37.

53. Eg Commission *Communication on the Elderly* COM(90) 80 final; Decision 91/49/EEC on Community actions for the elderly OJ 1991 L 28/29; Decision 91/554/EEC on the Liaison Group on the Elderly OJ 1991 L 296/42; Decision 93/512/EEC on a Community technology initiative for disabled and elderly people OJ 1993 L 240/42; *Social Policy Programmes, Networks and Observatories* (European Commission, 1996) p 55.

54. Youth for Europe III (1995–99) Decision 818/95/EC OJ 1995 L 87/1. See *Social Policy Programmes, Networks and Observatories* (European Commission, 1996) p 103. Projects are to have 'pedagogical orientation and openness towards other cultures'; also an 'innovative approach with European dimension'. For examples of projects, see *Youth for Europe: Compendium 1995* (European Commission, 1997). One might also consider Directive 94/33/EC OJ 1994 L 216/12 on the protection of young people at work. Although this provision is mainly concerned with the health and safety of young people in the workplace, it also includes provisions for the protection of young people's social and educational development, see Articles 1(3) and 8. This measure goes further than promoting voluntary convergence, requiring Member States to ensure specific, legally guaranteed protections for young people at work.

55. There are around 18 million people in the EU without a job. One half of those are 'long-term unemployed', that is, unemployed for more than a year. The 'Ergo' Community programme was launched in 1988, with the objectives of increasing awareness of policy makers of particular problems of the long-term unemployed; studying actions taken to combat long-term unemployment and bringing model actions to the attention of the EU institutions. The second stage of Ergo was launched in 1993. Twenty-eight projects were financed (at a rate of 75%) by the EU. The objectives of Ergo II were to determine how positive practices may develop as guidelines to policy; promote dialogue between actors in the field (local authorities, national managers, employment agencies) and to bring good practice to attention of the EU institutions. The Ergo II programme has now ended, but the Commission has stated it will continue with the process; see (1996) 5 Social Europe Magazine 12–13.

plicitly reflected a concern that differences between Member States in social protection and social assistance for persons such as those with disabilities might affect the establishment and functioning of the internal market.[56] Whether or not this was the case, as early as the 1974 SAP, the Commission was advancing measures to promote vocational and social rehabilitation of people with disabilities. From these very modest beginnings, the first Community Action Programme on the Integration of Handicapped People was agreed in the early 1980s.[57]

This First Programme was expressed to be concerned with the 'social integration' of people with disabilities, but was in effect focused on economic integration, especially employment and training. Information about technical products to help people with disabilities was to be provided on a European level,[58] and a network of local projects was sponsored.[59] The First Programme was followed by Helios I (1988–1991)[60] and Helios II (1992–96).[61] These action programmes are based on Articles 128 EEC and 235 EEC; as Waddington explains, progress towards raising the standard of living for citizens of the EU with disabilities can only be undertaken by taking a broad view of their economic and social exclusion.[62]

In conjunction with these direct expenditure action programmes, the impetus for EC soft law provisions concerning provision for people with disabilities has grown. In the employment sphere, Council enacted a Recommendation and Guideline on the Employment of Disabled People in the EC in 1986.[63] This recommendation aimed to promote 'fair opportunities' for disabled people. The attached guideline, which Member States are recommended to consider when drawing up their own codes of good

---

56. Hantrais, *supra* n 4, p 125.
57. First Action Programme 1983–1988; OJ 1981 C 347/1.
58. Handynet – a CD ROM database of technical aids for disabled people available in the EU (eg wheelchairs, adaptations of motor vehicles) is now fully operational. Handynet also provides details on procedures of how to buy, hire or borrow a technical aid, in the context of national social policies. (1996) 4 Social Europe Magazine 24.
59. Hantrais, *supra* n 4, pp 127–8.
60. 'Handicapped People in the European Community Living Independently in an Open Society'; OJ 1988 L 104/38.
61. Decision 93/136/EEC OJ 1993 L 56/30. See further Waddington, *Disability, Employment and the European Community* (Blackstone Press, 1995) pp 97–131.
62. Waddington, *supra* n 61, p 111.   63. OJ 1986 L 225/43.

practice, provided a statement of good practice and a framework for positive action to promote the employment and training of disabled people.

The Community Charter of Fundamental Social Rights 1989, point 26 provides that 'all disabled workers ... must be entitled to additional concrete measures aimed at improving their social and professional integration'. As explained above, the Charter does not confer rights on individuals, nor yet provide a separate legal basis for further action of the EU institutions, but it does provide a statement of principle underpinning any action within Community competence.[64]

Moving beyond soft law measures on the entitlements of *workers* with disabilities, to more general measures, Recommendation 92/442/EEC recommends that Member States should adapt and develop their social protection systems to 'guarantee a minimum means of subsistence to disabled persons legally resident within their territories', to foster social integration of persons with disabilities, and to ensure they enjoy a reasonable standard of living.[65] The Interim Evaluation report on Helios II noted that Helios II[66] was based on the principle of equal rights (not special assistance) for people with disabilities. Taking advantage of the observation that there were differing views of what this approach entailed,[67] the Commission proposed a common frame of reference, to serve as a guide for introduction and evaluation of activities under any new European-level programme, and implicitly (as it was also to promote continued debate) to provide a standard for assessment of national policies.

The new approach of the EU institutions on the issue of integration of people with disabilities is expressed in the Commission's Communication on Equality of Opportunity for People with Disabilities,[68] adopted by Council Resolution in early 1997.[69] The Council's Resolution is based on the respect for fundamental human rights, as a general principle of the EU,[70] point 26 of the

---

64. Waddington, *supra* n 61, pp 128–9.   65. Section I B 4.

66. COM(96) 8 final.

67. Eg lack of precise definitions of terms such as 'equal opportunities' and 'integration'.

68. COM(96) 406 final.

69. Resolution of Council and Representatives of the Governments of the Member States meeting within Council on equality of opportunity for people with disabilities. OJ 1997 C 12/1.

70. Article F2 TEU.

Community Charter and the United Nations General Assembly Resolution on Equal Opportunities.[71] The new approach involves a much stronger emphasis on identifying and removing barriers to equal opportunities and full participation for people with disabilities in all aspects of life: including education, work,[72] mobility and access,[73] and housing, in addition to welfare systems.[74]

The Council Resolution calls on Member States to consider national policies which will empower people with disabilities to participate in society,[75] and charges both the Member States and the EU to 'mainstream' disability issues, that is, to take disability issues into account where relevant in all areas of policy development.[76] The Commission is also charged with the usual information dissemination, reporting and evaluation role.[77]

The Commission Communication and Council Resolution appear to have the aim of giving renewed impetus to a 'rights-based' equal opportunities approach to protection of people with disabilities. Although at present the European-level measures are enacted as provisions of soft law, and thus cannot form the basis of individually enforceable rights, it may be that the groundwork for measures of 'hard law', along the lines of the harmonisation measures ensuring equal opportunities on grounds of sex and nationality, has been laid. The Treaty of Amsterdam will add a new Article 6a EC to form a legal basis for Council (acting unanimously) to take action, within the limits of the powers conferred on it by the Treaty, to combat discrimination based, *inter alia*, on disability. However, without a general legal basis for European-level harmonising activity in the social welfare field, this is only likely to have a significant impact in the area of equal opportunities for people with disabilities in employment, and not more generally.

As with the general provisions, the structural funds also support activities to help specific excluded groups.[78] For example, the 'Employment-Horizon' strand of the 'Employment' initiative is

---

71. Resolution 48/46 of 20 Dec 1993.
72. For statistics on people with disabilities and the labour market, see Doyle, *Disability, Discrimination and Equal Opportunities: A Comparative Study of the Employment Rights of Disabled Persons* (Mansell, 1995) pp 10–18.
73. Eg to transport systems and public buildings.
74. According to the Commission, these 'generally provide a minimum of support which is often insufficiently tied to the goal of facilitating participation'.
75. Section II 1.   76. Section II 1, Section III.   77. Section III.
78. See Chapter 9.

concerned with 'the enhancement of employment prospects for disabled people and other disadvantaged groups'.[79]

Conclusions

Although the EU has taken some action aimed at promoting social assistance or social welfare, and participates in the eradication of poverty and social exclusion, it is important to remember that the activities of the EU are minimal, to say the least. The budgets for direct action programmes remain a fraction of national social welfare budgets. None of the relevant measures of EC law is aimed at harmonisation (either positive or negative) by regulation, through the supremacy of European Community law. In this 'multi-level' policy process, the main base of competence to act on poverty and social exclusion remains with the Member States. However, the fact that the EU institutions have taken some action on such a limited legal basis may be regarded as evidence that the Member States see long-term solutions to the problems of poverty and social exclusion as something which may come out of concerted action.[80] Moreover, the EC's minimal soft law and direct expenditure actions may have prompted some convergence in national policies.

The EC's recent activity in the social assistance field tends to be focused on employment, rather than directly on welfare or poverty. This is exemplified in the 1996 Council Resolution on the role of social protection systems in the fight against unemployment.[81] This Resolution refers to Recommendation 92/441/EEC, but reflects a different general thrust to that Recommendation. Member States are called upon to incorporate the objectives of combatting unemployment and social integration of the unemployed into their social protection policies;[82] to organise their social protection systems to contribute to reintegration of the unemployed;[83] to seek a balance between sufficient resources for social protection systems and 'the need to avoid possible detrimental impact on employment

---

79. *Community Social Policy Programmes, Networks and Observatories* (European Commission, 1996) p 18.
80. Hantrais, *supra* n 4, p 155.
81. Resolution of Council and Representatives of the Governments of the Member States meeting within Council on the role of social protection systems in the fight against unemployment OJ 1996 C 386/3.
82. Section I 1.   83. Section I 2.

arising from excessive charges and taxes on labour';[84] and to promote systems of benefits and taxation to provide a clear incentive to work.[85]

The link between combatting social exclusion and (re)employment is quite different from the concept of 'Europe-wide solidarity', which is said to underpin social inclusion in the Commission's White Paper on Social Policy 1994.[86] Walker and Simpson note that the word 'poverty' has all but disappeared from official European parlance, being replaced by the more neutral 'social exclusion'. There is a danger here, they point out, as 'poverty' suggests a level of suffering which necessitates urgent action, whereas 'exclusion' may underplay the seriousness of the problem.[87] Moreover, focusing on (re)employment in the formal labour market as the most appropriate, or even the only, solution to the problems of poverty or social exclusion may be regarded by some as falling short of the moral requirements of social justice, and the guarantees which social citizenship and solidarity should provide. In particular, such an employment-centred position may reveal an underpinning of commodification of human beings, and may be insufficiently flexible to deal with the complex social and economic structures which make those in certain groups more vulnerable to exclusion. In its action programmes and soft law measures focused on these vulnerable groups, the EU has acted with sensitivity to these processes. It would therefore be a step backwards, in terms of promoting social citizenship in the EU, if the EU were to retreat to a narrower reconceptualisation of social protection.

---

84. Section I 4. 85. Section I 6.
86. European Commission (1994) *White Paper, European Social Policy: A Way Forward for the Union* COM(94) 333 final, p 37.
87. Moreover, some language versions may resonate with criminality or near criminality, for instance, in French the term is associated with drug addicts and prostitutes; Walker and Simpson, *supra* n 50, pp 109–10. See also Spicker, 'Exclusion' (1997) 35 JCMS 133–143, p 134.

CHAPTER NINE

The European Community structural funds

Introduction

The last four chapters have been primarily concerned with European Community deregulation, re-regulation and coordination of matters affecting social policy. It has also been seen that the EU institutions affect social policy matters by financing certain types of activities, for instance in the fields of health[1] and education.[2] This chapter focuses more firmly on the EC's financing of social policy measures, by considering the structural funds, which are the basis for (modest) European-level redistribution of resources from richer to poorer groups, defined either geographically or socially.[3]

On a national level, social policies contain provisions aiming to promote the 'inclusion' of groups 'excluded' from society socially or economically. These provisions are designed to promote generalised welfare,[4] in the sense of being aimed at redistribution of resources to groups, rather than to individuals. Of course, there is likely to be an overlap in actual policy provision between individual and generalised welfare measures.

National redistributive social policies are often expressed to be based on ideas of social justice,[5] rather than on arguments from economic efficiency, although these may also be persuasive.[6]

[1.] Eg the 'Europe Against Cancer', and AIDS programmes.
[2.] Eg the Socrates programme.
[3.] See Commission *First Cohesion Report* COM(96) 452 final.   [4.] See Chapter 1.
[5.] They may also be based on protecting cultural identity, eg language, ethnicity; Nevin, 'Regional Policy' in El-Aagra (ed), *The Economics of the European Community* (Philip Allan, 1990) p 327.
[6.] Nevin, *supra* n 5, pp 325–7; also Marks, 'Structural Policy in the EC', in Sbragia (ed), *Euro-Politics* (Brookings, 1992) p 195 ff; Wise and Gibb, *Single Market to Social Europe: The European Community in the 1990s* (Longman, 1993) p 200; Harrop, *Structural Funding and Employment in the European Union: Financing the Path to Integration* (Edward Elgar, 1996) p 48.

Furthermore, these policies are based on the shared identity of the citizens of the state, which underpins solidarity or 'cohesion' – the binding together of those who are part of the state by mutual duties of support – implied by these policies. This 'cohesion' justifies the redistribution of resources, financed through taxation, which is necessitated by social policy.

The groups whose welfare is to be promoted may be defined by identification of a particular characteristic (eg disability, race, religion, sex, age) which causes or exacerbates exclusion of those in the group, or may be defined spatially (all those living in deprived geographical areas). Promotion of welfare of groups of people defined spatially is usually termed 'regional policy'. National regional policy is aimed at redistributing economic activity within a state, to alleviate poverty and exclusion in declining or depressed regions. National governments may use various types of measures to provide incentives for firms to set up in depressed regions, such as interest-related subsidies, tax concessions, depreciation allowances, labour subsidies and capital grants.[7] Investment in infrastructure, such as communications, and in education and training may also be provided by the state.

There are some equivalent policies – at least apparently aiming to promote group welfare – at the European level. These are the structural funds: the European Regional Development Fund (ERDF), the European Social Fund (ESF) and the European Agricultural Guidance and Guarantee Fund (Guidance Section) (EAGGF). The ERDF is the EC's main regional policy instrument, the expressed intention of which is 'to help to redress the main regional imbalances in the Community through participation in the development and structural adjustment of regions whose development is lagging behind'.[8] However, some commentators[9] consider that the ERDF, especially before 1989, was in effect more concerned with distribution of finance between Member States than between regions. The ESF is concerned with the development of human resources, its aim being 'to render the employment of workers easier and to increase their geographical and occupational mobility within the Community'.[10] The EAGGF seeks to promote inclusion

7. Harrop, *supra* n 6, p 49. These measures may contravene EC competition law measures concerning 'state aids' to industry (Article 92 EC); see below.
8. Article 130c EC.
9. De Witte, 'The Reform of the European Regional Development Fund' (1986) 23 CMLRev 419–440.
10. Article 123 EC.

of those excluded by restructuring of the agricultural sector. However, within the context of the Common Agricultural Policy as a whole, the guidance section of the CAP budget is insignificant (no more than 5% of the total) compared to the guarantee section, which forms the basis of the price support mechanism for farmers in the EU. The price support mechanism favours large agri-business, in areas which are already wealthy; not smaller, poorer farmers in the southern Member States and in hill farm areas.[11]

The EC also operates other redistributive financial mechanisms, such as the European Investment Bank and the Cohesion Fund. The European Investment Bank (EIB) grants loans, on a non-profit-making basis, to help finance projects to promote 'the balanced and steady development of the common market in the interest of the Community'.[12] In particular, the EIB may help finance projects for developing under-developed regions; projects for modernising firms or developing new economic activities, or pro-jects 'of common interest' where the size or nature of the project necessitates European-level action.[13] The Cohesion Fund con-tributes to the financing of environmental and transport projects in 'Member States with a per capita GNP of less than 90% of the Community average which have a programme leading to the fulfil-ment of the conditions of economic convergence' for the purposes of economic and monetary union (EMU).[14]

At the European level, in contrast with the national level, the justification for these redistributive policies has tended to be expressed rather more in terms of economic integration. The idea is that disparities in wealth, for instance between regions, in the EU should be tackled because they hinder further integration, not because they promote social injustice. It is recognised that perfect competition, and perfect mobility of the factors of production, especially labour, do not exist outside of neoclassical economic models. In a single market, such as in the EC, regions on the

[11]. Scott, *Development Dilemmas in the European Community: Rethinking Regional Development Policy* (Open University Press, 1995) pp 102–104; Armstrong, 'Community Regional Policy', in Lodge (ed), *The European Community and the Challenge of the Future* (Pinter, 1993) p 149.

[12]. Article 198e EC.

[13]. Article 198e(a)–(c) EC. See Allen, 'Cohesion and Structural Adjustment', in Wallace and Wallace (eds), *Policy-Making in the European Union* (OUP, 1996) p 215.

[14]. Article 130d EC; Protocol on Economic and Social Cohesion, annexed to ToR by TEU.

periphery may be disadvantaged, for instance because of their distance from markets, or because they lack quality infrastructure, or are technologically backward. These disadvantages arising from economic integration should therefore be corrected, and all regions should be enabled to compete in the single internal market.[15]

However, there are also social and political motivations for redistributive and structural policies at European level. These have become more important as economic integration of the Member States shades into social and even political integration. The EU institutions are concerned to promote support for the integration project among those in disadvantaged groups or within regions who may suffer in the competitive climate of the internal market, without national protective measures, which, if they hinder trade, must be removed in accordance with membership of the EU. The institutions, and especially the European Parliament and Commission, are also concerned to promote a 'European' identity, and to ensure equity and 'cohesion' between Europeans. These concerns provide the social justice or moral basis for European-level redistributive policies.[16] The Commission's First Cohesion Report[17] conceptualises 'quality of life' policies and European citizenship as 'dimensions of cohesion'. The ideas of 'economic and social cohesion' at European level have taken on an increasing importance since the Treaty of Maastricht, as they are directly related to economic convergence and economic and monetary union.

Since the 1970s, the proportion of the EC budget devoted to structural fund spending has increased from less than 5% to an expected 35% in 1999.[18] Overall, during the period 1994–99, the EC will devote 141,471 million ecu (at 1992 prices) to structural fund spending.[19] It is important to note that this remains only a fraction of national redistributive spending on regional and social policies.[20] The EC can in no way be said to be taking over from the

15. Keating, 'Europeanism and Regionalism', in Jones and Keating (eds), *The European Union and the Regions* (Clarendon, 1995) pp 4, 18; Harrop, *supra* n 6, p 1.

16. Marks *supra* n 6, p 206; Harrop, *supra* n 6, p 2; Keating, *supra* n 15, p 18.

17. COM(96) 452 final.

18. Scott, *supra* n 11, p 17; Allen, *supra* n 13, p 209.

19. Regulation 2081/93/EEC, Article 12(1).

20. Even in the Member States where the structural funds represent the highest proportion of total investment (Greece, Portugal and Ireland), the proportions are 11%, 8%, and 7% respectively; Laffan and Shackleton, 'The Budget', in Wallace and Wallace, *Policy-Making in the European Union* (OUP, 1996).

governments of the Member States the role of a 'social state' in its structural fund provision. However, in so far as the EC does undertake structural fund redistribution, the EC at least appears to be taking on the role of supplementary provider of generalised welfare, and in this case can be submitted to examination of its policies in a comparable manner to a national government making such provision.

The relevant legislation: context

The underlying basis of the EC's structural policies is expressed in the Commission's 1992 review of structural policies[21] to be equality of opportunities, that is, competition on a fair basis, as opposed to free competition. Disadvantaged groups of people, be that on a regional basis, or on the basis of defining characteristics, should be enabled to enjoy the benefits of European integration on the same basis as advantaged groups. This is a particular form of the concept of 'cohesion'; firmly based in the competitive economy, but aiming to correct some of the more threatening dislocative or excluding aspects of economic integration. In this context, cohesion is at odds with some other EC policies, for instance competition policy based on Articles 85 and 86 EC.[22] Frazer maintains that the primacy of the cohesion aim over the free competition aim of the EC's and EU's policies may be justified by a schematic reading of the Treaties, especially Article B TEU.[23]

The historical development of the EC's structural funds is often described as a consequence of the need, as part of the intergovernmental bargain at times of Treaty reform, to make 'side payments' or bribes to economically weaker Member States, as a price for further economic integration.[24] However, the role of the institutions, in particular the Commission, in developing the details of

---

[21.] COM(92) 84.

[22.] Frazer, 'The New Structural Funds, State Aids and Interventions on the Single Market' (1995) 20 ELRev 3–19, p 8.

[23.] 'The objectives of the Union (a wider form of integration and cooperation than the Community) and the principal means by which they are to be achieved, must clearly be the superior provisions of the Union constitution. The absence of any mention of the regulation of competition in such provisions is significant', Frazer, *supra* n 22, p 14.

[24.] Allen, *supra* n 13; Marks, *supra* n 6, p 194; Lange, 'The Politics of the Social Dimension', in Sbragia (ed), *Euro-Politics* (Brookings, 1992) pp 250–1; but see Marks, *supra* n 6, p 201.

the policy, and especially its implementation, within the framework set out in intergovernmental deals is also significant.

The preamble to the original Treaty of Rome suggests that the founding states felt that economic integration would produce improvements across the whole EEC by and large unaided. However, the ESF was set up as a response to declining industries, for instance in coal and steel, as a result of the greater concentration brought about by establishing the single internal market. It was not until the enlargement of the EEC to include the UK, Ireland and Denmark that the first significant development of European Community regional policy took place. Following the Paris Summit in 1972, the Regional Policy Commissioner produced a report[25] calling for the establishment of a European Community regional policy based not only on the economic imperatives of integration, but on the need to promote the EC as a meaningful community for the peoples of Europe, by convergence of standards of living throughout its territory. The ERDF was subsequently established[26] as a means of channelling EC finances into regional development programmes.[27]

By the mid-1980s, the EEC had undergone a further enlargement, increasing the disparities in standards of living within its territory. The existing redistributive mechanisms were inadequate to deal with the situation in which whole Member States, such as Greece and Portugal, were 'under-developed' when compared to richer Member States.[28] In the context of the 1992 programme, aimed at completing the internal market, it was feared that the removal of non-tariff barriers necessitated by the 1992 programme would have a disproportionately disadvantageous effect on poorer regions (and indeed Member States), because of their inadequate infrastructure, higher unemployment, lower skill levels and lower productivity.[29] The amendment to the Treaty of Rome introduced by the Single European Act 1985 included, as a quid pro quo for completion of the internal market, a new Title V, Articles 130a–130e EEC, reforming the structural funds.[30] Article 130d EEC

25. Commission *Thomson Report on the Regional Problem in the Enlarged Community* COM(73) 550 final.
26. Regulation 724/75 OJ 1975 L 73/1, Article 235 EEC legal basis.
27. Harrop, *supra* n 6, p 52; Nevin, *supra* n 5, p 337; Scott, *supra* n 11, p 16; Wise and Gibb, *supra* n 6, p 201.
28. Scott, *supra* n 11, p 20; Wise and Gibb, *supra* n 6, p 201.
29. Cecchini Report; Padua-Schioppa Report; Scott, *supra* n 11, p 21; Wise and Gibb, *supra* n 6, p 229.
30. Scott, *supra* n 11, p 20; Wise and Gibb *supra* n 6, p 201; Harrop, *supra* n 6, p 6.

provided that proposals for reform of the structural funds should be submitted to Council on the initiative of the Commission. Thus, the details of the reform were not part of the (intergovernmental) Treaty amendment, but were left to be agreed later within the EC institutions.[31] The amounts of finance to be given over to the reformed funds were eventually agreed – after extensive arguments between the governments of the Member States – as part of the 'Delors-1 Package'.[32]

Reform of the structural funds was enacted in a series of regulations in 1988. The 'Parent Regulation' 2052/88/EEC[33] and the 'Coordination Regulation' 4253/88/EEC[34] were supplemented by specific implementing regulations for each fund.[35] The overall effect of the policy as reformed was to transfer resources from Belgium, Denmark, Germany, France and the Netherlands to Greece, Spain, Ireland, Italy and Portugal, with the UK remaining more or less unaffected.[36] The most important feature of the new approach was the removal of national quotas, expressing a commitment to take a EC-level view of areas in need of investment.[37] To ensure efficiency, structural funding was to accrue through integrated programmes, rather than individual projects, and monitoring and assessment procedures were to be improved.

The Treaty amendments effected at Maastricht saw a further refocusing of the EC's structural funds, although not as far-reaching an amendment as that in 1988 following the Single European Act. The new focus in the TEU is largely driven by EMU. This is most forcefully expressed in the Protocol on economic and social cohesion, which restates the objectives of cohesion through the structural funds, and provides a new financial instrument in the Cohesion Fund, available only to those economically weaker Member States which are aiming to meet the convergence criteria set out in Article 104c EC, that is, Spain, Greece, Portugal and Ireland. These are the Member States which are likely to be disadvantaged by the deeper integration implied by EMU.[38] Amendments to Article

---

31. Allen, *supra* n 13, pp 214–15.
32. Laffan and Shackleton, *supra* n 20, pp 79–81.
33. OJ 1988 L 185/9.   34. OJ 1988 L 374/1.
35. ERDF Regulation 4254/88/EEC OJ L 1988 L 374/15; ESF Regulation 4255/88/EEC OJ L 1988 L 374/22; EAGGF Regulation 4256/88/EEC OJ L 1988 L 374/25.
36. Marks, *supra* n 6, p 194.   37. Scott, *supra* n 11, p 22.
38. Allen, *supra* n 13, pp 217–18; Frazer, *supra* n 22, p 7; Scott, *supra* n 11, pp 38–40; Shaw, 'Twin-track Social Europe – The Inside Track', in O'Keeffe and

130a-e provided for a further reform of the structural funds,[39] which followed in 1993.[40] These regulations redefine the objectives of the EC's structural funds, and attempt to ensure greater transparency, more flexible procedures and rigorous financial control, in the application of the principle of subsidiarity to the administration of the funds.[41] The TEU also established the new Committee of the Regions, which plays an advisory role in the formation of regional policy in the EC.[42]

One significant new concern for the EC which will be introduced by the Treaty of Amsterdam is unemployment.[43] However, the new employment title does not envisage formal reforms to the structural funds, but is a 'flanking policy' aimed at coordination of national policies, with incentive measures financed by the EC. The Commission has prepared its 'Agenda 2000' opinion,[44] which covers, among other things, the development of the EC's structural policies, and the future financial framework of the EC, beyond 1999. The context of 'Agenda 2000' is the planned accession of Central and East European states, a further enlargement of the EU which is bound to have profound effects on its structural policies. 'Agenda 2000' will form the basis for Council's deliberations at the Luxembourg Summit in December 1997.[45]

The principles of EC structural policies

The EC's structural funds are based on four principles: concentration of resources on priority objectives; financing on the basis of

Twomey (eds), *Legal Issues of the Maastricht Treaty* (Wiley, 1994) pp 306–7; 'Committee for the Study of EMU Luxembourg 1989', cited in Armstrong, 'The Role and Evolution of European Community Regional Policy', in Jones and Keating (eds), *The European Union and the Regions* (Clarendon, 1995) p 23.

39. Article 130d EC.
40. Framework Regulation 2081/93 OJ 1993 L 193/5; Coordination Regulation 2082/93 OJ 1993 L 193/20; Regulation 2083/93 (ERDF) OJ 1993 L 193/34; Regulation 2084/93 (ESF) OJ 1993 L 193/39; Regulation 2085/93 (EAGGF) OJ 1993 L 193/44; Regulation 2080/93 (FIFG – financial instrument of fisheries guidance) OJ 1993 L 193/1.
41. Allen, *supra* n 13, p 223; Frazer *supra* n 22, p 5.
42. Article 198a EC.
43. New title on Employment to be inserted after Title VI.
44. Commission Communication Doc 97/6, 15 July 1997.
45. Conclusions of the Presidency, Amsterdam European Council, 17 June 1997: http://www.bz.minbuza.nl/europa97/frameset/fs-nieuws.html.

programmes, not individual projects; additionality in spending over and above national spending; and partnership between EU institutions, national governments and regional authorities. These principles were established in 1988 and maintained in the 1993 reforms, and are reflected in the regulations governing the operation of the structural funds.

Concentration

Regulation 2081/93/EEC, amending Regulation 2052/88/EEC, sets out in Article 1 the five priority objectives for EC action through the structural funds and other financial instruments. These are as follows:

Objective 1: 'promoting the development and structural adjustment of regions whose development is lagging behind' ('objective 1 regions');

Objective 2: 'converting the regions ... (including employment areas and urban communities) seriously affected by industrial decline';

Objective 3: 'combatting long-term unemployment and facilitating the integration into working life of young people and of persons exposed to exclusion from the labour market';

Objective 4: 'facilitating the adaptation of workers ... to industrial changes and to changes in production systems';

Objective 5(a): promoting development of rural areas by speeding up structural adjustment in the context of reform of the common agricultural and fisheries policies;

Objective 5(b): 'facilitating the development and structural adjustment of rural areas'.

A new objective 6, for promoting development of the Nordic countries and thinly populated areas, was added on the accession of Finland and Sweden.

A significantly larger proportion of the total structural fund expenditure – around 70% – accrues to objective 1 regions than to the other objectives.[46] This therefore is the main area of EC structural spending, and the one to which most attention will be

46. Regulation 2081/93/EEC, Article 12(2).

devoted in this chapter. Around 21.5% of the entire EU population lives in objective 1 regions.[47] The ERDF, ESF and EAGGF all contribute to objective 1 spending.[48] Objective 1 regions are defined in Regulation 2081/93/EEC, Article 8 as 'regions ... whose per capita GDP ... is less than 75% of the Community average'. These include the whole of Greece, Portugal and Ireland, much of Spain[49] and the Italian Mezzagiorno.[50] In addition to this economic definition, various other regions are also included 'for special reasons', some at least apparently more for political reasons.[51] Scott is critical of the reliance on GDP to determine the priority objectives for EC structural funds. Reliance on GDP shows an 'unimaginative' concept of development, rooted in quantity of capital and commercial activity, not quality of life.[52]

The ERDF is to provide support for productive investment to create employment, creating or modernising infrastructure to contribute to regional development, measures exploiting potential for internally generated development, and investment in education and health in objective 1 regions.[53] The addition of health and education to the original priorities, which are based on capital investment, may be evidence of a rather more balanced approach to development, to include quality of life issues, such as social conditions.[54] The ESF's main task is in objectives 3 and 4, that is, combatting unemployment and assisting workers to adjust to technological and industrial changes, but the ESF also provides support for objectives 1, 2 and 5(b), which can include support for job creation schemes.[55] The EAGGF is concerned with development of

47. Scott, *supra* n 11, p 23.
48. Regulation 2052/88/EEC, as amended by Regulation 2081/93/EEC, Article 2(1).
49. Excluding Aragon, Cataluña, Madrid, Navarra, Pais Vasco and Rioja.
50. A list of objective 1 regions is given in Regulation 2081/93/EEC, Annex I.
51. Such as Northern Ireland (UK), the French overseas departments, and, from 1993, Hainaut (Belgium), former East Germany, Flevoland (Netherlands), arrondisements of Avesnes, Eouai, and Valenciennes (France), Merseyside and the Highlands and Islands Enterprise Area (UK). Scott, *supra* n 11, p 33; Allen, *supra* n 13, p 225.
52. Scott, *supra* n 11, pp 29, 42–4.
53. Regulation 2052/88/EEC, as amended by Regulation 2081/93/EEC, Article 3(1); Regulation 4254/88/EEC OJ 1988 L 374/15, as amended by Regulation 2083/93/EEC, Article 1.
54. Kenner, 'Economic and Social Cohesion – The Rocky Road Ahead' (1994) LIEI 1–37, p 27.
55. Regulation 2052/88/EEC, as amended by Regulation 2081/93/EEC, Article 3(2).

agricultural regions, especially diversification. The EAGGF may also contribute to environmental projects, which again may improve the quality of life for those in the relevant regions in a social, rather than an economic, sense.

Objective 2 of the structural funds, concerned with combatting industrial decline and high unemployment, gains 11% of the total structural funding, and is financed by ERDF and ESF.[56] Objectives 3 and 4, which are the sole preserve of the ESF, attract 11% of the structural funding between them. The ESF's objectives were significantly reformed by Regulation 2081/93/EEC, with an expansion of objective 3 to include more categories of groups excluded from employment. These include disabled persons, women (especially single parents), young people, the homeless, ex-prisoners, refugees and immigrants. The ESF is primarily concerned with reintegrating the long-term unemployed into the labour market. It may support programmes of vocational training at various different levels, guidance and counselling for those seeking to enter or re-enter the employment market, and even provision of care services for dependants of excluded workers.[57] Objective 5a and 5b account for 4% of the structural funds, and objective 6 accounts for the remaining 3%.

Programming

The EC's structural funding finances multi-annual, multi-task, and occasionally multi-regional programmes, which are packages of various types of measures, financed through one or several funds, designed to achieve one of the priority objectives.[58] The principle of programming was initiated in the mid 1980s,[59] and aims to ensure greater efficiency, coordination and coherence in allocation of funds. Previously funds were granted to individual projects, formulated on the basis of national criteria.

The procedure for allocation of structural funding shows a

---

56. Regulation 2052/88/EEC, as amended by Regulation 2081/93/EEC, Article 2(1).
57. Harrop, *supra* n 6, pp 138–9.
58. Regulation 2052/88/EEC, as amended by Regulation 2081/93/EEC, Article 5(5); Scott, *supra* n 11, p 24; Allen, *supra* n 13, p 223; Marks, *supra* n 6, p 209. Coordination between the funds is governed by Regulation 4253/88/EEC, as amended by Regulation 2082/93/EEC.
59. Although in 1984 only 20% of ERDF was allocated to such packages; Scott, *supra* n 11, p 19.

balance of decision-making power between national governments and the Commission. Before 1993, the procedure was rather cumbersome. The governments of the Member States submitted to the Commission 'regional development plans' for objective 1 regions, including details on the current economic situation in the region, results of previous EC structural support, a description of the strategy to achieve the objectives concerned, an environmental impact assessment, and a description of proposed national and EC financial provisions.[60] These regional development plans covered a period of six years and were updated annually.[61] Member States were permitted to submit a single 'overall regional development plan' for all their objective 1 regions.[62] The Commission appraised the regional development plans, and in consultation with the national government, and with 'economic and social partners ... designated by the Member State at national, regional or local level',[63] drew up the Community Support Framework. The Community Support Framework is a document specifying development objectives, progress to be achieved, monitoring and assessment procedures, forms of assistance to be given by the structural funds, and an indicative financial plan, setting out amounts of assistance and specifying their source.[64] Since 1993, the procedure has been streamlined. Member States may now submit a 'Single Programming Document', which in effect combines the Community Support Framework (no longer pre-negotiated with the Commission) and proposals for particular programmes to receive financial assistance.[65]

In implementing the structural funds, the Commission is assisted by a number of committees composed of representatives of the governments of the Member States.[66] For objective 1 funding,

60. Regulation 2052/88/EEC, as amended by Regulation 2081/93/EEC, Article 8(4).
61. Regulation 2052/88/EEC, as amended by Regulation 2081/93/EEC, Article 8(3); Regulation 4253/88/EEC, as amended by Regulation 2082/93/EEC, Article 6; Regulation 4254/88/EEC, as amended by Regulation 2083/93/EEC, Article 2(2).
62. Regulation 2052/88/EEC, as amended by Regulation 2081/93, Article 8(4); Regulation 4253/88/EEC, as amended by Regulation 2082/93, Article 5(1).
63. Regulation 2052/88/EEC, as amended by Regulation 2081/93/EEC, Article 4(1).
64. Regulation 2052/88/EEC, as amended by Regulation 2081/93/EEC, Article 8(5); Regulation 4253/88/EEC, as amended by Regulation 2082/93/EEC, Article 8(2).
65. Allen, *supra* n 13, pp 223–4.
66. Regulation 2052/88/EEC, as amended by Regulation 2081/93/EEC, Article 17.

an advisory committee has been set up, chaired by a Commission representative. The Commission presents draft decisions on the measures it seeks to effect under the Single Programming Documents to the advisory committee. The Commission is required to 'take the utmost account' of the advisory committee's opinion,[67] although it is not formally required to follow that opinion. However, failure to take the opinion of the advisory committee into account would constitute a ground for review of the Commission decision.[68]

Most of the structural funding is administered according to programmes initiated by the Member States, as outlined above. However, 9% of the available structural funding is for Community programmes initiated by the Commission, with the agreement of the Member State or states concerned.[69] These 'own-initiative' programmes are multi-national, and are aimed at tackling problems shared by several Member States.[70] The Commission proposes a draft of 'own-initiative' programmes to the management committee for Community initiatives, made up of Member States' representatives and chaired by a Commission representative. If the management committee supports the proposal by a qualified majority,[71] the measures are adopted. If the management committee does not support the proposal, the matter is referred to Council, which may make a different decision to that proposed by the Commission, within a specified time-period, by qualified majority.[72] The role of the management committee ensures a significant influence of national governments over this area of potential Commission autonomy.[73] The lack of transparency of proceedings within the management and advisory committees, and the fact that local and regional actors are not represented within them, raise questions about the democratic legitimacy of EC regional policy.

'Own-initiative' programmes of the EC include, for example, STAR, which provides grants for advanced telecommunications services; RECHAR which aims to diversify the economic base of coal mining areas; and programmes concerned with vocational

---

67. Regulation 4253/88/EEC OJ 1988 L 374/1, as amended by Regulation 2082/93/EEC, Article 27.
68. Article 173 EC, 'infringement of an essential procedural requirement'; see Decision 87/373/EEC OJ 1987 L 197/33.
69. Regulation 2052/88/EEC, as amended by Regulation 2081/93/EEC, Article 5(5), Article 12(5).
70. Sçott, *supra* n 11, p 19.   71. Article 148(2) EC.
72. Regulation 2082/93/EEC, Article 29a.   73. Allen, *supra* n 13, p 227.

training in the EU as a whole, such as Euroform, NOW and Horizon.[74]

Additionality

The principle of additionality aims to ensure that EC funds provide extra support for development programmes, and do not simply substitute for national funding which would have been provided in any case, thereby subsidising national development budgets. This is reflected even in the early legislation, such as the preamble of Regulation 724/75: 'the Fund's assistance should not lead the Member States to reduce their own regional development efforts but should complement these efforts.' It is also inherent in the rules concerning the maximum ceilings (as a proportion of total costs) set out in Regulation 2081/93, Article 13. However, enforcement of the principle in practice has proved elusive, and suspicions remain concerning whether EC structural funding is truly additional to national funding.[75]

The difficulty of ensuring additionality in the application of EC structural funds was exacerbated in the past by the almost total control enjoyed by national governments in selecting the projects and programmes to be financed. So, for instance, in accordance with Regulation 274/75/EEC, Article 2, a specific quota of structural funding was reserved for each Member State. National governments could therefore use the ERDF and other structural funds to finance (or at best to consolidate) their own regional development priorities.[76] The removal of these quotas, a reform process begun in the mid-1980s,[77] should help to ensure that European-level priorities are pursued by the structural funds, and consequently should help ensure true additionality. However, as shown above, the national governments still maintain a significant influence over setting of priorities for structural fund spending, in that they

74. Euroform OJ 1990 C 327/3 – training needs arising from the completion of the internal market and introduction of new technologies; NOW OJ 1990 C 327/5 – training for women; Horizon OJ 1990 C 327/9 – training for people with disabilities. See Kenner, *supra* n 54, pp 16–17; Marks, *supra* n 6, pp 209–10.
75. Scott, *supra* n 11, p 17; Wise and Gibb, *supra* n 6, p 213; Nevin, *supra* n 5, p 338; Armstrong, *supra* n 11, p 146; Allen, *supra* n 13, p 223.
76. Scott, *supra* n 11, pp 17–18; Mosley, 'The social dimension of European integration' (1990) 129 International Labour Rev 147–163, pp 151–2.
77. Regulation 1787/84 OJ 1984 L 169/1 reform introduced 'indicative ranges' 'which established a minimum and maximum allocation to each Member State'. These had a mainly symbolic value: Scott, *supra* n 11, p 19.

initiate the development programmes for 91% of funding, and control the remaining 9% through the management committee procedure.

As a matter of law, additionality is required by Regulation 2082/93, Article 9(1), which provides that the EC structural funds and other financial instruments 'may not replace public expenditure on structural or comparable expenditure undertaken by the Member State in the whole of the territory eligible under an objective'. The Commission and the Member State agree procedures for verifying additionality, and national governments are required to 'provide the relevant financial information to the Commission at the time of the submission of the plans and regularly during the implementation of the Community support frameworks'.[78]

Partnership

The principle of partnership, in the context of EC structural funding, is defined as: 'close consultations between the Commission, the Member State concerned, and the competent authorities and bodies – including within the framework of each Member States' national rules and current practices, the economic and social partners, designated by the Member State at national, regional or local level, with all parties acting as partners in pursuit of a common goal.'[79] The idea behind the principle of partnership is to involve regional and local bodies in the planning, implementation, monitoring and assessment of development programmes relevant to their localities.[80] Various mechanisms are used to promote the principle of partnership, for instance regional or local authorities are involved in drafting regional development plans and may play a significant role in regional monitoring committees. The 'social partners' (representatives of labour and corporate management) also play a role in monitoring and assessment.[81]

[78.] Regulation 4253/88/EEC, as amended by Regulation 2082/93/EEC, Article 9(3).

[79.] Regulation 2052/88/EEC, as amended by Regulation 2081/93/EEC, Article 4(1).

[80.] Commissioner Bruce Millan: 'It means the close involvement of regional and local bodies with the Commission and national authorities in planning and implementing development measures', cited in Scott, *supra* n 11, p 26; Armstrong, *supra* n 11, p 143; Kenner, *supra* n 54, p 14; Allen, *supra* n 13, p 223.

[81.] Scott, *supra* n 11, p 26.

Application of the principle of partnership has allowed the Commission to form direct links with regional and local tiers of government, and to formulate aspects of EC structural and regional policy at least to some extent outside the control of central governments. These networks of information exchange, influence and gradual policy development may be regarded as an example of multi-level governance. However, the influence of these technocratic networks is limited to implementation of the broad policy deals agreed in the committees, at Council and at European Council summit meetings, fora at which national governments remain in control. The Commission is not legally competent to respond alone to requests for specific funding emanating from regional or local levels, no matter how close the networks of influence have become.[82] Moreover, in terms of the partners' monitoring role, it is national governments who designate who is to be a member of the relevant monitoring committees, which, even at regional level may include significant representation of national ministers.[83]

In terms of policy making, the influence of the partners at regional and local level is severely restricted. As Scott points out, following the principle of partnership to its logical conclusion would imply devolving power and autonomy to regional and local levels. Given the disparity of traditions, organisation and influences within different regions in the EU, a wide variety of regional development programmes and projects with differing aims, objectives and means to reach those aims would develop throughout the EU. This would be in direct conflict with the idea of a unified, coherent *European* regional development policy, which underpins the structural funds.[84] In fact, political authorities and other partners not at the level of national governments enjoy only a very limited discretion in the implementation of the EC's structural funds. Partnership is therefore really an issue of management, and also largely symbolic.[85]

Implementation and enforcement

As far as implementation and enforcement of the EC's structural funds (as opposed to policy development) is concerned, it is

---

82. Marks, *supra* n 6, pp 212, 213 ff; Keating, *supra* n 15, p 14; Allen, *supra* n 13, p 216.
83. Allen, *supra* n 13, p 224.
84. Scott, *supra* n 11, p 30; Allen, *supra* n 13, p 228.
85. Scott, *supra* n 11, p 31; Allen, *supra* n 13, p 228.

difficult to draw a sharp line distinguishing between European Community law and domestic law.[86] Programmes are approved by Commission decision, but are implemented on the ground by acts of national administrations.[87] This may raise difficulties in terms of control over legality of acts implementing EC structural policy. The relevant Commission decisions are addressed to the Member State concerned, not to any local beneficiaries of the funding or, perhaps more importantly, those who fail to benefit from EC funds. According to Article 173 EC, individuals are limited in their ability to challenge Commission decisions which are not addressed to them.[88] More significantly, the legal acts granting support to individual *projects*, in implementing programmes supported by the structural funds are taken at national level, therefore there is no 'act of the Commission' to challenge under Article 173 EC.[89]

State aids rules

As pointed out above, the cohesion aims of the EC's structural funding are in conflict with the free competition ideas which underpin other EC policies, in particular competition policy. The conflict is not so much over general objectives – both the structural funds and the rules in Articles 85 and 86 EC aim to complete the internal market – but over priorities and methods.[90]

The EC's regulation of competition also regulates national development measures if these distort or prevent competition in the internal market. Measures taken by national governments to aid economic development in declining regions may have such a distorting effect. These state aids measures are 'incompatible with

---

86. Scott, *supra* n 11, p xii; Scott, *EC Environmental Law* (Longman, 1998) Chapter 7.

87. Therefore, the viability of mounting a legal challenge to the legitimacy of structural fund measures will depend on national remedies and procedures. Scott, *supra* n 11, p xii.

88. See, in general, Case 25/62 *Plaumann* [1963] ECR 95; Case C-309/89 *Cordoniu* [1994] ECR I-1853; and, in particular, Case C-291/89 *Interhotel* [1991] ECR I-2257 and Case C-304/89 *Isidoro Oliveira* [1991] ECR I-2283, in which successful applicants named in the decision making a grant under the ESF were permitted to challenge Commission decisions requiring repayment of part of the funds. See also Case T-432–4/93 *Socurte* [1995] ECR II-503 and Case C-143/95 P *Socurte* [1997] ECR I-1. Scott, *supra* n 11, p 71.

89. Case T-461/93 *An Taisce* [1994] ECR II-733, Case C-325/94P *An Taisce* [1996] ECR I-3727. See Scott (1998), *supra* n 86.

90. Frazer, *supra* n 22, pp 9–10.

the common market'[91] and are subject to review by the Commission, which may require a national government to abolish or alter the relevant state aid.[92] However, some state aids, although distorting competition, may nonetheless be justifiable, as they serve another objective of the EC, such as tackling unemployment, promoting an 'important project of common European interest' or promoting conservation of heritage and culture.[93] In particular, under Article 92(3)(a) EC, 'aid to promote the economic development of areas where the standard of living is abnormally low' may be compatible with EC law.[94] In order to justify a state aid, it must also be shown that market forces alone would not in the short or medium term achieve the aim of the aid.[95] Justifiable state aids must be administered in a transparent manner, and no subsidies for current operations are permitted.[96]

The Commission's implementation of the structural funds (DG XVI) and enforcement of the state aids rules (DG IV) are coordinated to some extent. A common calendar operates for determining eligibility under both the structural funds and the state aids provisions. Article 92(3)(a) applies to 'regions ... where the per capita GDP does not exceed 75% of the Community average'.[97] However, problems remain, especially in the application of state aids rules to less prosperous regions within more prosperous Member States who can afford to subsidise their weaker regions. This national state aid provision is at odds with EU-wide redistributive policies.[98]

Conclusions

The EC's structural funds are a limited social policy instrument of redistribution of resources at European level, by the EU institutions

---

91. Article 92(1) EC.   92. Article 93 EC.   93. Article 92(3).
94. Wise and Gibb, *supra* n 6, p 236; Nevin, *supra* n 5, p 332.
95. See Case 730/79 *Philip Morris* [1980] ECR 2671; Commission's 14th Report on Competition Policy, point 202; Frazer, *supra* n 22, p 10.
96. Community guidelines on state aid for rescuing and restructuring firms in difficulty OJ 1994 C 368/12; Nevin, *supra* n 5, p 334.
97. Commission Communication on the application of Article 92(3)(a) and (c) to regional aid OJ 1988 C 212/2; Commission's 18th Report on Competition Policy, point 167; Wishlade, 'Competition Policy, Cohesion and the Coordination of Regional Aids in the EC' (1993) 14 European Competition Law Rev 143–150, pp 144, 148; Frazer, *supra* n 22, p 11.
98. Kenner, *supra* n 54, pp 33–4.

and governed by European Community legal principles. The funds are spent largely on basic infrastructures, for instance in roads, water and energy. Statistics suggest that economic growth (although not necessarily employment, welfare or quality of life), has improved in objective 1 regions.[99] The Commission's First Cohesion Report[100] reveals, for instance, that over the past decade regional differences in unemployment levels have increased, regional income disparities have widened and that the number of people living 'below the poverty line' has increased in several Member States, especially the UK, Italy and France.

'Development', in the sense of the structural funds, is *economic* development first and foremost. An underlying assumption of the legislation governing the structural funds is that social improvements will come about through reintegration of excluded groups into economic activity; hence the stress on training and retraining, with a view to entry or re-entry into the employment market, and with a view to attracting investment from companies looking for skilled workforces.[101] An emphasis on economic diversification is also evident, particularly in the EAGGF, with development of tourist facilities in rural economies being supported by EC financing.[102] There is little EC expenditure devoted to social welfare (or 'quality of life') infrastructure, such as housing, non-vocational education, or cultural or leisure facilities,[103] although health and vocational training may now be financed. Scott describes this as 'commodification of nature and culture, as well as people', and suggests that it indicates a tendency of the EC 'to conflate "life space" and "economic space"'.[104] Moreover, as Majone has pointed out, reducing inequality between regions does not necessarily reduce inequality between individuals. Sometimes, the main beneficiaries of structural funds are actually relatively well-off individuals in poor regions.[105]

The future of the EC structural funds is likely to be affected by the two main items on the EU's agenda for the short to medium term: enlargement to include Central and Eastern European states, and EMU. Enlargement to include even the most economically

---

99. Harrop, *supra* n 6, pp 150–1; Commission *First Cohesion Report* COM(96) 452 final, chapter 2.
100. COM(96) 452 final.   101. Scott, *supra* n 11, pp 46–8.
102. Harrop, *supra* n 6, pp 82–85.   103. Scott, *supra* n 11, pp 50–2.
104. Scott, *supra* n 11, p 134.
105. Majone, 'The European Community: Between Social Policy and Social Regulation' (1993) 31 JCMS 153–169, p 163.

developed Central European states will involve a significant increase in the proportion of the total EU population living in objective 1 regions as currently defined.[106] The new Member States are likely to expect equal treatment with existing Member States; their accommodation within the existing structural fund system will be politically delicate to say the least.[107] The Commission's 'Agenda 2000' envisages reform of the structural funds, and in particular the concentration of objective 1 and 2 funding on 35–40% of the Union's population by the year 2006, rather than the current 51%. Whether agreement to this effect can be forged between the governments of the Member States remains to be seen. EMU will prevent Member States from depreciating their exchange rates to help less competitive industries and firms within less developed areas to compete more effectively.[108] At the same time, short term consequences of EMU for employment may increase pressures for development aid within less developed areas. However, at present it is difficult to see a significant expansion of the EC structural funds to meet these problems. There is, currently at least, no feeling of 'cohesion' among European populations, no feeling of European citizenship and solidarity, which would make the significant redistribution of resources implied by a major expansion of the EC structural funds politically acceptable.[109]

The future of the structural funds may also depend upon a resolution of their aims in principle. The economic principles underpinning the internal market and in particular the EC's competition law and policy suggest that the structural funds may be necessary market interventions in the short or even medium term, but that, in the long term, the market itself will ensure equalised standards, and increased welfare for all.[110] However, social or political rationales for continued intervention in terms of development funding may ensure that the EC's structural funds continue to play a role, whether that be conceptualised as introducing equality of opportunity to compete in the internal market, in accordance with neoliberal models, or as ensuring greater welfare for those groups of

---

106. Marks, *supra* n 6, p 219.
107. Allen, *supra* n 13, p 231; Kenner, *supra* n 54, pp 34–6.
108. Harrop, *supra* n 6, p 53.
109. Marks, *supra* n 6, p 220. By way of contrast, the 'cohesion' of Germans – the idea of 'German-ness' – made politically feasible the significant development funding for former East Germany.
110. Allen, *supra* n 13, p 211; Armstrong, *supra* n 11, p 52; Harrop, *supra* n 6, p 52.

individuals (defined regionally or by membership of an excluded group) who are less able to compete in accordance with models of social cohesion or social justice.

CHAPTER TEN

Conclusions: the law of a 'people's Europe'?

Introduction

> Europe is a social entity. One of the things each of the Member
> States introduces into the European integration process is a sense
> of responsibility for the needs of its citizens.[1]

European social policy is developing in the multi-level system of
governance constituted in interactions within and between national, sub-national and European policy and law makers. The
value of the contribution of the EU to the development of European social policy is at present difficult to assess. This book has
taken the view that where EU-level action affects social policy provision in the Member States, it should meet the standards of social
cohesion or social justice. European social policy appears to offer
the potential to do so, by building a future 'people's Europe',
based on solidarity, social citizenship and social inclusion. However, a continuing emphasis on the creation of an internal market
for the benefit of 'Europeans' would point, inevitably, to a narrow
and frustratingly exclusive conception of European social policy.

Within the multi-level system of governance constituted between the EU and its Member States, social policy has taken on a
unique complexion. Actors at EU, national and regional level in-
teract to create and implement law and policy with social significance; for instance, coordination of social security provision for
migrants, standards for the recognition of vocational training
qualifications, promotion of development of language skills, controls over medical products, promotion of programmes to alleviate

---

1. Forword, Comité des Sages, 'For a Europe of Civic and Social Rights' (Brussels,
Oct 1995 – Feb 1996).

poverty and provision of structural funding. As different actors seek to enhance their influence, European social policy may develop in new or even surprising directions; for example, towards a broad 'education' rather than a narrow 'vocational training' policy, or perhaps towards a 'health policy' rather than 'competition policy' basis for regulation of pharmaceuticals. Courts, especially the European Court of Justice, may play a significant role in social policy development, as imaginative litigants seek to enforce entitlements in EC law – for example, non-discriminatory entitlement to 'social advantages', or freedom of establishment for social service providers, or free movement of capital for pensions. Any of these may have profound effects on national social policies. Governments, institutions and other actors may seek to challenge the legality of acts in the social policy sphere taken by the EU institutions. European Community law is not simply a neutral device for implementing policy choices, but is an inherent part of the reflexive process of policy formation. Community law contributes to the shape of European social policy, by opening opportunities for development in particular directions – for example by allocating competence to different actors or combinations of actors – or by closing off potential developments by rendering them inconsistent with Community law, in accordance with the Member States' 'duty of fidelity' expressed in Article 5 EC.

For lawyers, one of the most important concerns in tracking the development of European social policy is the legality of action of the EU institutions in the social field. New legal basis provisions, inserted into the Treaty of Rome at times of Treaty reform, have opened fresh avenues for social policy measures. The ability of litigants to challenge acts of the EU institutions on the grounds of lack of competence or incorrect legal basis is an important safeguard for the legality of EU action. This is particularly so given the well-known problems of democratic deficit and lack of transparency which characterise policy-making processes at EU-level. However, in practice, it is generally the privileged litigants of the EU institutions and governments of the Member States, and not individuals, who are most likely to be able to establish *locus standi* to challenge acts of the institutions.[2]

Moreover, it is not enough simply to ensure legality of regulatory acts of the EU institutions. 'Horizontal' relationships (as op-

---

[2.] Article 173 EC; see Chapter 3, n 101.

posed to the 'vertical relationship' of top-down regulatory harmonisation) in the multi-level system of governance within the EU are likely to take on increasing significance in the formation of European social policy.[3] For instance, if welfare providers begin to trade with each other across borders, applying the EC's internal market law to 'welfare goods and services', this will affect the ability of national governments to keep welfare provision exclusively under their national regulatory controls and even to keep welfare spending within their borders. 'Privatisation' of provision of social benefits can only enhance this process. Cross-border welfare trade has taken place (at least in the past) on a relatively small scale, for example Kent County Council is contracting with Calais region for the provision of some welfare services.[4] Creation of new European-level standards, and mutual recognition of professional qualifications, including those of the caring professions, is likely to facilitate this type of cross-border activity. More significantly, new networks of social actors and new agencies, created and sustained by EC funding, and liaising with the Commission, are proliferating. Their influence in both the national social policy sphere and the debate concerning the social dimension of the process of European integration is likely to change the direction of EU-level developments, and may promote convergence of national social policy regimes without the need for top-down regulatory harmonisation. Because of the potential of these newly (or differently) empowered actors to prompt policy changes in European social policy, it may become increasingly important to ensure the legality of Commission action granting financial support, and to raise questions concerning its legitimacy or appropriateness. As explained in Chapter 9, the current administrative structure of the EU's structural funding effectively precludes judicial review of Commission action in the detailed instances of granting finance for specific projects (where it counts). This is on the grounds that no 'Community act' sanctioning the finance exists.[5]

---

3. Streek, 'Neo-Voluntarism: A New European Social Policy Regime?' (1995) 1 ELJ 31–59, p 34.
4. Room, 'European Social Policy: competition, conflict and integration' (1994) 6 Social Policy Rev 17–35, pp 25–31.
5. Case T-461/93 *An Taisce* [1994] ECR II-733; Case C-325/94P *An Taisce* [1996] ECR I-3727; Scott, *EC Environmental Law* (Longman, 1998).

Policy incoherence

One of the principal features of multi-level European social policy is its lack of policy coherence, as demonstrated in Chapters 5–9. The EC has enacted some of its own social policy measures, and has affected social policy provision in the Member States through its deregulatory, re-regulatory and coordinating laws, and through provision of financial support for certain social policy activities. However, these provisions do not amount to an EU-level social policy, in the sense of a series of measures meeting the responsibilities of a state for its citizens and others lawfully resident within its territory. In particular, they do not provide a complete system of support for individuals who need it, or redistribute resources according to principles of social justice, social citizenship and cohesion.

EC laws and other measures which affect social policy provision within the EU are often based on a mixture of social and economic objectives, sometimes with economic objectives taking predominance. Economic aims, such as completing the internal market in labour, or ensuring level playing fields of competition for firms in different Member States or different regions within the EU often underpin ostensibly social measures, or at least provide a partial justification for their enactment. The mixed aims behind policy provisions may contribute to the lack of overall policy coherence. This characteristic of European social policy is exacerbated by the different underlying models – neo-liberal, convergence, social cohesion and social justice – for appropriate social policy provision at large in the EU. No political consensus exists EU-wide on the fundamental basis for social policy provision. In order to forge agreement, Commission documents and even Treaty provisions (including legal basis provisions) often use extremely flexible language to combine statements of principle which are fundamentally incompatible.[6] Small wonder, then, that European social policy as an entity is incomplete and incoherent, characterised by tensions and unresolved contradictions.

The deregulatory forces of the EC's internal market law have the potential to disrupt or undermine the coherence of national social cial policies, especially if 'regulatory gaps' appear where the application of national laws is inconsistent with EC law, and no

---

6. Deakin, 'Labour Law as Market Regulation', in Davies et al (eds), *European Community Labour Law: Principles and Perspectives* (Clarendon, 1996) pp 64, 84.

re-regulation at EU level takes place. This phenomenon of competition between different regulatory regimes may increase pressure for re-regulation at EU-level, either from those who stand to lose from such regulatory competition, or from those who believe that important interests are not adequately protected within it. The institutional structure of the EU is such that it is very difficult to agree regulatory norms concerned with social policy in Council. Furthermore, the welfare regimes of Member States differ widely. Given these institutional structures, the mechanisms of coordination and financial support are probably more likely to have a significant long-term impact on the process of integration of social policy provision through a rather haphazard convergence of national regimes in the European Union, than by coherent 'top-down' harmonisation by regulation. Policy incoherence, therefore, seems set to remain a feature of European social policy.

Convergence?

It is difficult to say whether integration of national social policies through convergence is already taking place within the EU. Some research points to at least weak trends of convergence in social welfare policies in the Member States.[7] This is not surprising, as all the Member States are facing similar problems in terms of demographic changes, such as ageing populations, changing family structures and the widespread entry of women into the paid labour market. All of these problems jeopardise the traditional post-war settlement which forms the basis of the Member States' welfare systems. However, convergence of problems does not necessarily imply convergence of solutions.[8] Although there appears to be a more or less general agreement among the Member States that restructuring of social welfare systems is needed to cope with demographic changes, there remain significant differences in the details of changes, actual and proposed.

One of the most significant factors contributing to convergence

---

7. Taylor-Gooby, 'The Response of Government: Fragile Convergence?', in George and Taylor-Gooby (eds), *European Welfare Policy: Squaring the Welfare Circle'* (Macmillan: 1996) pp 216–17; Hantrais, *Social Policy in the European Union* (Macmillan, 1995) p 139; Taylor-Gooby, 'Paying for Welfare: The View from Europe' (1996) 67 PQ 116–126.

8. Room, *supra* n 4, p 23.

trends is the attraction in most, if not all, Member States of cost containment policies, and indeed 'privatisation' of at least some aspects of social welfare provision. In research interviewing policy makers and politicians in EU states about welfare issues, Taylor-Gooby found particular interest among powerful Member States (especially Germany) in cost containment in welfare spending.[9] There is a general pattern in the Member States of retrenchment in provision of benefits, and also a trend of increased efforts to raise additional income, for instance through adjusting state pension entitlements.[10] Although this trend may be largely attributable to more general factors, and not limited to Member States of the European Union, the EU institutions may channel the direction of change in the Member States through its various harmonisation mechanisms, including soft law, and the provision of funding.

There is also some evidence that convergence of national social policies is taking place on the basis of a 'northern European' conception of poverty and social exclusion. In the northern Member States, such as Germany, France and the UK, the connection between non-participation in the labour market and poverty and exclusion is much stronger than in the south. If the labour market disintegrates in these northern states, large disparities between people's material and social situations follow almost automatically.[11] Much of the EC's activity in the areas of poverty and social exclusion is focused upon reintegration into the labour market of those 'excluded' from it. This method of tackling social exclusion, if successful, has the additional bonus of reducing financial burdens on systems providing welfare benefits, and so fits with aims of cost containment. Moreover, the idea that the only appropriate method for tackling social exclusion is to reintegrate individuals into the formal labour market fits relatively comfortably with the (predominantly) economic aims of the Treaty of Rome.

Legitimacy

These trends towards 'cost containment' and reconceptualisation of social welfare on the basis of re-employment policies, possibly

---

[9.] Taylor Gooby, *supra* n 7, pp 116–26.

[10.] Taylor-Gooby, in George and Taylor-Gooby *supra* n 7, p 216.

[11.] Paugam, 'Poverty and Social Disqualification: A Comparative Analysis of Social Disadvantage in Europe' (1996) 6 JESP 287–303, p 298.

at least in part prompted by EC action, have led some commentators to be extremely critical of the activities of the EU institutions in the social welfare area.[12] Through its direct applicability in the legal regimes of the Member States, EC law is seen by them as undermining national-level social policy provision reached through national democratic processes in which the relevant interests are represented and social actors are consulted. The policy making process at EU level is not regarded as safeguarding those interests. These concerns were reflected, for example, in the Scandinavian women's movement's opposition to membership of the EU.

Indeed, at the current stage of the integration process, it is not possible to identify a political or social community which could legitimate EU-level intervention in social policy, however well the relevant interests were represented there. There can be no 'solidarity' on an EU-wide basis, as there is no 'European people' on which such cohesion – essential for a legitimate social policy settlement – could be based. Nor is there ever likely to be such solidarity in the EU, which consists of various communities, defined in various ways, and overlapping in their membership. Questions may therefore be raised about the legitimacy of EU-level action in the field of social policy. Might not national, or even regional or local, levels – where there is solidarity and cohesion – be a more appropriate place to take social policy decisions, concerned with the provision and redistribution of social goods, the regulation of their providers, and the welfare of a community and its members?

If one takes the view that social policy provision should meet the requirements of social cohesion and social justice, in order to ensure fairness, equality and above all personal dignity, then European social policy, at least in its current form, may well fall short of those requirements. One possible solution to this shortfall would be for the EU to withdraw from the social policy field, and leave Member States to make their own social policy provision, unaffected by their membership of the EU. There is a problem, however, for those who see withdrawal of the EC's competence to affect national social policy provision, and its restoration to national (or indeed regional or local) levels as the solution to the lack of legitimacy of European social policy. They must maintain

---

12. Schulte, 'Guaranteed minimum resources and the European Community', in Simpson and Walker (eds), *Europe: for richer or poorer?* (CPAG, 1993); Simpson, and Walker, 'Conclusion: whose Europe?', in Walker and Simpson (eds), *Europe: for richer or poorer?* (CPAG, 1993).

that it is possible for Member States to retain different social provisions at the same time as their commitment to the internal market and in the near future, at least for some Member States, to
economic and monetary union. Given that economic and social
phenomena are essentially interconnected, a total withdrawal of
the EU from all actions with consequences for national social
policies would jeopardise the EU's processes of economic integration. Moreover, and more importantly, all Member States are facing
global trends which profoundly affect their abilities to determine or
control social and welfare policies within their borders. The 'welfare capitalism' settlements of the 1950s and 1960s are now under
pressure from reductions in amounts of revenue available for welfare spending, drives towards economic efficiency and moves towards individualisation and privatisation of welfare provision.[13]

The view that economic integration will shade into social integration, and that the two cannot be kept separate, has led some
commentators critical of the current position to call for *more*, not
less, involvement by the EU institutions in social policy. It is felt
that a common 'European model' of social policy may be best
placed to withstand global trends threatening welfare provision in
the European Union. The EU has therefore been called upon to
take a much more pro-active role, and set a minimum floor of social standards which all Member States must meet. This view may
be supported either from the conservative social cohesion standpoint (that some minimum harmonisation is necessary to prevent
'welfare dumping'[14]) or from a social justice or social citizenship
standpoint (that all people lawfully resident within the EU should
be entitled to share in the basic standard of living that human dignity
requires).[15] Within the current Treaty framework, the only legal
basis for minimum harmonisation provisions would be Article 235
EC, and intervention by the EC in the social welfare field would
require considerable re-conceptualisation of the 'aims and objectives of the Treaty', not to mention the requirements of subsidiarity. If the Amsterdam amendments are ratified, the new social
chapter provisions might provide a legal basis for such action, although in most cases action would require unanimity of Council,
which is likely to militate against significant EU-level provision.

13. See Chapter 4.
14. Migration within the EU by people attracted to Member States with the most
generous welfare systems.
15. Schulte, *supra* n 12, pp 48–9.

Of course, the view that the EU should take on more responsibilities in the social field, perhaps even to the extent of developing its own minimum standards for social welfare, is open to the criticism that the EU lacks the political community necessary to legitimate such a policy. It would require another entire book to do justice to the question of the legitimacy of European social policy. It would seem, at least for those who maintain the position that the social justice model is the most appropriate basis for social policy, that an appropriate basis for the EU's contribution to European social policy lies somewhere in between the two positions outlined. This would entail a division of competences through application of the flexible doctrine of subsidiarity, and, crucially, a more explicit recognition that the EU has developed beyond a 'purely economic' Community, and so it may be appropriate for its policies to pursue social objectives, without necessarily being underpinned by some sort of economic basis.

A European workers' Europe, or a people's Europe?

Many aspects of European social policy – especially those emanating from the EU level – seem to be constrained, at least at present, in two directions. European social policy seems to be limited, first, by a focus on employment and, second, by the restriction of entitlements to citizens of the EU (as currently constituted), that is, nationals of the Member States. For instance, the provisions on social security for migrants are predicated upon there being a migrant EUC worker by whom and through whom entitlements to social security and social assistance are gained. Commission documents concerning education policy are concerned with 'lifelong learning' and training to create a competitive labour force for the EU. Full free movement entitlements for those in higher education are limited to migrant EUC workers; migrant students have a 'third class' status in EC law. Recent soft law measures on convergence of social welfare systems stress the link between pressures on welfare systems, incentives to re-enter the labour market, employment levels, and taxation burdens on employers and employees. There are indications that the focus on (re)employment in the EC's policies aimed at combatting social exclusion is likely to become even stronger. In a speech in January 1997, Social Affairs Commissioner Flynn stated that a 'new social model' is needed for the EU, showing that social policy is a productive factor, and in particular that structural reforms are needed to help more people enter the job market.[16]

This focus on employment may be largely to do with the context in which EU-level social policy measures are enacted, implemented and construed – that of the neo-liberal market ideology of the creation of the internal market and economic integration. EC law and policy often proceed on the basis of commodification of individuals: it is not people but 'workers' (and their families) who have social security rights if they move around the EU, education is training for proto-workers, 'social inclusion' turns out to mean economic inclusion in the labour market, and 'development' turns out to be measured in terms of economic growth, not enhancement of people's quality of life.

Turning to the second limitation, the hierarchy of entitlements in EC law to social protection, and access to social benefits such as social security, education and health benefits, is based on an extremely diluted EU-level version of social citizenship, which places a strong premium on the notion of belonging or being an 'insider'. Third country nationals, even those who are lawfully resident within the territory of the EU, are largely absent from EU-level social policy provision. This absence possibly lays European social policy open to charges of indirect racial discrimination, or at the very least an inappropriate failure to reflect the experiences and needs of some of the more vulnerable members of the EU's multi-cultural population. There is a danger that EU-level social policy provision will simply replicate aspects of national social policy provision which themselves fall short of the requirements of social cohesion and social justice. Redrawing the boundaries of who may benefit from social policy provision from 'nationals' to 'citizens of the European Union' does not meet universalist social justice standards. These are based on notions of common humanity, solidarity, and the responsibilities of states, or other systems of governance, such as the EU, towards individuals within their territories. The EU, as a system of governance which affects individuals' welfare, shares these responsibilities.

However, the aim of reducing social exclusion need not necess-

---

16. Flynn at Amsterdam Conference on Social Policy and Economic Performance Agence Europe No 6899, 24 Jan 1997.

arily be based on this rather narrow and commodifying notion of individuals as 'European workers'.[17] If the concept of citizenship of the EU were to be developed to include social citizenship entitlements in the Marshall sense, this would open up the potential for European social policy to promote social and even political and cultural inclusion, in addition to economic inclusion, and to do so on a basis not determined by nationality, but by status in the EU's legal and social order. Entitlements to social benefits, such as to education in its broad cultural sense, and health protection and quality of life, could be promoted by the EU institutions. This need not necessarily be through 'European Union welfare entitlements' established by legally enforceable regulation, but by EU funding and financial support and by provisions of soft law encouraging the development of national social policies in those directions. What is particularly appealing about a potential European social policy based on social citizenship is that 'citizenship' here would not be exclusively applicable to nationals of the Member States, but could be extended to include those third country nationals who 'belong' to the EU through their economic, cultural and social participation in its community or communities. This could truly be the basis for the law of a people's Europe.

17. Shaw, *Citizenship of the Union: Towards Post-National Membership?* (Academy of European Law, 1995); Barnard and Deakin, 'Social Policy in Search of a Role' in Caiger and Floudas (eds), *1996 Onwards: Lowering the Barriers Further* (Wiley, 1996), pp 194–5; Bercusson et al, 'A Manifesto for Social Europe' (1997) 3 ELJ, 189–205, pp 196–8, 200–2, although there the focus is on people as workers, albeit 'decommodified workers'.

Further reading

For a good short introduction to the subject, see Catriona Carter (1996) 'The European Union Social Policy Debate' in Philippe Barbour (ed) *The European Union Handbook* (London and Chicago: Fitzroy Dearborn). Stephan Leibfried and Paul Pierson (eds) (1995) *European Social Policy: Between Fragmentation and Integration* (Washington: Brookings) and Allan Cochrane and John Clarke (eds) (1993) *Comparing Welfare States: Britain in International Context* (London: Open University Press) are longer collections on social policy dealing with the European Union. Longer legal texts include Ruth Nielsen and Erika Szyszczak (1997) *The Social Dimension of the European Union* (Copenhagen: Handelshojskolens Forlag) and Catherine Barnard (1996) *EC Employment Law* (London: Wiley), especially the more general introductory chapters.

For a brief introduction to the regulation issues surrounding social policy, see G. Majone (1996) 'A European regulatory state?' in Jeremy Richardson (ed) *European Union: Power and Policy-making* (London: Routledge) and Simon Deakin (1996) 'Labour Law as Market Regulation: the Economic Foundations of European Social Policy' in Paul Davies, Antoine Lyon-Caen, Silvana Sciarra and Spiros Simitis (eds) *European Community Labour Law: Principles and Perspectives* (Libor Amicorum Lord Wedderburn of Charlton) (Oxford: Clarendon).

Further details on specific policy areas may be found in the following:

Social Security
Catherine Barnard (1996) *EC Employment Law* (London: Wiley) Chapter 3.
Caroline Laske (1993) 'The Impact of the Single European Market on Social Protection for Migrant Workers' 30 CMLRev 515–539.

Education
Paul Craig and Gráinne de Búrca (1995) *EC Law: Text, Cases and Materials* (Oxford: Clarendon Press) Chapter 15.

Ruth Nielsen and Erika Szyszczak (1997) *The Social Dimension of the European Union* (Copenhagen: Handelshojskolens Forlag) Chapter 3.
Jo Shaw (1992) 'Education and the Law in the European Community' 21 *Journal of Law and Education* 415–442.

Health
Martin McKee, Elias Mossialos and Paul Belcher (1996) 'The Influence of European Law on National Health Policy' 6 JESP 263–286.

Social assistance and poverty
Robin Simpson and Robert Walker (eds) *Europe: for richer or poorer?* (London: CPAG).
Linda Hantrais (1995) *Social Policy in the European Union* (London: Macmillan).

Structural funding
Joanne Scott (1995) *Development Dilemmas in the European Community: Rethinking Regional Development Policy* (Buckingham: Open University Press).

Bibliography

Abel-Smith B., J. Figueras, W. Holland, M. McKee and E. Mossialos (eds) (1995) *Choices in Health Policy: An Agenda for the European Union* (Aldershot: Dartmouth).

Abel-Smith, Brian (1991) *Cost Containment and New Priorities in Health Care: A study of the European Community* (Aldershot: Avebury).

Admiraal, P. H. (1992) 'Introduction to Competition in Health Care' in H. E. G. M. Hermans, A. F. Casparie and J. H. P. Paelinck (eds) *Health Care in Europe After 1992* (Aldershot: Dartmouth).

Allen, David (1996) 'Cohesion and Structural Adjustment' in Helen Wallace and William Wallace (eds) *Policy-Making in the European Union* (Oxford: Oxford University Press).

Altenstetter, C. (1992) 'The Effects of European Policies on Health and Health Care' in H. E. G. M. Hermans, A. F. Casparie and J. H. P. Paelinck (eds) *Health Care in Europe After 1992* (Aldershot: Dartmouth).

Armstrong, Harvey (1995) 'The Role and Evolution of European Community Regional Policy' in Barry Jones and Michael Keating (eds) *The European Union and the Regions* (Oxford: Clarendon).

Armstrong, Harvey (1993) 'Community Regional Policy' in Juliet Lodge (ed) *The European Community and the Challenge of the Future* (London: Pinter).

Armstrong, Kenneth (1997) 'New Institutionalism and EU Legal Studies' in Paul Craig and Carol Harlow (eds) *Law-Making in the European Union* (Deventer: Kluwer).

Armstrong, Kenneth (1995) 'Regulating the Free Movement of Goods: institutions and institutional change' in Jo Shaw and Gillian More (eds) *New Legal Dynamics of European Union* (Oxford: Oxford University Press).

Barnard, Catherine (1997) 'The United Kingdom, the "Social Chapter" and the Amsterdam Treaty' 26 ILJ 275–282.

Barnard, Catherine (1996) *EC Employment Law* (London: Wiley).

Barnard, Catherine (1996) 'The External Dimension of Community Social Policy: the Ugly Duckling of External Relations' in N. Emiliou and D. O'Keeffe (eds) *The European Union and World Trade Law* (London: Wiley).

Barnard, Catherine (1995) 'A European Litigation Strategy: the Case of the Equal Opportunities Commission' in Jo Shaw and Gillian More (eds) *New Legal Dynamics of European Union* (Oxford: Oxford University Press).

Barnard, Catherine and Simon Deakin (1996) 'Social Policy in Search of a Role: Integration, Cohesion and Citizenship' in A. Caiger and D. A. Floudas (eds) *1996 Onwards: Lowering the Barriers Further* (Chichester: Wiley).

Begg, Iain and Francois Nectoux (1995) 'Social Protection and Economic Union' 4 JESP 285–302.

Bercusson, Brian, Simon Deakin, Pertti Koistinen, Yota Kravaritou, Ulrich Mückenberger, Alain Suipot, Bruno Veneziani (1997) 'A Manifesto for Social Europe' 3 ELJ 189–205.

Bercusson, Brian (1996) *European Labour Law* (London: Butterworths).

Berlin, A. (1992) 'Current Trends likely to Affect Health Care in Europe After 1992' in H. E. G. M. Hermans, A. F. Casparie and J. H. P. Paelinck (eds) *Health Care in Europe After 1992* (Aldershot: Dartmouth).

Beukel, Eric (1994) 'Reconstructing Integration Theory: The Case of Educational Policy in the EC' 29 *Cooperation and Conflict* 33–54.

Bieber, Roland (1988) 'On the Mutual Completion of Overlapping Systems' 13 ELRev 147–158.

Bovis, C (1996) 'Regulating the Public Markets of the European Union', in A. Caiger and D. A. Floudas (eds) *1996 Onwards: Lowering the Barriers Further* (Chichester: Wiley).

Bradley, K. St C. (1997) 'The European Parliament and Comitology: On the Road to Nowhere' 3 ELJ 230–254.

Buise, R. V. (1992) 'Harmonization of Medical Ethics; A Civil Servant's View' in H. E. G. M. Hermans, A. F. Casparie and J. H. P. Paelinck (eds) *Health Care in Europe After 1992* (Aldershot: Dartmouth).

Bulmer, Simon (1994) 'The Governance of the EU: A New Institutionalist Approach' 13 *Journal of Public Policy* 351–380.

Burrows, Noreen (1997) 'Non-Discrimination and Social Security in Co-operation Agreements' 22 ELRev 166–169.

Burrows, Noreen (1997) 'Opting in to the opt-out' *Web Law Journal*.

Burrows, Noreen and Jane Mair (1996) *European Social Law* (London: Wiley).

Cahill, Michael (1994) *The New Social Policy* (Oxford: Blackwell).

Caillods, Françoise (1994) 'Converging trends amidst diversity in vocational training systems' 133 *International Labour Review* 241–257.

Carter, Catriona (1996) 'The European Union Social Policy Debate' in Philippe Barbour (ed) *The European Union Handbook* (London and Chicago: Fitzroy Dearborn).

Chalmers, Damian (1995) 'The Single Market: From Prima Donna to Journeyman' in Jo Shaw and Gillian More (eds) *New Legal Dynamics of European Union* (Oxford: Oxford University Press).

Cochrane, Allan (1993) 'Comparative Approaches in Social Policy' and 'Looking for a European Welfare State' in Allan Cochrane and John Clarke (eds) *Comparing Welfare States: Britain in International Context* (London: Open University Press).

Collins, Doreen (1990) 'Social Policies' in Ali M. El Agraa (ed) *The Economics of the European Community* (London: Philip Allan).

Collins, Doreen (1986) 'Policy for Society' in Juliet Lodge (ed) *European Union: The European Community in Search of a Future* (London: Macmillan).

Comité des Sages (1996) *For a Europe of Civic and Social Rights* (Brussels: European Commission).

Coppel, Jason and Aidan O'Neill (1992) 'The European Court of Justice: Taking Rights Seriously?' 29 CMLRev 669–692.

Cornelissen, Rob (1996) 'The Principle of Territoriality and the Community Regulations on Social Security (Regulations 1408/71 and 574/72)' 33 CMLRev 439–471.

Craig, Paul and Gráinne de Búrca (1995) *EC Law: Text, Cases and Materials* (Oxford: Clarendon Press).

Cram, Laura (1997) *Policy-making in the EU: conceptual lenses and the integration process* (London: Routledge).

Cram, Laura (1994) 'The European Commission as a Multi-Organization: Social Policy and IT Policy in the EU' 1 JEPP 195–217.

Cram, Laura (1993) 'Calling the Tune without Paying the Piper? Social Policy Regulation: the Role of the Commission in European Social Policy' 21 *Policy and Politics* 135–146.

Crijns, L. H. J. (1987) 'The Social Policy of the European Community', in *Social Europe* No 1/79 (Brussels: Commission of the EC) 51–62.

Cross, Eugene (1992) 'Pre-emption of Member States' Law in the EEC: A Framework for Analysis' 29 CMLRev 447–472.

Crouch, Colin (1995) 'Organised interests as resources or as constraint: Rival logics of vocational training policy' in Colin Crouch and Franz Traxler (eds) *Organized Industrial Relations in Europe: What Future?* (Aldershot: Avebury).

Cullen, H. (1996) 'From Migrants to Citizens? European Community Policy on Intercultural Education' 45 ICLQ 109–129.

Daintith, Terence (ed) (1995) *Implementing EC Law in the United Kingdom: Structures for Indirect Rule* (London: Wiley)

Davies, L. (ed) (1992) *The Coming of Age in Europe* (London: Age Concern).

Deakin, Simon (1996) 'Labour Law as Market Regulation: the Economic Foundations of European Social Policy' in Paul Davies, Antoine Lyon-Caen, Silvana Sciarra and Spiros Simitis (eds) *European Community Labour Law: Principles and Perspectives* (Libor Amicorum Lord Wedderburn of Charlton) (Oxford: Clarendon).

de Búrca, Gráinne (1995) 'The Language of Rights and European Integration' in Jo Shaw and Gillian More (eds) *New Legal Dynamics of European Union* (Oxford: Oxford University Press).

de Búrca, Gráinne (1993) 'Fundamental Human Rights and the Reach of EC Law' 13 OJLS 283–319.

de Witte, Bruno (ed) (1989) *European Community Law of Education* (Baden-Baden: Nomos).

Dehousse, R. (ed) (1994) *Europe After Maastricht: An Ever Closer Union?* (München: Beck).

Dehousse, R. (1992) 'Integration v Regulation: On the Dynamics of Regulation in the European Community' 30 JCMS 383–402.

Dennett, J., E. James, G. Room and P. Watson (1982) *Europe Against Poverty: The European Poverty Programme 1975–1980* (London: Bedford Square Press).

Dorn, Nicholas (1993) 'Health Policies, Drug Control and the European Commmunity' in Charles E. M. Normand and J. Patrick Vaughan (eds) *Europe Without Frontiers: The Implications for Health* (London: Wiley).

Doyle, Brian (1995) *Disability, Discrimination and Equal Opportunities: A Comparative Study of the Employment Rights of Disabled Persons* (London: Mansell).

Drake, Helen (1996) 'Jacques Delors and the Discourse of Political Legitimacy' in Helen Drake and John Gaffney (eds) *The Language of Leadership in Contemporary France* (Aldershot: Dartmouth).

Drake, Helen (1995) 'Political Leadership and European Integration: the case of Jacques Delors' 18 *West European Politics* 140–160.

Eichenhofer, E. (1993) 'Coordination of social security and equal treatment of men and women in employment: recent social security judgments of the Court of Justice' 30 CMLRev 1021–1042.

Esping-Andersen, Gøsta (1990) *The Three Worlds of Welfare Capitalism* (Cambridge: Polity).

European Commission (1997) *Promoting Apprenticeship Training in Europe* COM(97) 300 final.

European Commission (1997) *Agenda 2000* Doc 97/6.

European Commission (1997) *Youth for Europe Compendium* (Luxembourg, European Commission).

European Commission (1996) *Interim Evaluation Report on Helios II* COM(96) 8 final.

European Commission (1996) *Communication on Equality of Opportunity for People with Disabilities* COM(96) 406 final.

European Commission (1996) *Communication on the Development of Social Dialogue at Community Level* COM(96) 448 final.

European Commission (1996) *First Cohesion Report* COM(96) 452 final.

European Commission (1996) *Learning in the Information Society: Action plan for a European education initiative 1996–98* COM(96) 471 final.

European Commission (1996) *Social Policy Programmes, Networks and Observatories* (Luxembourg, European Commission).

European Commission (1995) *Proposal for a Council Directive amending Directive 86/378/EEC* COM(95) 186 final.

European Commission (1995) *Social Protection in the European Community* COM(95) 457 final.

European Commission *Proposal for a European Parliament and Council Directive on the legal protection of biological inventions* COM(95) 661 final.

European Commission (1995) *Teaching and Learning: Towards the Learning Society* COM(95) 950 final.

European Commission (1994) *Communication and Proposal for a European Parliament and Council Directive adopting a programme of Community action on health promotion, information, education and training* COM(94) 202 final.

European Commission (1994) *White Paper, European Social Policy: A Way Forward for the Union* COM(94) 333 final.

European Commission (1994) *Proposal for an action plan on unemployment* COM(94) 529 final.

European Commission (1993) *Proposal for a Medium-term Action Programme to Combat Exclusion and Promote Solidarity (1994–1999)* COM(93) 435 final.

European Commission (1993) *Communication Concerning the Application of the Agreement on Social Policy* COM(93) 600 final.

European Commission (1993) *White Paper on Growth, Competitiveness and Employment* COM(93) 700 final.

European Commission (1992) *Communication on Community Structural Policies: Assessment and Outlook* COM(92) 84 final.

European Commission (1991) *First Report on the application of the Community Charter of the Fundamental Social Rights of Workers* COM(91) 511 final.

European Commission (1990) *Communication on the Elderly* COM(90) 80 final.

European Commission (1989) *Preliminary Draft of the Community Charter of Fundamental Social Rights* COM(89) 248 final.

European Commission (1988) *Report on the implementation of Directive 77/486/EEC on the education of children of migrant workers* COM(88) 787 final.

European Commission (1983) *Proposal for a Council Directive on parental leave and leave for familly reasons* COM(83) 686 final.

European Commission (1976) *Proposal for a directive concerning the progressive implementation of the principle of equality of treatment for men and women in matters of social security* COM(76) 650 final.

European Commission (1975) *Communication on equal treatment between men and women* COM(75) 36 final.

European Commission (1973) *Thomson Report on the Regional Problem in the Enlarged Community* COM(73) 550 final.

Fitzpatrick, Barry (1992) 'Community Social Law after Maastricht' 21 ILJ 199–213.

Flynn, James (1988) 'Vocational Training in Community Law and Practice' 8 YEL 59–85.

Frazer, Tim (1995) 'The New Structural Funds, State Aids and Interventions on the Single Market' 20 ELRev 3–19.

Freedland, M. (1996) 'Vocational Training in EC Law and Policy - Education, Employment or Welfare' 25 ILJ 110–120.

Gardner, John S. (1996) 'The European Agency for the Evaluation of Medicines and European Regulation of Pharmaceuticals' 2 ELJ 48–82.

George, Vic (1996) 'The Future of the Welfare State' in Vic George and Peter Taylor-Gooby (eds) *European Welfare Policy: Squaring the Welfare Circle'* (London: Macmillan).

George, Vic and Peter Taylor-Gooby (eds) (1996) *European Welfare Policy: Squaring the Welfare Circle'* (London: Macmillan).

Ginsburg, Norman (1992) *Divisions of Welfare* (London: Sage).

Gold, Michael and David Mayes (1993) 'Rethinking a Social Policy for Europe', in Robin Simpson and Robert Walker (eds) *Europe for richer or poorer* (London: CPAG).

Gomà, Richard (1996) 'The Social Dimension of the European Union: a new type of welfare system?' 3 JEPP 209–230.

Graf von Schulenberg, (1992) 'Competition, Solidarity and Cost Containment in Medical Care' in H. E. G. M. Hermans, A. F. Casparie and J. H. P. Paelinck (eds) *Health Care in Europe After 1992* (Aldershot: Dartmouth).

Green, N., T. Hartley and J. Usher (1991) *The Legal Foundations of the Single Market* (Oxford: Oxford University Press).

Hagen, Kåre (1992) 'The Social Dimension: A Quest for a European Welfare State', in Z. Ferge and J. E. Eivind (eds) *Social Policy in a Changing Europe* (Boulder: Westview).

Handoll, John (1989) 'Foreign Teachers and Public Education' in Bruno de Witte (ed) *European Community Law of Education* (Baden-Baden: Nomos).

Hancher, Leigh (1991) 'Creating the Internal Market for Pharmaceutical Medicines – An Echternach Jumping Process' 28 CMLRev 821–853.

Hantrais, Linda (1995) *Social Policy in the European Union* (London: Macmillan).

Harrop, Jeffrey (1996) *Structural Funding and Employment in the European Union: Financing the Path to Integration* (Cheltenham: Edward Elgar).

Hermans, H. E. G. M., A. F. Casparie and J. H. P. Paelinck (eds) (1992) *Health Care in Europe After 1992* (Aldershot: Dartmouth).

Hervey, Tamara (1998) 'Buy Baby: The European Union and regulation of human reproduction' (forthcoming 1998 OJLS).

Hervey, Tamara and David O'Keeffe (eds) (1996) *Sex Equality Law in the European Union* (London: Wiley).

Hix, Simon (1995) 'Parties at the European Level and the Legitimacy of EU Socio-Economic Policy' 33 JCMS 527–554.

Hochbaum, E. (1989) in Bruno De Witte (ed) *European Community Law of Education* (Baden-Baden: Nomos).

Holloway, Richard (1981) *Social Policy Harmonisation in the European Community* (London: Gower).

Hopkins, Nicholas (1996) 'Recognition of Teaching Qualifications: Community law in the English Context' 21 ELRev 435–448.

Hopkins, Nicholas (1996) 'Education and the children of migrant workers: once a child always a child' 18 JSWFL 114–118.

Hoskyns, Catherine (1996) *Integrating Gender* (London: Verso).

Hoskyns, Catherine and Linda Luckhaus (1989) 'The European Community Directive on Equal Treatment in Social Security' 17 *Policy and Politics* 321–355.

Houghton-James, Hazel (1993) 'The Implication for Member States of the development of an education policy by the Court of Justice' 5 *Education and the Law* 85–93.

Joerges, Christian (1994) 'European Economic Law, the Nation-State and the Maastricht Treaty' in R. Dehousse *Europe After Maastricht: An Ever Closer Union?* (München: Beck).

Jones, Nigel (1996) 'The New Draft Biotechnology Directive' 6 *European Intellectual Property Review* 363–365.

Kahn Freund, O. (1974) 'On Uses and Misuses of Comparative Law' 37 MLRev 1–27.

Kaufer, Erich (1990) 'The Regulation of New Product Development in the Drug Industry' in G. Majone (ed) *Deregulation or Re-regulation? Regulatory Reform in Europe and the United States* (London: Pinter).

Keating, Michael (1995) 'Europeanism and Regionalism' in Barry Jones and Michael Keating (eds) *The European Union and the Regions* (Oxford: Clarendon).

Kendall, Vivien (1994) *EC Consumer Law* (London: Wiley Chancery).

Kenner, Jeff (1994) 'Economic and Social Cohesion – The Rocky Road Ahead' LIEI 1–37.

Keohane, Robert O. and Stanley Hoffmann (eds) (1991) *The New European Community: Decisionmaking and Institutional Change* (Boulder: Westview Press).

214

Kleinman, Mark and David Piachaud (1993) 'European Social Policy: Conceptions and Choices' 3 JESP 1–19.

Korpi, Walter (1983) *The Democratic Class Struggle* (London: Routledge and Kegan Paul).

Kuper, Bernd-Otto (1994) 'The Green and White Papers of the European Union: The Apparent Goal of Reduced Social Benefits' 4 JESP 129–137.

Laffan, Brigid and Michael Shackleton (1996) 'The Budget' in Helen Wallace and William Wallace *Policy-Making in the European Union* (Oxford, Oxford University Press).

Lange, Peter (1992) 'The Politics of the Social Dimension' in A. M. Sbragia (ed) *Euro-Politics: Institutions and Policy-Making in the 'New' EC* (Washington: Brookings).

Laske, Caroline (1993) 'The Impact of the Single European Market on Social Protection for Migrant Workers' 30 CMLRev 515–539.

Lasok, D. (1994) *Lasok and Bridge's Law and Institutions of the European Union* (London: Butterworths).

Leibfried, Stephan (1993) 'Towards a European Welfare State?' in Catherine Jones (ed) *New Perspectives on the Welfare State in Europe* 133–156 (London: Routledge).

Leibfried, Stephan and Paul Pierson (1996) 'Social Policy' in Helen Wallace and William Wallace (eds) *Policy-Making in the European Union* (Oxford: Oxford University Press).

Leibfried, Stephan and Paul Pierson (eds) (1995) *European Social Policy: Between Fragmentation and Integration* (Washington: Brookings).

Leibfried, Stephan and Paul Pierson (1995) 'Semisovereign Welfare States: Social Policy in a Multitiered Europe' in Stephan Leibfried and Paul Pierson (eds) *European Social Policy: Between Fragmentation and Integration* (Washington: Brookings).

Leibfried, Stephan (1992) 'Towards a European Welfare State? On integrating poverty regimes in the European Community' in Z. Ferge and J. E. Eivind (eds) *Social Policy in a Changing Europe* (Boulder: Westview).

Leidl, Reiner (1993) 'EC Health Care Systems Entering the Single Market' in Charles E. M. Normand and J. Patrick Vaughan (eds) *Europe Without Frontiers: The Implications for Health* (London: Wiley).

Lenaerts, K. (1994) 'Education in European Community Law after Maastricht' 31 CMLRev 7–41.

Lewis, Jane (1996) *Women and Social Policies in Europe* (Aldershot: Edward Elgar).

Lewis, Jane (1992) 'Gender and the Development of Welfare Regimes' 2 JESP 159–173.

Lonbay, Julian (1989) 'Education and Law: The Community Context' 14 ELRev 363–387.

Luckhaus, Linda (1997) 'Privatisation and Pensions: Some Pitfalls for Women?' 3 ELJ 83–100.

Luckhaus, Linda (1995) 'European Social Security Law' in A. I. Ogus and N. J. Wikeley (eds) *The Law of Social Security* (London: Butterworths).

Ludlow, Peter (1991) 'The European Commission' in Robert O. Keohane and Stanley Hoffmann (eds) *The New European Community: Decisionmaking and Institutional Change* (Boulder: Westview Press).

Maduro, Miguel Poiares (1997) 'Reforming the Market or the State? Article 30 and the European Constitution: Economic Freedom and Political Rights' 3 ELJ 55–82.

Maher, Imelda (1995) 'Legislative Review by the EC Commission: Revision without Radicalism' in Jo Shaw and Gillian More (eds) *New Legal Dynamics of European Union* (Oxford: Oxford University Press).

Majone, G. (1996) 'A European regulatory state?' in Jeremy Richardson (ed) *European Union: Power and Policy-making* (London: Routledge).

Majone, G. (1996) 'Which social policy for Europe?' in Yves Meny, Pierre Muller and Jean Louis Quermonne (eds) *Adjusting to Europe: The impact of the European Union on national institutions and policies* (London: Routledge).

Majone, G. (1993) 'The European Community: Between Social Policy and Social Regulation' 31 JCMS 153–169.

Majone, G. (1991) 'Cross-National Sources of Regulatory Policy-making in the European Community and the United States' 11 JPP 79–106.

Majone, G. (1990) *Deregulation or Reregulation? Regulatory Reform in Europe and the United States* (London: Pinter).

Marks, Gary (1992) 'Structural Policy in the EC' in A. M. Sbragia (ed) *Euro-Politics: Institutions and Policy-Making in the 'New' EC* (Washington DC: Brookings).

Marshall, T. H. (1975) *Social Policy* (London: Hutchinson).

McKee, Martin, Elias Mossialos and Paul Belcher (1996) 'The Influence of European Law on National Health Policy' 6 JESP 263–286.

Miller, G. (1993) *The Future of Social Security in Europe in the context of EMU* (Report to the EC Commission, Brussels: Observatoire Social Européen).

Milner, Susan (forthcoming) 'Training Policy: Steering between divergent national logics' in H. Kassim, A. Meron and D. Hire (eds) *Beyond the Market: The European Union and National Social, Environmental and Consumer Protection Policy* (London: Routledge).

Montanari, Ingalill Järensjö (1995) 'Harmonization of social policies and social regulation in the European Community' 27 *European Journal of Political Research* 21–45.

Moore, Matthew (1997) 'Case C–308/93 *Cabanis-Issarte*' 34 CMLRev 727–739.

Moravcsik, A. (1995) 'Liberal Intergovernmentalism and Integration: a rejoinder' 33 JCMS 611–620.

Moravcsik, A. (1993) 'Preferences and Power in the EC: A Liberal Inter-governmentalist Approach' 31 JCMS 473–524.

Morgan, Marilynne A. (1987) 'A Review of the Case Law of the Court of Justice on Migrant Workers and Social Security' 24 CMLRev 483–507.

Mosley, Hugh (1990) 'The social dimension of European integration' 129 *International Labour Review* 147–163.

Moxon-Brown, Edward (1993) 'Social Europe', in Juliet Lodge (ed) *The European Community and the Challenge of the Future* (London: Pinter).

Munroe, J. G. (1990) 'A Review of the Case Law of the Court of Justice on Migrant Workers and Social Security' 27 CMLRev 547–571.

Neill, Patrick (1994) *The European Court of Justice: A Case Study in Judicial Activism* (Conference Paper, Brasenose College Oxford 16 Sept 1994).

Neuwahl, Nanette and Allan Rosas (eds) (1995) *The European Union and Human Rights* (The Hague: Martinus Nijhoff).

Nevin, E. T. (1990) 'Regional Policy' in Ali M. El-Aagra (ed) *The Economics of the European Community* (New York: Philip Allan).

Nielsen, Ruth and Erika Szyszczak (1997) *The Social Dimension of the European Union* (Copenhagen: Handelshojskolens Forlag).

Normand, Charles E. M. and P. Vaughan (eds) (1993) *Europe Without Frontiers: The Implications for Health* (Chichester: Wiley).

Ogus, A. (1994) *Regulation: Legal Form and Economic Theory* (Oxford: Clarendon Press).

O'Keeffe, David and Patrick Twomey (eds) (1994) *Legal Issues of the Maastricht Treaty* (London: Wiley Chancery).

O'Keefe, David (1996) 'The Uneasy Progress of European Social Policy' 2 *Columbia Journal of European Law* 241–263.

O'Keeffe (1992) 'Free Movement of Persons and the Single Market' 17 ELRev 3–19.

O'Keeffe, David (1985) 'Equal Rights for Migrants: the Concept of Social Advantages in Article 7 (2), Regulation 1612/68' 5 YEL 93–123.

Oliver, Peter (1996) *Free Movement of Goods in the European Community* (London: Sweet and Maxwell).

Paugam, Serge (1996) 'Poverty and Social Disqualification: A Comparative Analysis of Social Disadvantage in Europe' 6 JESP 287–303.

Peers, Steve (1997) '"Social Advantages" and Discrimination in Employment: Case Law Clarified and Confirmed' 22 ELRev 157–165.

Peters, B. Guy (1992) 'Bureaucratic Politics and the Institutions of the European Community' in A. M. Sbragia (ed) *Euro-Politics: Institutions and Policymaking in the 'New' EC* (Washington: Brookings)

Petersen, Jorn Henrik (1991) 'Harmonization of Social Security in the EC revisited' 29 JCMS 505–536.

Phelan, Diarmuid R. (1992) 'Right to Life of the Unborn v Promotion of

217

Trade in Services: The European Court of Justice and the Normative Shaping of the European Union' 55 MLRev 670–689.

Pierson, Paul and Stephan Leibfried (1995) 'Multitiered Institutions and the Making of Social Policy' in Stephan Leibfried and Paul Pierson *European Social Policy* (Washington DC: Brookings).

Pieters, Danny (ed) (1990) *Introduction into the Social Security Law of the Member States of the European Community* (Brussels: Bruylant).

Pochet, Philippe et al (1996) 'European Briefing' 6 JESP 61–68; 163–168; 241–246; 329–335.

Rainbird, H. (1993) 'Vocational education and training' in M. Gold (ed) *The Social Dimension* (London: Macmillan) 184–202.

Ramprakash, Deo (1994) 'Poverty in the Countries of the European Union: a synthesis of Eurostat's statistical research on poverty' 4 JESP 117–128.

Rasmussen, H. (1986) *On Law and Policy in the European Court of Justice* (Dordrecht: Martinus Nijhoff).

Rees, A. M. (1985) *T. H. Marshall's Social Policy in the Twentieth Century* (London: Hutchinson),

Room, Graham (ed) (1991) *Towards a European Welfare State* (Bristol: SAUS).

Room, Graham (1994) 'European Social Policy: competition, conflict and integration' 6 *Social Policy Review* 17–35.

Roscam Abbing, H. D. C. (1992) 'European Community and the Right to Health Care' in H. E. G. M. Hermans, A. F. Casparie and J. H. P. Paelinck (eds) *Health Care in Europe After 1992* (Aldershot: Dartmouth).

Ross, George (1995) *Jacques Delors* (Cambridge: Polity).

Ryba, R. (1992) 'Toward a European Dimension in Education: Intention and Reality in EC Policy and Practice' 36 *Comparative Education Review* 10–24.

Sauer, F. (1992) 'The European Community's Pharmaceutical Policy' in H. E. G. M. Hermans, A. F. Casparie and J. H. P. Paelinck (eds) *Health Care in Europe After 1992* (Aldershot: Dartmouth).

Scharpf, Fritz (1996) *A New Social Contract? Negative and Positive Integration in the Political Economy of European Welfare States* (Florence: EUI Working Paper RSC 96/44).

Schulte, Barnd (1993) 'Guaranteed minimum resources and the European Community' in Robert Walker and Robin Simpson (eds) *Europe: for richer or poorer?* (London: CPAG).

Scott, Joanne (1998) *EC Environmental Law* (London: Longman).

Scott, Joanne (1995) 'The GATT and Community Law: rethinking the "regulatory gap"' in Jo Shaw and Gillian More (eds) *New Legal Dynamics of European Union* (Oxford: Oxford University Press).

Scott, Joanne (1995) *Development Dilemmas in the European Community: Rethinking Regional Development Policy* (Buckhingham: Open University Press).

Scott, Joanne and Wade Mansell (1993) 'European Regional Development Policy: Confusing Quantity with Quality?' 18 ELRev 87–108.

Scott, Colin (1995) 'Changing Patterns of European Community Utilities Law and Policy: An Institutional Hypothesis' in Jo Shaw and Gillian More (eds) *New Legal Dynamics of European Union* (Oxford: Oxford University Press).

Shanks, Michael (1977) 'The Social Policy of the European Communities' 14 CMLRev 375–383.

Shaw, Jo (1996) *Law of the European Union* (London: Macmillan).

Shaw, Jo (1995) *Citizenship of the Union: Towards Post-National Membership?* (Florence: Academy of European Law).

Shaw, Jo (1994) 'Twin-track Social Europe – The Inside Track' in David O'Keeffe and Patrick Twomey (eds) *Legal Issues of the Maastricht Treaty* (London: Wiley) 295–311.

Shaw, Jo (1993) *European Community Law* (London: Macmillan).

Shaw, Jo (1992) 'Education and the Law in the European Community' 21 *Journal of Law and Education* 415–442.

Simpson, Robin and Robert Walker (1993) 'Conclusion: whose Europe?' in Robin Simpson, and Robert Walker (eds) *Europe: for richer or poorer?* (London: CPAG).

Slot, Piet Jan (1996) 'Harmonisation' 21 ELRev 378–397.

Sohrab, Julia (1996) *Sexing the Benefit: Women, Social Security and Financial Independence in EC Sex Equality Law* (Aldershot: Dartmouth).

Spicker, Paul (1997) 'Exclusion' 33 JCMS 133–143.

Spicker, Paul (1995) *Social Policy: Themes and Approaches* (London: Prentice Hall/Harvester Wheatsheaf).

Spicker, P. (1993) 'Can European social policy be universalist?' 5 *Social Policy Review* 207–226.

Spicker, Paul (1991) 'The Principle of Subsidiarity and the Social Policy of the European Community' 1 JESP 3–14.

Sprokkereef, A. (1993) 'Developments in European Community education policy' in Juliet Lodge (ed) *The European Community and the Challenge of the Future* (London: Pinter).

Steiner, Josephine (1996) 'The principle of equal treatment for men and women in social security' in Tamara Hervey and David O'Keeffe (eds) *Sex Equality Law in the European Union* (London: Wiley).

Steiner, Josephine (1992) 'Social Security for EC Migrants' JSWFL 33–47.

Storey, Hugo (1994) 'United Kingdom Social Security Law: European and International Dimensions' 1 *Journal of Social Security Law* 110–132 and 142–154.

Streek, Wolfgang (1995) 'Neo-Voluntarism: A New European Social Policy Regime?' 1 ELJ 31–59.

Szyszczak, Erika (forthcoming) *EC Labour Law* (London: Longman).

Szyszczak, Erika (1995) 'Social Rights as General Principles of Community Law' in Nanette Neuwahl and Allan Rosas (eds) *The European Union and Human Rights* (The Hague: Martinus Nijhoff).

Taylor, David G. (1993) 'Europe Without Frontiers? Balancing Pharmaceutical Interests' in Charles E. M. Normand and J. Patrick Vaughan (eds) *Europe Without Frontiers: The Implications for Health* (London: Wiley) 283–294.

Taylor-Gooby, Peter (1996) 'Paying for Welfare: The View from Europe' 67 PQ 116–126.

Taylor-Gooby, Peter (1996) 'The Response of Government: Fragile Convergence?' in Vic George and Peter Taylor-Gooby (eds) *European Welfare Policy: Squaring the Welfare Circle*' (London: Macmillan).

Temple Lang, J. (1991) 'The Sphere in which Member States are obliged to comply with General Principles of Community Law' 1991 LIEI 23–35.

ter Kuile, B. H., F. M. du Pré and K. Sevinga (1992) 'Health Care in Europe after 1992: the European dimension' in H. E. G. M. Hermans, A. F. Casparie and J. H. P. Paelinck (eds) *Health Care in Europe After 1992* (Aldershot: Dartmouth).

Titmuss, Richard (1974) *Social Policy* (eds Abel-Smith and Titmuss) (London: Allen and Unwin).

Verkerk, M. A. (1992) 'Introduction to Medical Ethics' in H. E. G. M. Hermans, A. F. Casparie and J. H. P. Paelinck (eds) *Health Care in Europe After 1992* (Aldershot: Dartmouth).

Vogel-Polsky, Elaine (1990) 'What Future is there for a Social Europe Following the Strasbourg Summit?' 19 ILJ 65–80.

Vos, Ellen (1997) 'The Rise of Committees' 3 ELJ 210–229.

Waddington, Lisa (1995) *Disability, Employment and the European Community* (London: Blackstone Press).

Walker, Robin and Robert Simpson (eds) (1993) *Europe: for richer or poorer?* (London: CPAG).

Wallace, Helen and William Wallace (eds) (1996) *Policy-Making in the European Union* (Oxford: Oxford University Press).

Watson, Philippa (1993) 'Social Policy after Maastricht' 30 CMLRev 481–513.

Watson, Philippa (1991) 'The Community Social Charter' 28 CMLRev 37–68.

Weatherill, Stephen (1996) *EC Consumer Law and Policy* (London: Longman).

Weatherill, Stephen (1995) *Law and Integration in the European Union* (Oxford: Clarendon).

Weatherill, Stephen (1994) 'Beyond Preemption? Shared Competence and Constitutional Change in the European Community' in David O'Keeffe and Patrick Twomey (eds) *Legal Issues of the Maastricht Treaty* (London: Wiley Chancery).

Weatherill, Stephen and Paul Beaumont (1995) *EC Law* (Harmondsworth: Penguin).

Weiler, J. H. H. (1997) 'The EU Belongs to its Citizens: Three Immodest Proposals' 22 ELRev 150–156.

Weiler, J. H. H. and Nicolas Lockhart (1995) '"Taking Rights Seriously" Seriously: The European Court and its Fundamental Rights Jurisprudence' 32 CMLRev 51–94 and 579–627.

Wellens and Borchardt (1989) 'Soft Law in European Community Law' 14 ELRev 267–321.

White, Alan W. (1996) 'Whither the Pharmaceutical Trade Mark?' 8 *European Intellectual Property Review* 441–445.

Whiteford, Elaine (1996) 'Occupational Pensions and European Law: Clarity at Last?' in Tamara Hervey and David O'Keeffe (eds) *Sex Equality Law in the European Union* (London: Wiley).

Whiteford, Elaine (1995) 'W(h)ither Social Policy?' in Jo Shaw and Gillian More (eds) *New Legal Dynamics of European Union* (Oxford: Oxford University Press).

Whiteford, Elaine (1993) 'Social Policy after Maastricht' 18 ELRev 202–222.

Wikeley, N. J. (1988) 'Migrant Workers and Unemployment Benefit in the European Community' *Journal of Social Welfare Law* 300–315.

Williams, Fiona (1997) 'Contestations of Gender, 'Race'/Ethnicity and Citizenship in EU Social Policy' paper presented to European Sociological Association Conference, 29 August 1997.

Williams, Fiona (1993) 'Gender, Race and Class in British Welfare Policy' in Allan Cochrane and John Clarke (eds) *Comparing Welfare States: Britain in International Context* (London: Open University Press).

Wilson, Michael (1993) 'The German Welfare state: A Conservative Regime in Crisis' in Allan Cochrane and John Clarke (eds) *Comparing Welfare States: Britain in International Context* (London: Open University Press).

Wincott, Daniel (1995) 'Political Theory, Law and European Union' in Jo Shaw and Gillian More (eds) *New Legal Dynamics of European Union* (Oxford: Oxford University Press).

Wise, Mark and Richard Gibb (1993) *Single Market to Social Europe: The European Community in the 1990s* (Harlow: Longman).

Wishlade, Fiona (1993) 'Competition Policy, Cohesion and the Coordination of Regional Aids in the EC, 14 *European Competition Law Review* 143–150.

Wyatt, Derrick and Alan Dashwood (1993) *European Community Law* (London: Sweet and Maxwell).

Zilioli, Chiara (1989) 'The Recognition of Diplomas and its Impact on Educational Policies' in Bruno De Witte (ed) *European Community Law of Education* (Baden-Baden: Nomos).

Index